Luke Harding is an award-winning foreign correspondent with the *Guardian*. He has reported from Delhi, Berlin and Moscow and has also covered wars in Afghanistan and Iraq. He is the co-author of two previous books, written with David Leigh, *WikiLeaks: Inside Julian Assange's War on Secrecy* (2011) and *The Liar: The Fall of Jonathan Aitken* (1997), nominated for the Orwell Prize. The Hollywood studio DreamWorks has bought film rights to *WikiLeaks*. He has also written for the magazine *Granta*. He lives in Hertfordshire with his wife, the freelance journalist Phoebe Taplin, and their two children.

Praise for *Mafia State*

'*Mafia State* deals with many aspects of Russian life, from the Russian-Georgian war to the rise of the far Right, from Putin's wealth to rural poverty. [Harding's] reports are clear, precise and up-to-the minute' *Spectator*

'Russia laid bare in an absorbing account of four years spent as head of the Guardian's Moscow bureau ... There is now a vast literature describing the hard reality of Putin's Russia, but what Harding adds to our awareness is a sense of what it is like to live that reality every day. He does this by relating tragedies and absurdities through a series of vivid and often moving encounters ... The author's descriptive powers and his insights into the mentality and techniques of Putinism are enough to make *Mafia State* an essential read' David Clark, *New Statesman*

'The importance of Luke Harding's book lies in its first-hand account of a relatively mild but telling bout of state sponsored harassment, of a kind that, like much else in Russia, is intentionally opaque and deniable' AD Miller, *Guardian*

'Uncertainty, fear and understandable paranoia permeate this book. But this does not cloud the analysis. Harding's description of the rise of Russia's racist right ... is deeply troubling. He suggests it is the one political force which threatens Putin's mafia state ... Harding's book makes it clear that Russia has sunk once again into a deep political and social malaise that is going to make the immense challenges facing all of us despite the current crisis tougher, not easier' Misha Glenny, *Irish Times*

'Both intriguing and highly pertinent to understanding current issues ... Harding is relentless in his pursuit of the truth and delineates sharply the social conditions and attitudes in Russia ... [his] style is informed but informal and yet brings into focus contemporary Russia' *bookbag.co.uk*

'*Mafia State* is full of all possible clichés concerning Russian life ... However, the sex manual left by a KGB agent in Luke Harding's bedroom in order to "demoralise him" gives the author a right to say (and a reader a reason to believe) that these clichés are still true' *Oxonian Review*

'Extensive and often insightful ... [it] does bring to light many important events that might otherwise have been hushed up' *Russia Profile*

Mafia State

How one reporter became an
enemy of the brutal new Russia

Luke Harding

guardianbooks

Published by Guardian Books 2012

4 6 8 10 9 7 5 3

First published in Great Britain in 2011 by

Guardian Books
Kings Place, 90 York Way
London N1 9GU

www.guardianbooks.co.uk

A CIP catalogue record for this book is available from the British Library

ISBN 9780852652497

Text design by seagulls.net
Cover design by Two Associates

Printed and bound by CPI Group (UK) Ltd, Croydon, CR0 4YY

CONTENTS

The Break-in

Flat 49-50, House 8, Fifth Voikov Drive, Voikovskaya, Moscow
28 April 2007

*Harassing activity against all embassy personnel has spiked
in the past several months to a level not seen in many years.
Embassy personnel have suffered personally slanderous and falsely
prurient attacks in the media. Family members have been the victims
of psychologically terrifying assertions that their USG [United States
government] employee spouses had met accidental deaths. Home
intrusions have become far more commonplace and bold, and activity
against our locally engaged Russian staff continues at a record pace.
We have no doubt that this activity originates in the FSB.*

JOHN BEYRLE, US AMBASSADOR IN MOSCOW, CONFIDENTIAL
STATE DEPARTMENT CABLE, 9 NOVEMBER 2009

Someone has broken into my flat. Three months after arriving in Russia as
the *Guardian*'s new Moscow bureau chief, I return home from a dinner
party. It's late. I turn the key. At first, everything appears normal. Children's
clothes lie in the corridor, books are piled on the living room floor; there is
the comforting debris of family life. And then I see it. It is a strange detail.
The window of my son's bedroom is wide open.

I am certain it wasn't open when I'd left five hours previously, taking my
two children with me. We live on the 10th floor of one of Moscow's post-
communist-era apartment blocks, an ugly orange-brick tower. It overlooks

a park of silver birches and deep green firs, in the Moscow suburb of Voikovskaya. We keep our windows shut. The danger of a child falling out is too obvious. To open the window you have to twist the white plastic handle downwards 90 degrees. Two handles, in fact. This is possible only from the inside; it couldn't have blown open.

But the window *is* open, almost provocatively, defiantly so – a statement, even. "Has there been a burglar?" my six-year-old son asks, peering out of the open window and down at the frozen courtyard one hundred metres below. It is a reasonable question. It's a small step from his bed to the window. "I don't know," I reply. "It's a mystery. Perhaps someone managed to climb up the outside. Maybe it was Spiderman." In our spare room, with its unused exercise bike and lurid tropical plant, I discover a cassette tape hissing in our music player. I hadn't put the tape on either. My wife, Phoebe Taplin, is away for the weekend. So someone else has put the tape on.

Several hours later, while trying to suppress a feeling of – what? – horror, alarm, incredulity, bafflement, a kind of cold rational rage, a tightening fury, I wake up. An unknown alarm clock is going off somewhere in the flat. The noise is unfamiliar. I go into the living room and turn on the lights. A clock – left behind by my Russian landlord, Vadim, who had moved out two weeks earlier – is beeping loudly. I turn it off, fumblingly. I hadn't set it. But someone else has – to go off at 4.10am. I look at the date. It's Sunday 29 April 2007. I go back to bed. I sleep fitfully.

It's clear, then, that this is no orthodox break-in. Nothing has been stolen; nothing damaged. Several thousand dollars lazily concealed in a kitchen drawer, next to an egg whisk, are untouched. (The money is next month's rent. Two decades after communism and the alleged end of the cold war, Russia is still a cash economy. The preferred currency is dollars, though euros are also acceptable.) I can discount Vadim as the culprit, since his only interests appear to be venal ones.

The intruders' aim seems merely to have been to demonstrate that they had been there – and to show, presumably, that they can come back, if the mood takes them. They have apparently entered through the front door. The locks don't seem to have troubled them much. They have opened a window, set an alarm, and probably hidden a few bugs. Then they are gone.

I can't help wondering whether a recording device has been concealed in the marital bedroom. This isn't a thought I want to pursue.

The dark symbolism of the open window in the children's bedroom is not hard to decipher: take care, or your kids might just fall out. For any child, the 10-storey drop would be deadly. Mission accomplished: the men – I assume it is men – have vanished like ghosts. I find myself in a new world. It is a place of unknown rules, of thuggish adversaries. I lack the vocabulary to explain what has just happened to us: a burglary, a break-in, an intrusion? Suddenly, it appears we have become the objects of a malign psychological exercise, a dark experiment on the human soul. Our souls. I hug my son close. But who are these ghosts? And who sent them?

CHAPTER 1

Sword and Shield

Room 306, FSB Investigation Bureau, Lefortovo prison, Moscow
23 May 2007

*Freedom of speech, freedom of conscience, freedom of
mass media, property rights – all those basic elements of a
civilised society will be safely protected by the state.*
ACTING PRESIDENT VLADIMIR PUTIN, 31 DECEMBER 1999

In fact, I pretty much knew the identity of my ghosts – or at least of the
agency that had sent them. Fifteen days earlier, on 13 April 2007, the
London-based Russian oligarch and Kremlin critic Boris Berezovsky gave
an interview to my newspaper, the *Guardian*, in which he called for the
violent overthrow of Vladimir Putin's regime. My name was on the
Guardian's front-page story, together with that of two London-based
colleagues; I am, as far as Russia's vigilant security services are concerned,
fair game. From now on, Russia's Federal Security Service, or FSB – the
main successor agency to the KGB – takes a keen interest in me.

Three weeks after the *Guardian* interview with Berezovsky appears in
print, I receive a surprising phone call. It is the FSB. They want to see me.
The story has caused a furore inside Russia. It has led the bulletins of
Russia's government-controlled Channel One and Rossiya stations – which
normally extol Vladimir Putin in every broadcast. It also provokes outraged
commentary in the tabloid newspapers, whose contents have been
described, fairly I think, as "Putin plus boobs". The *Guardian*'s report even

pricks parliamentarians from Russia's normally muted Duma to demand Berezovsky's extradition from Britain, where he has been in hiding since 2003, something Britain's judicial system has consistently refused to do.

In May 2007 the FSB opens a criminal investigation into the *Guardian* story. Russia's chief prosecutor, Yuri Chaika, had already charged Berezovsky with fraud – accusing him of stealing £4.3m from the Russian state airline Aeroflot. But it is clear that additional criminal charges would bolster the prosecutor's case and might just embarrass the British government, one of Russia's least favourite European partners.

The man from the FSB who calls my office number doesn't identify himself. "You have to come and see us," he says. His tone is polite but adamant. It carries a flavour of subterranean menace. He explains I am being summoned as a "witness" in a criminal case into the Berezovsky story and need to report directly to the FSB. The conversation is as follows. My assistant, Yulia Molodstova, translates (in these early days my Russian was still halting):

Yulia:　　So you want to interview Luke Harding as a witness in a criminal case? We need the number of the case to tell our legal department in London.

Officer: Number 432801.

Yulia:　　We need more detail.

Officer: We will tell you everything here.

Yulia:　　Can you tell us what the investigation is, who is conducting it?

Officer: No, because this is secret information. As soon as your witness comes to us, we will tell him as much as he should know.

At this point the officer turns his attention to Yulia. In unmistakeably sinister tones, he makes clear he knows who she is:

Officer: I perfectly understand. You are, as I understand, Yulia Vladimirovna?

Yulia:　　No, not Vladimirovna.

Officer: Your last name is Molodstova?

Yulia: Yulia Sergeyevna.

Officer: Yulia Sergeyevna, can you please ask your boss to choose a time from Wednesday to Friday next week to come and see us. He is invited as a witness.

I explain that the transcript of the interview with Berezovsky is available on the *Guardian* website and there is little I can add to it. My own role in the Berezovsky story had been modest, I say. I had merely phoned the Kremlin's urbane, English-speaking spokesman Dmitry Peskov and asked him if he had a reaction. This is perfectly true. But it fails to deflect him. "You will come and see us," he says. "I suggest you bring a lawyer."

The agency also writes us a letter in Russian:

Federal Security Service
Russian Federation
Investigation agency
04.05.07 No 6/2-1053

To the Head of the Moscow bureau of the *Guardian*, 123056 Moscow, Gruzinsky per 3, 75-76

The investigation directorate of the Federal Security Service of the Russian Federation is probing a charge No 432801 concerning Berezovsky BA who is being imputed with activities aimed at taking over power in Russia, which is a crime described in the article 278 of the Criminal Code of the Russian Federation.

On 13 April 2007, the *Guardian* newspaper published an article, "I am plotting a new Russian revolution" by Ian Cobain, Matthew Taylor and Luke Harding. This article contains information about taking over of state power in Russia.

With regard to that and according to part 4, article 21 of the Criminal Code of the Russian Federation, we ask you to inform us about the following (the address is 11116 Moscow, Energeticheskaya St 3a):

Where, when and under what circumstances and on whose initiative the interview with Berezovsky was taken ...

Who was present at that interview?

Was there a recording of the interview made using technical equipment? If yes, what kind of equipment and has the recording been saved?

Chief investigator on cases of especial importance of the Investigation agency of Federal Security Service of Russia

Law enforcement major

AV Kuzmin

[Andrey Vyacheslavovich Kuzmin]

Three weeks after this call I find myself outside Lefortovo prison – a drab, yellow, three-storey building lined with spiralling razor wire, and close to the centre of Moscow and an attractive leafy park. In the era of Peter the Great, this had been the foreigners' quarter, where the young tsar held all-night drinking parties with his Swiss mercenary friend and mentor, Franz Lefort. The jail was founded in 1881 and used for tsarist prisoners. In communist times Lefortovo was the KGB's most notorious detention centre. It was a place where those who had offended the state were taken for interrogation and isolation; and put in "psychic" cells.

Its former inmates are an illustrious bunch. In the 1930s "enemies of the state" such as Yevgenia Ginzburg were held here before being taken to camps in Siberia. Later inmates included the Soviet dissident Vladimir Bukovsky, who now lives in Britain. The novelist Alexander Solzhenitsyn wrote about Lefortovo in *The Gulag Archipelago*. He described its "psychological cells" like No 111. It was "painted black and ... had a day-and-night 25-watt bulb, but was in all other respects like every other Lefortovo cell: asphalt floor; the heating valve out in the corridor where only the guards had access to it". From the neighbouring hydrodynamics institute came "an interminable irritating roar", a "roar which would make a bowl or cup vibrate so violently that it would slip off the edge of the table". Another inmate was Alexander Litvinenko, who was held for eight months in 1999 before he fled to Britain. Litvinenko was on friendly terms with Lefortovo's prison director; he kept in shape by exercising furiously inside his cell.

Litvinenko was averse to cigarette smoke; the FSB gave him a chain-smoking informer cell-mate.

Lefortovo isn't a place where journalists are normally admitted, especially foreign ones. The prison, on Energeticheskaya Street, is not marked on any map. It is hidden behind a row of dull apartment blocks. A solitary plane tree grows in the courtyard. As I stand with my lawyer, Gari Mirzoyan, a veteran of Moscow's criminal circuit, the sun comes out. My mood brightens. This feels absurd. I'm waiting in the sun to go and see the FSB, an organisation that is supposed to exist, like some kind of nocturnal rodent, in darkness. We phone AV Kuzmin, the major who has summoned us; he is ready to see us.

Gari presses the entrance bell. A large reinforced metal door swings open. Inside is a waiting room, bleak, empty and apparently without chairs or tables; next to it is a small reception area. The reception itself is hidden by a one-way silvered mirror: the officer on duty can see us, we can't see him. In fact that isn't strictly true – a disembodied hand appears briefly. The hand takes away my passport and phone; the hand is hairy, I note. I ask for my mobile phone to be returned – a pointless gesture since I strongly suspect it is already bugged. The owner of the hand agrees. *Khorosho*, he says – *good*. The hand returns the phone. Gari slips out and puts it in his car. Five minutes pass. We are given permission to proceed upstairs – though a corridor decorated with a worn red-green carpet. We go past a strange Victorian-style lift. The lift has old-fashioned prison bars; it is, in effect, a moving cage. It appears to descend to Lefortovo's lower depths, an internal K-shaped prison where a small number of detainees, mostly political prisoners, are kept. The oligarch Mikhail Khodorkovsky – once Russia's richest man – was held downstairs, following his arrest in 2003 and before his politically driven conviction for fraud and his banishment, like the Decembrists who rebelled against Nicholas I, to Siberia.

Old-fashioned video cameras record our movements from the stairwells; the corridor is lined with a series of identical anonymous wooden doors. With its atmosphere of shabby menace and institutional gloom, Lefortovo looks very much like the Berlin headquarters of the Stasi – East Germany's secret police. If anything has changed here since Soviet times, I am at a loss to identify it. We arrive at Room 306 and knock. Major AV

Kuzmin answers. He invites us inside. To my surprise, he is a young man – 29, 30, perhaps – wearing a dark olive-green FSB uniform. His hair is blond and cut short; his expression inscrutable and blandly handsome. I expected someone older.

The fact that he is investigating the Berezovsky case – at the behest of the presidential administration – suggests that he is already moving rapidly up the FSB's career ladder. His office gives little away: there are no family photos; a couple of tiny green spider plants perched on top of a wardrobe are the only hints of warmth. On the table stands fizzy mineral water and three glasses – engraved with *ЧК-ОГПУ-КГБ-ФСБ*, the initials of Russia's secret spy organisations, beginning with the "Cheka", the communists' first secret police force, founded in 1917 by Felix Dzerzhinsky, a fanatical Bolshevik and friend of Lenin.

The initials suggest a sort of secret brotherhood, it strikes me – and a continuity of mentality and methods. Despite the fall of communism the FSB clearly sees itself carrying out the same holy mission as its KGB predecessor: to protect the state and to smite its enemies.

Kuzmin begins. Lying on his desk is a high-quality colour photocopy of the *Guardian*'s Berezovsky front page. He tosses it to me. He speaks in Russian.

"Could you confirm who you are?"

"Luke Daniel Harding," I say.

"How long have you been in Moscow?"

"Four months."

"Where did you go to university?"

"Oxford."

"Are you married?"

"Yes."

"Can you tell me the circumstances in which your interview with Berezovsky took place?"

"It took place in London."

"How do you know this?"

"The *Guardian*'s legal department told me. As you know, I've never met Mr Berezovsky."

"Is the tape recording of his remarks genuine?"

"As far as I know, yes."

And so on. His questions are strikingly pointless. At first it seems that this isn't really an interrogation, but a piece of bureaucratic book-keeping designed to place on the record my acknowledged minor role in the Berezovsky drama. It's only later it dawns on me that the point of this official summons isn't to unravel a crime: it's to intimidate me. Kuzmin's absurd questions – and my answers – are a deliberate irrelevance. His actual goal is to arouse insecurity, bewilderment and even fear in someone whom the FSB has – provisionally at this point – identified as an "enemy". The tactic has clearly worked on others in the past. My legal team – found with great difficulty, since none of Moscow's legal firms wanted to take on the Berezovsky brief – had advised me to keep my answers short. Kuzmin taps my answers two-fingered into his desktop computer. He seems satisfied with my minimalist replies.

I realise, of course, that he knows the answers in advance. By this point, the FSB has apparently broken into my flat, bugged my phone and hacked into my email account. There isn't much that will surprise them. Since a formal investigation has been opened against me, their activities may even be "legal" – though legal doesn't mean much in a state that uses politically susceptible courts to enforce its wishes. After 55 minutes Kuzmin announces that our interview is over. It is 11.10am. He gives me my witness statement. I sign it. The atmosphere inside the room has become drowsy, and somnolent. I have heard no noise at all – no footsteps outside, and certainly no laughter, merely a strange and unsettling silence penetrating Lefortovo's etiolated corridors. I want a drink. But I decline to touch the fizzy water, fearing – unreasonably, I'm sure – it may have been tampered with.

For a moment, I'm tempted to ask Kuzmin questions of my own. Principally: did you order the break-in at my flat? Whom did you send? Is there now a bug in my bedroom? And do you have children yourself? Kuzmin is businesslike. He shakes me by the hand. He even gives me a gift. It is a 2007 FSB calendar. There are no pictures – this isn't the FSB's style. But the words "Investigations department, Lefortovo prison" are written above the months of the year in clear silver capitals against a deep purple background. The calendar includes the FSB's escutcheon-like crest: a sword and shield, in scarlet, decorated with the two-headed Romanov eagle. The sword and shield is the same motif as the KGB's; the Russian Federation imperial eagle has updated the KGB's hammer and sickle. It looks as if the organisation sees itself as involved in some kind of heraldic mission, a bit like the Knights Templar or the Masons, I think.

I return to the *Guardian*'s dilapidated office-kitchen, and cook myself some gooseberries. The gooseberries are one of many seasonal fruits sold by the *babushkas*, or old ladies, outside my metro station. They also trade in women's jumpers, leather gloves and warm socks. I hang the calendar in our small corridor next to the kitchen. Maybe the calendar will give me protection in the months ahead. It turns out I will need it.

Vladimir Putin succeeded Boris Yeltsin in 2000. Swiftly, he created a pastiche neo-Soviet Russia. The FSB became the pre-eminent power in the land – a huge, secret, prodigiously resourced organisation that operates outside the framework of the law according to its own set of (also secret) rules. After the collapse of the Soviet Union, the KGB had been dissolved. But it didn't disappear: it simply got a new name. In 1995 most of the KGB's operations were transferred to the new FSB. The FSB is Russia's main domestic spy agency and state security organisation. Nominally, it carries out the same functions as the FBI and other western law enforcement agencies – criminal prosecution, organised crime and counter-terrorism. But its most important job is counter-espionage.

This means Russia's tiny and demoralised band of opposition politicians, who remain on the margins of public life until mass protests against Putin begin in 2011. It means human rights activists; workers for foreign NGOs; and ambitious billionaire tycoons like Khodorkovsky who fail to observe the Putin regime's rules – obey the state and stay out of politics. It means foreign diplomats, especially American and British ones. And it also appears to mean troublesome western journalists.

Most dangerously, though, it means traitors. It appears clear to me – and, as leaked US diplomatic cables subsequently show, to the British and US governments as well – that there had been an FSB dimension to the murder in London of Litvinenko, a Russian dissident. Litvinenko died in a London hospital in November 2006, three weeks after sipping a cup of green tea poisoned with radioactive polonium-210. Litvinenko was a former FSB officer. So is his alleged killer, Andrei Lugovoi.

By the time of Litvinenko's murder, former KGB agents – part of a powerful group of officers with intelligence or military backgrounds known as the *siloviki* – had risen to key positions inside Putin's Kremlin. Putin had retired as a KGB agent in 1991. His own KGB career had been undistinguished. He had reached the rank of lieutenant colonel, and had served in the KGB's foreign intelligence unit. The collapse of the Soviet bloc found him stranded in the unglamorous East German town of Dresden, where he worked undercover in the Soviet Union's cultural institute.

Apparently Lieutenant-Colonel Putin had made several blunders. He had been recalled from Dresden to work as an assistant to the deputy rector of Leningrad University, an obscure and humiliating demotion. It was at this point, however, that Putin's fortunes changed. He began work for Anatoly Sobchak, St Petersburg's liberal mayor, a fierce enemy of the KGB and one of Russia's leading democrats. Putin prospered.

By 1999 he had become head of the FSB. In the summer of 1999 President Yeltsin picked the obscure Putin to become prime minister – endorsing him as his successor just months later. Once president, Putin elevated trusted members of Russia's security services into the governorships of Russia's provinces, into ministries, and into the directorships of Russia's state-owned companies. Putin's former spy cronies from St Petersburg were running the country, despite having little or no competence in economic matters. The KGB, then, were back.

But there were important differences. As the journalists Andrei Soldatov and Irina Borogan note, the Soviet-era KGB was subordinate to the political will of the Communist party. The party was in control of every KGB directorate, department or division. The FSB, by contrast, is "a remarkably independent entity, free of party control and parliamentary oversight", they write. The service enjoys extraordinary autonomy and freedom – even to the point of plotting and carrying out assassinations abroad of alleged Kremlin enemies.

Soldatov and Borogan call their 2010 study of the FSB and the restoration of the security services under Putin *The New Nobility*. The title is apt. The phrase comes from a speech made by Nikolai Patrushev, who in 1999

9

succeeded Putin as FSB director. It alludes to the enormous influence and wealth accrued by the agency's shadowy personnel. The FSB differs from its western counterparts and its immediate predecessor, the Soviet secret service. "In some ways the FSB most closely resembles the ruthless *mukhabarat*, the secret police of the Arab world: devoted to the protection of authoritarian regimes, answering only to those in power, impenetrable, thoroughly corrupted, and unopposed to employing brutal methods against individuals suspected of terrorism or dissent," the authors, later good friends, write.

Privately, US diplomats offer a different analogy. They liken the agency to Russia's pre-revolutionary secret police. In a classified 2009 cable to FBI director Robert S Mueller, ahead of Mueller's visit to Moscow, the US ambassador John Beyrle compares the FSB to the secret agents who once worked for the Russian empire. The FSB's imperial predecessor was responsible for fighting leftwing revolutionary activity and political terror. Its tactics included undercover agents and covert operations. "Despite the changes since the collapse of the Soviet Union, Russia's security services more closely resemble the model of the tsarist-era *Okhrana* (secret police) than western law-enforcement institutions," Beyrle tells the FBI.

Beyrle also references two other modern agencies responsible for state security: the SVR, Russia's foreign intelligence service; and the MVD, the interior ministry, with more than 190,000 soldiers in its internal security division. All three agencies are embroiled in the Kremlin's political battles, he says, and often compete for influence against each other, "with shadowy conflicts occasionally bubbling to the surface". Their enthusiasm for pursuing investigations depends directly on political factors. All use the courts as a weapon against political enemies.

Their chief objective, however, is to protect Russia's ruling power elite. This task has become more pressing following the pro-western "colour revolutions" in Georgia and Ukraine. Beyrle correctly points out that the security services blame the US and other western powers for inciting the demonstrations and the overthrow – in 2003 and 2004 respectively – of governments in Tbilisi and Kiev. "State security remains the services' primary responsibility and all three organisations devote considerable attention and resources to counter-intelligence and domestic intelligence work," Beyrle tells Washington.

Given his KGB background, it's not surprising that Putin has remade the government in his own image. Sociologists estimate that in 2003 the number of senior Kremlin officials with a security/military background was 25%. By 2007 it is 42%. The figure includes only known former agents. It excludes those whose KGB activity was disguised with a "legend" – the spy world's shorthand for a cover story. By 2006 the figure for "affiliated" *siloviki* – including both official and unofficial agents – is an astonishing 77%. Over the past decade the FSB has acquired new responsibilities. Its budget has grown. The exact size of the agency is a closely guarded state secret. But Soldatov and Borogan estimate the FSB now has more than 200,000 agents. In February 2010 US defence secretary, Robert Gates, observes that democracy in Russia has practically vanished. Instead, the country is an "oligarchy run by the security services".

Beyrle's deputy, Eric Rubin, ponders the FSB's ideological outlook in another dispatch. He describes the heads of Russia's modern security services as "pragmatic hardliners":

[They] share a worldview of Soviet xenophobia and distrust of the west that portrays the US as actively working to destabilise Russia. At the same time, they appreciate the benefits that co-operation with the US provides, not only in achieving their assigned missions, but also in enhancing their country's position internationally.

The *siloviki*, or power guys, view the demise of the Soviet Union as a humiliating disaster – in the words of Vladimir Putin, "the greatest geopolitical catastrophe of the 20th century". Their "historic" mission – as they see it – is to restore Russia's lost greatness. It is to assert the country's resurgent international power and its new economic might, derived from a massive increase across the early part of the 21st century in global oil and gas prices.

I arrive in Moscow in January 2007. At this moment Russia isn't quite a superpower again, despite President Putin's best efforts to throw his weight around on the international stage, and his undoubted gift at G8 gatherings and other top-level get-togethers for sardonic repartee mixed with snide remarks about western hypocrisy and double-dealing. Critics see Russia as domestically repressive and internationally dangerous. True or not,

Russia leads the global community in one respect. It has become the world's foremost spy-state. Its obsession with spying can reach ridiculous heights. In December 2008 legislators in North Ossetia even name a peak in the Caucasus after Russia's brave spies. The previously unnamed mountain, towering 3,269 metres in the Sugansky Ridge, close to the border with Georgia, is called the Peak of Russian Counterintelligence Agents.

The summons to Lefortovo is one outward aspect of my strange new Moscow life. The other is more furtive and unpleasant: pernicious official snooping by a state that has no compunction in rifling through my correspondence, bugging phones, and invading our privacy. Within hours of publication of the *Guardian*'s Berezovsky story someone has hacked into my email account. Emails tagged with the name "Berezovsky" mysteriously reappear in my inbox, only to vanish again minutes later. Someone else claiming to be from the "president's office" calls demanding my private mobile phone number. I tell them to ring the office. A middle-aged woman, casually dressed and with – I note – a rather bad 1970s-ish haircut, rings the street bell outside my Voikovskaya flat at 7am. I don't buzz her in. Somehow she finds her way up to the 10th floor and knocks on my door. I open it. She examines me closely and leaves.

There are further examples of weirdness, verging on the surreal. On 15 April 2007, I fly from Moscow to London on Aeroflot for a family funeral. I walk through the last security gate. As I go to pick up my belt and laptop, someone slaps me, hard, on the left shoulder, from behind. I turn round. There is a young man, with slick-backed dark hair wearing a leather jacket – the unmistakeable uniform of the KGB spook. He is smirking. "There is something wrong with your jacket," he says, speaking in English with a strong Russian accent. "No there isn't," I reply testily. The man nods, slips to the front of the queue, and disappears. I look for him on the plane but cannot see him.

After take-off, I make my way to the Aeroflot bathroom. I take off my jacket and shirt. I peer at my shoulder. Nothing there. At least nothing I can see. But I wouldn't actually know what a recording or tracking device looks like, I reflect. Back in Moscow a few days later, I get my first taste of old-fashioned KGB-style surveillance. I arrange to meet the BBC's delightful Moscow correspondent, Richard Galpin, for a drink; we agree to rendezvous at the Winston Churchill pub in Sokol, a suburb not far from my Moscow home. Fearing unwanted company, we meet outside and move off instead to a nearby Moscow coffee bar.

We sit in the basement. The cafe is deserted. We are the only customers. After 20 minutes, two men in leather jackets appear. They appear to be junior agents. One of them inquires politely, *Mozhno?* – may I? – and sits down next to me on a low wooden bench. His thigh is one inch from my thigh. He puts a holdall next to us, presumably containing a listening device. As undercover agents, the pair come across as the most bungling in history, more Chief Inspector Jacques Clouseau than KGB. It's only later I learn that the agents are engaged in *demonstrativnaya slezhka* – demonstrative pursuit. Their goal isn't so much intelligence gathering as low-level harassment and general irritation. Richard and I laugh, pay the bill, and depart – leaving our new friends behind. The encounter is nearly funny. But, I reflect, these provincial thugs may be the same ones who broke into our flat and opened my son's window, with its long, unambiguous plunge to the courtyard below.

A few days later I find myself sitting in a comfy upstairs meeting room at the British embassy in Moscow. The room differs from others inside the embassy building in one important respect: it doesn't exist. At least not officially. The embassy's security officer fixes me with a friendly smile; next to him is Britain's deputy ambassador in Moscow, Sian MacLeod. Before entering I had solemnly stuffed my mobile in a cabinet outside.

The room is the only part of Her Majesty's embassy in Moscow not bugged by the Russians, the officer explains ruefully. "Everywhere else isn't safe," he admits. Inside, the room looks a bit like a music recording studio; it has padded soundproof walls, a long conference table, chairs, and a large map of the Russian Federation. It feels like the sort of emergency meeting room familiar to fans of *Doctor Who*. The officer explains that I'm not the first person to suffer at the hands of the FSB's notorious "burglary squad". Its existence is Moscow's worst kept diplomatic secret, he says. The agency has broken into the flats of numerous other western diplomats and local Russian staffers; the ritual is almost an accepted part of Moscow embassy life.

The FSB's tactics are bizarre. After breaking in, agents often turn off freezers; they defecate in loos (which they then don't flush); and – on occasion – they pocket the TV remote control. They return it weeks later. Another favourite tactic is to introduce an item of low value – a cuddly toy or squishy elephant – that hadn't been there before. The aim is psychological: to harass the victim and perhaps even to persuade them that they are going quietly bonkers. "We don't talk about it publicly. But, no, you are not going mad. There's no doubt the FSB broke into your flat. We have a file this thick of similar cases," the officer says, conjuring with his hands a five- or six-inch deep pile. "Generally we don't make a fuss about it."

The officer gives me several tips. One of the most important is to steer clear of femmes fatales, he says – a ploy from the KGB's playbook but still very much in use by its modern successor. "First, avoid Moscow's numerous attractive young women: the many strip-bars, nightclubs, and honey-pots in Moscow where you can easily become the victim of an FSB set up." He also confirms that my flat will now be bugged. "There isn't much you can do about this. Trying to identify or remove the bugs will merely trigger the FSB's return," he says, helpfully.

Nor is there any point in changing the locks; the FSB dispatch professionals who can slip through any door with ease. If there is anything sensitive I want to discuss, I should write it down in felt-tip pen. (Afterwards, the trick is to soak the conversation and flush it down the toilet. My wife and I try this for two days. I even draw myself being pursued by a long-toothed cartoon monster, beneath the words "Fascist Beast". But the novelty of felt-tip conversations quickly wears off. For the rest of my stay in Moscow Phoebe and I take a stroll in the garden instead.)

The officer has a few other pieces of advice. Though the FSB is well resourced, most of its agents can't speak English. "It is necessary for them to get close to you – close enough to make a decent audio recording of any conversation. The FSB don't like getting out of their cars and will rarely pursue you on the Moscow metro – though they can if they want. And there's no point in worrying about surveillance. The agency has a hundred different methods." The Russian security services' favourite gadget is distinctly practical: a man-bag – normally placed on a table close to where you are speaking. Finally, the officer explains that when making arrangements it takes a KGB-FSB surveillance team 20 minutes to get into position. "If you've got anything important to say, do it in the first five minutes."

I leave the embassy. I set off home. The conversation has been enlightening. There's clearly no point in looking for the bugs. Nor is there any sense in complaining to the Russian police about the intrusion at my family home. Any complaint is likely simply to elicit a polite response from the officers on duty that I am suffering from paranoia. The non-burglary burglaries, then, have a kind of brutal logic to them. How do you officially complain to a state about a break-in, when the culprits are working for – and sent by – the state?

The FSB's invisible presence continues; the agency becomes an intangible part of my Moscow life. The city's late spring turns into a hot, sticky summer. After work I go for dips in the pond just behind our suburban tower-block home, jogging through the pine trees down to a small wooded shrine and spring, where pensioners fill bottles full of holy water, wheeling them carefully home. From here I run along a little boggy track and past banks of purple flowering Himalayan balsam. Fishermen dressed in green hunting jackets sit contentedly on the banks of the lake; sometimes they catch a small carp-like fish. Next to them volleyball players gather under the birch trees.

Politically, in late 2007, there is only one question of significance: who will Vladimir Putin nominate to be his successor? Or will he, as is commonly assumed, continue to run the world's biggest country through some extralegal route? After eight years in office, and two consecutive presidential terms, Putin is obliged by Russia's constitution to step down.

The Kremlin's rivalrous factions – and most Russian voters – would be happy to see him carry on. But this would mean sacrificing one thing that Putin seeks – international respect. Despite his anti-western outbursts, which become more frequent in 2007, Putin enjoys schmoozing President George W Bush and other world leaders. An unconstitutional third term would make him little better than Islam Karimov or Nursultan Nazarbayev – neighbouring Central Asian despots who maintain their presidential rule indefinitely "at the will of the people". It would also invite analogies with Alexander Lukashenko, the authoritarian multi-term president of neighbouring Belarus, and a leader so awful that the then-US secretary of state Condoleezza Rice dubs him Europe's last dictator. In the autumn of 2007, it's hard to discern what is going on inside the Kremlin – not just for western journalists, but even for those who work there.

At the same time, the FSB's campaign of harassment against me continues – always pettily, sometimes loudly, sometimes quietly, with someone in a backroom clearly turning the volume of minor persecution up and down. Russia has a long tradition of spying on its citizens – a practice defined in France in the 18th century as "perlustration". As US diplomats point out in classified cables, the "regrettable" habit of official snooping dates back to Catherine the Great; the empress had sequestered rooms at the post office for special services known as "black offices". "Soviet governments were less subtle; officials automatically examined all international correspondence, and a special perlustration division was housed in a building at the main centre for highway and rail transportation in Moscow," US diplomat Dave Kostelancik writes. The practice continues under Putin: in 2009 Russia's communications ministry issues a decree allowing eight law enforcement agencies including the FSB access to citizens' mail and electronic correspondence. In reality, the practice is already widespread.

That someone also listens to my phone calls is made clear most days. FSB agents cut the line whenever my conversation strays into sensitive areas. Mentioning words like "Berezovsky" or "Litvinenko" means the immediate end of any call. (For a while, I substitute the word "banana" for Berezovsky. Amazingly, this appears to work.) Discussions of Kremlin politics also end badly – with the frustrating "beep beep" of a disconnected line.

Sometimes more harmless subjects also provoke the wrath of my invisible listener – or listeners. Live interviews, in which I talked about Putin and the nature of the Russian state, are particularly liable to disruption. During one broadcast with Radio New Zealand the line is cut five times – a record. I feel almost proud of this. The conversation is terminated even when I talk about the recent discovery of a perfectly preserved baby woolly mammoth, dug up by a lucky reindeer herder in Russia's frozen Arctic north. How could a conversation about a 16,000-year-old extinct mammoth endanger the security of the Russian state? But who am I to judge what might compromise Russia's path back to greatness?

At first I wonder whether my silent listeners might not actually be real people but merely automated software, programmed to intervene when certain key words are spoken. Later, though, I grow convinced the listeners exist. They are real. But who are they? And who are the unseen ghosts who haunt our flat?

In early December 2007, I arrange a meeting with Olga Kryshtanovskaya, Russia's foremost expert on Kremlin elites, and a researcher at the institute of sociology at Russia's Academy of Sciences. Unusually for a sociologist, Kryshtanovskaya has feet in both camps: she has good contacts inside The Firm, as the FSB styles itself, but is also a reputable academic. I take the metro out to Kryshtanovskaya's home in the northern Moscow suburb of Medvedkovo.

Olga is a short, slightly plump woman of middle years, dressed in a burgundy jacket and with gold-rimmed glasses; her gaze is kindly, unblinking and ingenuous.

Sitting in her living room, and clad in a pair of her guest slippers, I ask Kryshtanovskaya about the FSB's methods. What she says is illuminating. The FSB maintains a listening station somewhere in Podmoskovie – in Moscow's suburbs, she says. Its existence, like everything connected to the agency, is a state secret. The FSB has its own special department for spying on foreign diplomats, Kryshtanovskaya adds; she thinks it probably has one for watching foreign journalists as well. The listeners are told whom they have to listen to – 24-hour surveillance is expensive but required in certain cases; other targets are listened to intermittently.

But isn't this rather boring work, I wonder? After all, who would want to eavesdrop on the inane traffic between the *Guardian*'s correspondents and its foreign desk in London? Or – as Neil Buckley, the bureau chief for the *Financial Times* in Moscow puts it – discussion of whether his infant son Alexander has done a poo that morning? "The special technical centre works on a shift system. Workers are normally on duty for an eight-hour shift. It's monotonous work. The workers are not creative. After each shift they write a report," Kryshtanovskaya tells me. She adds: "The thing that keeps them going is the idea that they are serving their country and defeating its enemies."

This patriotic instinct is key. She continues: "The FSB is a powerful organisation. Its recruits feel flattered to be serving the state, even in a lowly capacity." Typically, its personnel are drawn from the army – known in Russian as jackboots (*sapogi*). Others come from civilian life; they are known as the jackets (*pidzhaki*). The biggest distinction within the hidden world of Russia's security services is between intelligence and counter-intelligence operatives, Kryshtanovskaya says. Those who had worked in intelligence gathering – including Putin and Sergei Ivanov, Russia's hawkish former defence minister – tend to be brighter and more flexible. They know foreign languages (Putin German, Ivanov English and Swedish).

The most fanatical hardliners come from counter-intelligence, Kryshtanovskaya suggests. These officers she characterises as zombies. "These people were brought up in the Soviet Union. They were super-isolationist. They didn't know anything about the west. They were not allowed to travel abroad. They were fed zombie propaganda and ended up as orthodox fanatics. The intelligence agents who worked abroad had experience of the world. They were more liberal, more educated and more flexible." I like Kryshtanovskaya more and more. She speaks quietly, but with persuasive eloquence.

Despite its internal differences the FSB remains a remarkably homogenous organisation – with its own distinct *siloviki* mentality. This means, among other things: suspicion of everything; the conviction that Russia is surrounded by hostile enemies; the belief that the west and Nato are out to "destabilise" it. If Russia isn't surrounded by enemies then the FSB's rationale for existing would disappear, Kryshtanovskaya points out; the organisation would vanish in a puff of conspiratorial smoke. "No enemies means no KGB." This explains a lot.

As Russia moves towards parliamentary "elections" in December 2007, Putin's list of enemies grows steadily longer, I notice. In a pre-election speech in Moscow's Luzhniki football stadium, the president – dressed in a black polo-neck jumper – memorably denounces Russia's democrats as "jackals". The country's liberals are foreign agents, intent on wrecking Russia's carefully crafted stability, he tells a crowd of supporters from the pro-Kremlin United Russia party – borrowing a line from the Stalin era. He says the same thing four years later when tens of thousands of middle-class Russians turn out to protest against massive fraud in the 2011 poll. Not content with disparaging his opponents as western stooges, he suggests that the white ribbon worn by demonstrators looks like a condom.

The FSB remains an attractive employer. Membership of this most secret of clubs offers certain benefits – benefits that compensate for the relatively derisory level of pay. "If you work for the FSB you don't have to worry about the law. You can kill someone and nothing will happen," Kryshtanovskaya says. Mow down an old lady at a pedestrian crossing while drunk, or wipe out a business rival – the state will always protect you. "It's not surprising that FSB people have a special feeling. It's like being Superman," she says.

I ask Kryshtanovskaya about the 2006 murder of Alexander Litvinenko. Senior officers in the FSB had privately admitted to her that Litvinenko's assassination must have been an FSB operation, she says. They had no regrets whatsoever about the target – a traitor to Russia and someone who deserved to be murdered – but were unimpressed by the bungling and messy way his assassination was carried out. The KGB had murdered its enemies much more efficiently and tidily under Yuri Andropov – the former KGB chief, who succeeded Leonid Brezhnev in 1982 as general secretary of the Communist party of the USSR. Andropov is now revered in secret service circles: he is the hardliners' hardliner and the subject of a Putin propaganda campaign. There are Andropov scholarships to the FSB's Moscow training academy. As part of Andropov's posthumous rehabilitation, Putin in 1999 restored a memorial plaque to the KGB leader on the Lubyanka, the FSB's gloomy Moscow HQ.

"My FSB friends told me this [Litvinenko's bungled assassination] would never have happened under Andropov," Kryshtanovskaya says. "They told me that the KGB was much more efficient at murdering in those days."

I say goodbye. On her doorstep, I give her back the guest slippers. She gives me a word of advice.

"Be careful," she says.

"Why?"

"Because you are an enemy of Putin," she says, matter-of-factly.

CHAPTER 2

The Money Trail

The Academy Cafe, Bolshaya Bronnaya Street, Moscow
17 December 2007

*If you really want to understand the Putin regime in depth ...
go directly to the fiction department and take home
everything you can find by Mario Puzo.*
GARRY KASPAROV

The Academy Cafe is a short stroll from Moscow's Pushkin Square. It is a congenial place to meet. Here, lissom girls with ash-blonde hair flick through the latest copies of *Vogue*; a supercilious doorman takes your coat; outside, rows of black four-wheel-drives and luxury BMWs clog the icy pavement; inside, waitresses in smart white blouses glide among the tables. The cafe is a kind of junior common room for Russia's new modish rich. Its fashionably dressed denizens are the runaway winners in Putin's new Russia. Round the corner is the lilac-shaded boulevard ring, running along the line of Moscow's old city walls, past theatres, mansions, monuments and the yellow neoclassical church where the poet Alexander Pushkin was married.

Stanislav Belkovsky suggests we talk in the cafe. Belkovsky, a Russian political analyst and former speechwriter for Boris Berezovsky, is a man with influential contacts deep inside the Kremlin. Belkovsky has an astonishing tale to tell. In the summer of 2006 he published a book on Vladimir Putin's finances. In it, he alleged that the president has secretly accumulated a very large fortune. Belkovsky then went further. In an interview in November

2007 with the German newspaper *Die Welt* he claimed that the president's secret assets now amount to more than $40 billion – a figure that would make him the richest man in Russia – in Europe, indeed.

Putin is far wealthier than the billionaire oligarch Roman Abramovich, Belkovsky had claimed. In 2007, Abramovich, owner of the west London Chelsea Football Club, is – officially at least – Russia's richest individual, with a $19.2 billion fortune.

I am intrigued. Belkovsky turns up half an hour late; he's been stuck in one of Moscow's notorious traffic jams. Dressed in a smart black suit, and with a bushy beard and ample paunch, he resembles a prosperous, well fed, and highly intelligent medieval abbot. Belkovsky speaks impeccable English. He calmly explains that the aim of his publications is not to embarrass Putin but merely to rectify the west's erroneous image of him.

Over the past eight years, the west had been distracted by Putin's "neo-Soviet image", Belkovsky says. In reality, he is merely a "classic post-Soviet businessman", whose personal psychology was shaped while working under Anatoly Sobchak in the St Petersburg's mayor's office in the mafia-and-crime-ridden early 90s. Unlike Russia's former Soviet leaders, Putin and his inner circle have no ideology, he says. They are simply interested in making money. They are, in short, kleptocrats.

Over a cup of bitter espresso, I turn the conversation towards Belkovsky's sensational allegations. Does he have any proof? And who are his informants?

Citing as his sources senior figures inside the president's own administration, Belkovsky says that Putin owns vast holdings in three Russian oil companies. These are concealed behind a "non-transparent network of offshore companies". Putin "in effect" controls 37% of Surgutneftegaz, an oil exploration firm and Russia's third biggest oil producer, worth $20 billion, Belkovsky says. He also owns 4.5% of Gazprom, the state energy giant, and "at least 75%" of Gunvor, a mysterious Swiss-based oil trader, owned by Guennadi Timtchenko. Timtchenko is a St Petersburg friend from the early 1990s. Timtchenko, like Putin, is rumoured to have served in the foreign affairs directorate of the KGB – a claim he denies. Gunvor's turnover in 2007 is $48 billion, with profits of almost $500 million – an astonishing sum even by the galactic standards of the oil industry.

Our jaw-dropping conversation goes like this:

"How much is Putin worth?"

"I think at least $40 billion," Belkovksy says. "The maximum I cannot know. I suspect there are some businesses I know nothing about. Maybe more. Maybe much more. He's the richest man in Europe for sure. The King of Saudi Arabia has $21 billion, which is half of Putin's wealth."

"How is Putin's wealth concealed?"

"There's a non-transparent scheme of successive ownership of offshore companies and funds, with the final point in Zug [in Switzerland] and Liechtenstein. Putin should be the beneficial owner. It would be non-transparent for any company where he has some interests."

"Is there a way we can prove any of this?"

"It would be difficult. But maybe a little bit easier after Putin quits," Belkovsky says. He adds: "Putin's wealth isn't a secret among the elites. And you should note that Vladimir Vladimirovich has never sued me."

The story, it strikes me, is outlandish and extraordinary. But it is also highly plausible. As any motorist in Moscow can testify, corruption in Russia begins with the traffic police, the dreaded *gaishniki*, who routinely demand a 500 rouble (£10) bribe for imaginary traffic offences. This chain of corruption appears to stretch to the very top of the Kremlin.

The official rhetoric coming from the Kremlin during the mid Putin period is relentlessly anti-western: Russia routinely denounces the US administration's plans to site elements of its missile defence shield in central Europe. It disagrees with the international community on a host of other problems: Kosovo, whose independence Moscow bitterly opposes; Iran's nuclear programme, and what to do about it; and the disastrous US-led war in Iraq. It also skirmishes with the European Union over numerous other issues. Polish meat imports, for example; and an Estonian decision to shift a monument to a Red Army soldier, which in May 2007 prompts a massive cyber-attack by Kremlin hackers on the Estonian government.

Putin's anti-western campaign is much more equivocal, however, than it seems, Belkovsky and other equally thoughtful analysts suggest.

There is a compelling reason for this: under communism, a senior Politburo official could hope for a comfortable Moscow apartment, a luxurious *dacha* on the Black Sea and a holiday in Warsaw Pact Bulgaria. Now, however, the Russian elite has its wealth hidden in the west. In addition, it is immeasurably richer than in Soviet times. It does not want to reach the point in its dealings with the world that its Swiss bank accounts are frozen – or its officials put on visa blacklists. According to Belkovsky, Putin's primary concern is to legitimise his assets in the west – and those of his "team" – and to ensure that nobody takes them away from him when, and if, he ever leaves power.

But the need to safeguard one's private fortune is paramount. This is especially true if the fortune is in eight or more digits. Any political uncertainty, therefore, can lead to insecurity among Russia's elite, and even panic. (One US diplomat compares it to "a feeding frenzy among those currently in high positions who fear their snouts could soon be torn from the trough.") As Putin prepares in 2007 to vacate the Kremlin – enacting a stage-managed transfer the following May to the post of prime minister – nervousness within the Kremlin erupts into full-blown clan warfare. This vicious tribal rivalry blows up four years later when Putin successfully manoeuvres to get his old job as president back. In 2006, while a fellow at the Reuters Institute of Journalism at Oxford University, and while embarking on the long task of learning Russian, I ask one of the members of the Russian faculty what he thinks about the Putin regime. "Opaque nastiness," he replies.

But by the late autumn of 2007, some light is being shed into the Kremlin's normally dark corners. As well as claims about Putin's personal corruption – previously discussed only in whispers – other intriguing details begin to emerge of Kremlin business deals, involving Russia's giant state-run energy corporations and billions and billions of dollars. In November 2007 a previously obscure fund manager, Oleg Shvartsman, gives an interview to Russia's *Kommersant* newspaper, in which he claims that he manages the finances of a group of very senior FSB officers. Shvartsman explains that the group – which also includes members of the SVR, Russia's foreign intelligence service – are involved in what he calls "velvet re-privatisations". The term is a confusing one. But it refers to the model of state capitalism that Putin and his bureaucratic team has built up since 2000.

In the 1990s a small group of businessmen had, with the help of Boris Yeltsin, become billionaires when Russia's state-owned industries were privatised, invariably acquiring valuable national assets for obscenely small sums of money. During the post-Yeltsin era, however, Putin had re-asserted control over the country's strategic natural resources. Suddenly, it was the state, in the form of the Kremlin's top bureaucrats and the *siloviki*, who controlled Russia's vast oil and gas reserves. Putin's cronies and associates became directors of Russia's leading energy companies.

Igor Sechin, Putin's deputy chief of staff and the leader of the Kremlin's hardline *siloviki* faction is chairman of Russia's state oil company, Rosneft, a post he will hold till 2011. Dmitry Medvedev – an ex-lawyer and Kremlin insider whom Putin endorsed in December 2007 to succeed him as president – runs the state gas monopoly Gazprom. Other ministers control Russia's railways, a nuclear energy conglomerate, and the aerospace industry. It is, as Perry Anderson writing in the *London Review of Books* puts it, a uniquely Russian form of *cumul des mandats* – the accumulation of mandates. Others sum it up more pithily. They call it "Kremlin Inc".

But this system of state-managed bureaucratic capitalism can hardly be described as disinterested. The officials who manage Russia's strategic industries grow very rich indeed. According to Shvartsman, senior FSB officers are keen to become even richer – by forcibly "de-privatising" successfully run private firms, threatening their owners with dire consequences if they fail to co-operate, and turning the firms into larger, and much more inefficiently managed, state corporations.

Shvartsman's embarrassing revelations appear part of a wider power struggle within the Kremlin. They are clearly damaging to the *siloviki* Kremlin faction led by Sechin. This group is made up of Kremlin officials with backgrounds in Russia's military and its intelligence services, including the FSB. It includes Nikolai Patrushev, the FSB's director, deputy Alexander Bortnikov, who succeeds Patrushev in 2008 as FSB chief, and Putin's aide Viktor Ivanov. It also numbers Mikhail Fradkov, who in late 2007 swaps his job as prime minister to become the new head of the SVR, as well as Rashid Nurgaliyev, Russia's interior minister.

In WikiLeaks cables, US diplomats make much of this intra-elite battle. They depict it as a struggle for Russia's soul between the cold-war-obsessed *siloviki* and the more western-friendly modernisers. The *siloviki* are cast as the most influential opponents of Washington's engagement agenda with Moscow – a fact that diplomats attribute to their lack of experience of

Europe or the US. Bortnikov spends his entire career within the FSB working on economic issues, including a stint as head of the FSB's Economic Security Directorate. He also reputedly helps spearhead Putin's campaign against any possibly unreliable oligarchs. Fradkov, by contrast, a former Soviet intelligence agent in the 1970s, does at least have some connections abroad; he serves as Russia's ambassador to the EU between 2003 and 2004.

The White House views these divisions in ideological and conceptual terms. A cable from US ambassador John Beyrle to FBI director Robert Mueller describes the *siloviki* as a group that believes a strong state "exercising effective control is the answer to most political and economic problems". According to the ambassador, the *siloviki*'s main enemies are a group of "liberals" or modernisers. They include Medvedev, who, unusually for a senior Kremlin figure, has no background in Russia's repressive security services. Others in the Medvedev clan include Abramovich, who is close to both the Putin and the Yeltsin families, and Alisher Usmanov, the Uzbek-born billionaire and Arsenal FC shareholder. The US ambassador believes the modernisers "recognise that Russia's future depends on integration with the world economy and that confronting some of the country's most stubborn problems – such as corruption – requires transparency and the impartial application of the law".

Over a second cup of espresso, however, Belkovsky is snortingly dismissive of the Americans' good-guys-bad guys analysis. "There are many groups, not just two. I estimate there are some 15 groups [inside Russia's power structures]," he says. "They can be united around some big discussions. But there is no difference in ideology between them." He continues: "There are certainly no liberals or *siloviki*. It isn't a liberal/*siloviki* conflict. It's about money and security, and providing security for their money. Nothing more. They are business competitors with the same purposes and goals."

Money is what counts in Russia, according to Belkovsky. He describes Putin's team as "really devoted adherents to the money religion … This regime is a classical third world kleptocracy, established and governed and ruled by people with no metaphysical needs, and who believe there are no ideologies at all." Putin's preferred method of dealing with a political problem – indeed his solution to most of Russia's economic and social difficulties – is to throw money at it, Belkovsky says. Putin remains sceptical of liberal methods such as reform. "He's quite sure that money is a universal stimulus. For the past eight years in power Putin has got some proofs that this thesis [is correct]," Belkovsky concludes.

Like what, I ask. Belkovsky points to the fact that in 2005 Putin hired Gerhard Schröder – just out of a job as German chancellor – to become chairman of the controversial Nord Stream consortium, building a gas pipeline under the Baltic. (It turned out the chief executive of the project was none other than a former East German secret police officer whom Putin knew from his KGB days.) Belkovsky adds: "Putin's also bought Silvio Berlusconi. Ridiculous? Not if WikiLeaks cables published a couple of years later are to be believed.

In the autumn of 2007 Russia finds itself gripped by vicious intra-clan warfare. In October the FSB detains General Alexander Bulbov, the deputy head of the Federal Drugs Agency, and part of the "liberal" group. His arrest sees a surreal standoff between his personal bodyguards and FSB agents, who waggle their machine guns at each other. The following month the Sechin clan strikes again – when Russia's bearded deputy finance minister Sergei Storchak – another "liberal" – is arrested and charged with embezzling $43.4 million. His boss, finance minister Alexei Kudrin, part of the liberal clan, defends Storchak and says he is innocent. This isn't enough, however, to get Storchak out of Lefortovo prison – though he is eventually released. (I later meet Storchak at a party. I ask him why he was arrested. "No idea," he replies. He adds that he spent a lot of time in jail reading the Bible.)

In the dying days of 2007, then, the question of who will succeed Vladimir Putin as president preoccupies the Kremlin's twitchy elite. This isn't just a question of political preferences but of financial – possibly even personal – survival. In theory, any new president can take away the old elite's assets, just as Putin did with Yeltsin-era oligarchs like Khodorkovsky. Yeltsin was canny enough to strike a deal with Putin, his successor: Putin's first act as president was to grant Yeltsin and Yeltsin's family immunity from prosecution. "Once Putin leaves power he will be accused. Inevitably. It's the great tradition. When Putin quits he faces the question of how to legalise his funds, and all his friends' funds and assets in the west," Belkovsky says. "This is a very painful and sensitive question for Putin."

As WikiLeaks shows, this question is critical in determining whom Putin endorses as his Kremlin successor. For much of Spring 2007, the smart money is on Sergei Ivanov, the smooth, impressive, English-speaking first deputy prime minister. Ivanov is given star billing at the St Petersburg economic forum. But in the late autumn Putin plumps instead for Medvedev, a less charismatic and much weaker figure. At less than five feet and four inches tall, Medvedev has a stocky upper body and short legs. He is of even smaller stature than Putin, in a cabinet of already quite diminutive men. The choice is – on the face of it – a surprising one.

But for Putin, Medvedev's selection is entirely logical. In an illuminating WikiLeaks dispatch, the US deputy assistant secretary of state David Kramer refers to Putin's "hidden assets", and suggests that they play a crucial part in Russia's Byzantine succession process. Citing opposition sources, Kramer repeats the view that Putin won't stay on as president for an unconstitutional third term. Instead, Kramer writes to Beyrle, Putin "is nervously trying to secure his future immunity from potential law enforcement investigations into his alleged illicit proceeds".

The president's chief concern, as he prepares to exit the Kremlin, is to find a weak and, above all, loyal successor, Kramer writes, in a cable with some names redacted:

XXXXXXX said that popular opinion in Moscow believes that Sergei Ivanov is out of the running for president. He commented that Putin was afraid of Ivanov, deeply distrustful, and that he needed a weaker figure to succeed him instead. He argued that Putin understands that under the system he has created there is no real rule of law and that at any time anyone can be arrested or businesses destroyed. Since Putin reportedly had secret assets tied up abroad (working through proxies like oligarch XXXXXXX), he worried that with a strong successor like Ivanov the tables could be turned on Putin, making him the object of law enforcement investigations and Interpol warnings.

The question for me is what to do with this sensational story, alleging that Putin has secretly accumulated billions of dollars, and is one of the world's richest men. I'm conscious the leak about Putin's finances could be malicious and/or planted rumour. But Belkovsky is no maverick or crackpot: he is the head of a respected Moscow think tank, the National Strategy Institute. He is quoted frequently in the press, including in pro-Kremlin publications. He writes books, plays and commentaries. I later learn from WikiLeaks that he is a regular interlocutor for the US; embassy officials keenly seek out his views.

At the same time, others are also publicly comparing the Russian regime to a mafia organisation. I'm struck by a piece written by Garry Kasparov. Published in the *Wall Street Journal*, it appears four months before my meeting with Belkovsky. Kasparov, the former world chess champion, is a well-known critic of the Kremlin and an opposition leader. And yet it's hard to disagree with his logic. He describes the Putin government as "unique in history". It is, he writes, "part oligarchy, with a small, tightly connected gang of wealthy rulers", and a "partly feudal system, broken down into semi-autonomous fiefdoms in which payments are collected from the serfs, who have no rights".

He continues: "If you really want to understand the Putin regime in depth I can recommend some reading. No Karl Marx or Adam Smith. Nothing by Montesquieu or Machiavelli, although the author you are looking for is of Italian descent ... Instead, go directly to the fiction department and take home everything you can find by Mario Puzo."

Kasparov recommends that students of the Russian government should turn to *The Godfather* for enlightenment, while not leaving out Puzo's later titles such as *The Last Don*, *Omertà* and *The Sicilian*. I read: "The web of betrayals, the secrecy, the blurred lines between what is business, what is government, and what is criminal – it's all there in Mr Puzo's books ... A Puzo fan sees the Putin government [more] accurately: the strict hierarchy, the extortion, the intimidation, the code of secrecy and, above all, the mandate to keep the revenue flowing. In other words, a mafia." His commentary is titled "Don Putin".

Even with a team of legal experts, and reams of secret Kremlin documents, though, it would be almost impossible to untangle the president's finances. But, I conclude, there is enough material for a carefully written story, setting out what has been alleged. Belkovsky's claims, moreover, are already circulating on the web.

After my chat with Belkovsky, I interview several other analysts, including Elena Panfilova, the head of Transparency International in Moscow, and a formidably eloquent observer of Russia's political scene.

Panfilova confirms the general thesis. In normal times there is an "inter-vertical loyalty", as she puts it, that stops the Kremlin's rival influence groups from attacking each other. This has now broken down, she suggests. The Sechin-FSB group and a "liberal" Kremlin clan are furiously dishing the dirt about each other. These leaks are not designed to promote greater trans-parency but to influence Putin, whom Panfilova dubs "the ultimate reader".

I resolve to write a story for the *Guardian*. My article runs on 18 December 2007 on the *Guardian*'s front page, under the headline, "Putin, the Kremlin war, and a secret $40 billion fortune". It begins: "An unprece-dented battle is taking place inside the Kremlin ahead of Vladimir Putin's departure from office, the *Guardian* has learned, with alleged details being revealed of the president's billion-dollar fortune. Rival clans inside the Kremlin are embroiled in a struggle for the control of assets as Putin prepares to transfer power to his hand-picked successor, Dmitry Medvedev, in May."

By mid-morning more than a quarter of a million people across the world have read the story. I wait, fearing the worst. But from the Kremlin there is a perplexing silence. The Kremlin, and Dmitry Peskov, simply ignore the alle-gations, refusing to issue a denial or even to comment. Gunvor, the Geneva-based firm which Putin allegedly controls, is more forthcoming. The company's chief executive officer Torbjörn Törnqvist fires off a letter to the *Guardian* saying that it is "plain wrong" to suggest that Putin "owns any part of Gunvor, or is a beneficiary of its activities". He adds: "This company is majority owned by its founders, Guennadi Timtchenko and myself, with a minority of the shares held by a third investor. None of the shares in this organisation are held by President Putin or by anyone allied to him."

Törnqvist also claims that Gunvor's profits are "in the hundreds of millions, and not the billions", and that this is not unusual "for a business of our scale operating in this sector". He does, however, make one startling admission: Putin and Timtchenko were indeed friends, something Gunvor had never previously confirmed. "Mr Timtchenko did indeed know President Putin in the days before the latter became famous. However, suggestions that they share a KGB heritage or have been in business together are completely wide of the mark."

The US State Department, however, appears sceptical of the company's claims. Two WikiLeaks cables from the embassy in Moscow shed some light on Gunvor and on the murky practices of Russia's oil export industry. One, sent to Washington in November 2008, begins: "The oil trading business in Russia has long been opaque, benefiting politically connected firms such as the secretive oil trading firm Gunvor." Citing oil industry experts, the cable says Russia has "a reputation for secretive deals involving intermediary companies with unknown owners and beneficiaries". It continues: "Oil exports from state-owned or state-influenced oil companies have reportedly been funnelled through favoured oil traders, potentially yielding billions of dollars of profits for these companies. Of particular note in the Russian oil trading business is Gunvor. The company is rumoured to be one of the sources of Putin's undisclosed wealth, and is owned by Guennadi Timtchenko, who is rumoured to be a former KGB colleague of Putin's." The cable also references Surgutneftegaz. Amazingly, it is unclear who actually owns it. Surgutneftegaz is "another reported source of Putin's illicit wealth".

The Americans, however, acknowledge that it is impossible to discover the truth about an industry that gives away little or no information about itself. The same cable lauds efforts by the Russian anti-corruption campaigner and blogger Alexey Navalny to force Russian oil companies to make greater disclosures. Navalny, a minority shareholder, carries out a series of doomed legal actions against Russian oil companies. His aim is to force them to reveal volumes of oil and terms of trade. In 2007 Navalny is a largely obscure figure. But by 2011 Navalny has attracted a national following; he is arrested in December after leading protests against rigged parliamentary elections. Navalny, and his anti-graft website RosPil.info, are the biggest single threat to the Kremlin. His nickname for United Russia – "the party of thieves and crooks" – sticks. He is talked of as a future president.

Navalny estimates Gunvor "may control up to 50% of total Russian oil exports". The company itself, in its glossy but uninformative brochure, admits to handling "one third of Russia's seaborne oil exports". In 2010 its turnover goes from $53 billion to $65 billion, with exports of 104 million tons. Navalny tells the US embassy he doesn't believe that Putin owns either Surgutneftegaz or Gunvor. His reasoning is simple and persuasive: he "does not really need to have a direct link from an asset to benefit from it".

My own dogged attempts to obtain an interview with Timtchenko prove fruitless. The company hires a PR consultant in London, Michael Prescott, with whom I exchange cordial emails. I send Prescott a list of questions. Prescott agrees to answer them. He doesn't. Gunvor remains unwilling to divulge details of the exact nature of the association between Putin and Timtchenko, or explain how and where they first met. There is no invitation to meet Timtchenko, or perhaps take a stroll around his luxurious mansion in the picturesque Swiss canton of Zug, a popular destination for publicity-shy international businessmen.

It takes another two months before Putin gets round to issuing his own denial of allegations of personal corruption. The venue is the Kremlin; the occasion Putin's grandiose annual press conference. This is the largest set-piece event of the Kremlin's media year: some 2,000 journalists, most of them Russian, gather in a giant two-tiered Kremlin auditorium, and get to lob questions at the leader of the world's largest country. I had attended my first Kremlin press conference a year earlier, in 2007 – it had been notable for its length (three and a half hours), for the surreal range of questions (including on gardening, and how to bring up children), and for the fact that escape from the cavernous Kremlin hall is impossible. It was also clear that the Kremlin carefully vets all questions in advance: the press conference, like so much of Russia's democracy, has the feel of a giant facade.

Some two hours into the 2008 press conference, Douglas Birch, the American bureau chief of the Associated Press, stands up. Speaking in halting Russian, he asks Putin about the corruption allegations and whether he is indeed the richest man in Europe. Putin is ready for this one; his face lights up and he breaks into a sour half-smile. "My richness is simply the richness of the Russian people," he says, sonorously. He then launches into an earthy pre-rehearsed attack: "This is just rubbish, picked out of someone's nose and smeared on bits of paper. The claims are nonsense –

rubbish – the kind of shit that people write in their little newspapers. There is nothing to it."

Putin makes no attempt to address the specific allegations about his beneficial ownership. Nor does he explain the nature of his relationship with Timtchenko. There is also no explanation as to why the Kremlin had kept silent on the allegations for eight weeks. (One version is that Putin's terrified aides did not dare to show him the article. Unlike Medvedev, Putin doesn't read newspapers or use the internet; in the words of one observer he is "informationally isolated".) The following day the *Moscow Times* runs a front-page story on the press conference, which includes a rejoinder from Belkovsky. "Mr Putin makes lots of claims, including that Russia is a thriving democracy. Given this I don't think we should take his comments about his personal wealth too seriously," he observes wryly.

In April 2008, meanwhile, *Forbes Russia* publishes its annual list of Russia's top 100 wealthiest individuals. The list makes compelling reading. It reveals that Russia now boasts 110 billionaires, more than any other country apart from the United States, which has 469 of them. Roman Abramovich has slipped down from first to third place, and is now worth a mere $24.3 billion. Officially at least, Russia's richest man is now the aluminium tycoon Oleg Deripaska, with a $28.6 billion fortune, followed by the steel billionaire Alexei Mordashov, in second place with $24.5 billion. Intriguingly, Timtchenko features in the list for the first time as its highest new entrant, with a fortune put at $2.5 billion. Another friend of Russia's president, Yuri Kovalchuk, the owner of the Rossiya bank, is worth $1.9 billion. Many of those on the list lived in the same exclusive *dacha* collective in St Petersburg as Putin. Timtchenko is one of them.

Putin himself figures nowhere – but as *Forbes Russia*'s editor-in-chief Mikhail Kashulinsky explains, the list doesn't include "government workers" or "officials". Asked whether being a friend of Vladimir Putin helps make you a billionaire, Kashulinsky is succinct. "Probably," he admits. "If you look at other people who are not Putin's friends, they are not as rich."

CHAPTER 3

Death of a Spy

Nightingale Grove Motel, Engels Street, Kursk, western Russia
22 November 2007

*Fried, noting Putin's "attention to detail", questioned whether
rogue security elements could operate in the UK ... without Putin's
knowledge. Describing the current atmosphere as strange, he described
the Russians as increasingly self-confident, to the point of arrogance.*
SECRET CABLE FROM THE US EMBASSY IN PARIS, 12 DECEMBER 2006,
QUOTING US ASSISTANT SECRETARY OF STATE DANIEL FRIED

It isn't the most auspicious moment to arrive in Moscow as a correspondent for a British newspaper. Four months earlier, Alexander Litvinenko – a former FSB spy who had sought asylum in the UK after falling out with his bosses – had been murdered in London. It was the most brazen assassination of modern times. Seemingly, a three-man hit squad dispatched from Moscow had carried out the killing. The murder weapon was unusual. It was a rare radioactive isotope, polonium-210. The substance suggested Russian state involvement. The killing, with its flavour of international nuclear terrorism, caused headlines around the world. It was hard to think of a bigger story. Relations between Britain and Russia had already been frosty; after the Litvinenko scandal it is beginning to look like a bad-natured re-run of the cold war.

Before long, three suspects for the murder emerge: Andrei Lugovoi, Dmitry Kovtun and Vyacheslav Sokolenko. All three are ex-KGB agents. During my four years in Moscow I will come across Lugovoi – Litvinenko's

alleged assassin – several times. In May 2007 I attend a stormy press conference given by Lugovoi, soon after Britain's Crown Prosecution Service
charges him with murder. The packed venue is the Moscow office of the
private Russian news agency Interfax. (It was here, in 1998, that Litvinenko
denounced his FSB superiors, claiming they had secretly ordered him to kill
Boris Berezovsky. That accusation led to his arrest, exile to London, and
eventual gruesome murder.) Today's gathering is a theatrical event.

Flanked by Kovtun, Lugovoi says British special services bumped off
the FSB émigré. He claims Berezovsky, a "British agent", also took part. I
stand up. I ask Lugovoi if he has evidence for this. "*Yest!*" he says. "There
is!" He does not explain what that evidence is. And the question has irritated
him. He stares at me. "Your British citizenship is sold in the market like a
cheap Chinese T-shirt!" Afterwards, the Kremlin announces that Lugovoi's
accusations – a wild attempt to muddy the waters, in my view – are "worthy
of further investigation".

Four months later I meet Lugovoi again. He is on the campaign trail,
embarking on an unlikely political career as a deputy in Russia's parliament.
Lugovoi is number two on the federal list of the misleadingly named Liberal
Democratic Party of Russia (LDPR), a bizarre bunch of ultra-nationalists
and alleged gangsters who usually toe the Kremlin line. The party's leader,
Vladimir Zhirinovsky, is Russia's best known political clown and a purveyor
of xenophobia. (US diplomats describe one Zhirinovsky speech as "punctuated with the usual histrionics about western interference and perfidy".)
One source tells the Americans the Kremlin deliberately pushed Lugovoi
on to the LDPR's party list to provide him with immunity (as a deputy he
can't be prosecuted.) Another suggests it was Zhirinovsky's idea to recruit
Lugovoi to boost the party's image. The same source speculates that
Lugovoi enjoys "the personal protection of Putin".

US diplomats are bemused by the Russian establishment's support for
Lugovoi's new career. "It seems odd that the Kremlin, which presumably
would want to see the furore over the Litvinenko matter end as soon as
possible, has kept the matter front and centre by sanctioning Lugovoi's
entry into Russian politics," they cable home.

In the weeks before the December 2007 Duma election, I cover
Lugovoi's campaign as he makes an unlikely CV leap – from alleged assassin

to celebrity politician. He travels from Russia's far east, over the rugged Urals and back to the Ukrainian border. Everywhere he takes the same message: that Britain is a rogue state. It is also not very good at football, he points out. "We were joking on the plane over here whether we should congratulate the England team on their performance," he tells me, at a press conference in the town of Kursk, held in the rustic Nightingale motel.

Lugovoi's remarks on football follow England's 3-2 defeat to Croatia in the 2008 European championships qualifiers. The result means Russia qualifies at England's expense. Lugovoi claims that British agents spirited away video evidence from the Millennium Hotel in London, the scene of Litvinenko's poisoning, following a meeting between Litvinenko, Lugovoi and Kovtun. He repeats his claim that it was the British establishment who killed Litvinenko rather than him. "The Litvinenko affair is the greatest failure by the British security services," he says. Lugovoi demonstrates no sympathy for Litvinenko's widow, Marina: "I understand the wish of the relatives to find justice but someone is trying to politicise this. At the end of the day Litvinenko was a spy spying on his own country."

This is one of my more colourful reporting assignments. I follow Lugovoi to Manturovo, a village 60 miles outside Kursk, set in a rural landscape of crumbling *dachas*, snow-covered fields and silvery poplar trees. He visits a new state-of-the-art cowshed before dropping into an orphanage. After that he addresses party supporters in a pink-painted public hall decorated with a relief of Lenin and a small icon. The fur-coated locals listen politely. Several times they even applaud. Lugovoi is not a natural politician – though in Russia's manipulated political landscape this doesn't mark him out in any way – and cuts an incongruous figure: he's wearing a pinstriped suit, purple tie with geometric swirls and a pair of expensive crocodile-skin shoes. Lugovoi says the British are to blame for many of Russia's woes. The British invaded Crimea, forged the Zinoviev letter, and went on behaving as "Anglo-Saxon imperialists". "If you look at Russian-British relations the cold war never started and never ended," he insists.

I'm keen to gauge what the locals think of him. Do they really want to vote for someone famous for being – well – an international killer? "It's difficult to say," says Viktor Shumakov, a veteran of the Soviet war in Afghanistan. "In Russia many strange things happen all the time." He tells me: "Britain is a long way away. But I know you have nice apples." Most villagers appear more preoccupied with local issues – low pensions, high unemployment and the fact that half of the villagers are drunk. "Lots of people here are alcoholics. Most of the older men have died. And prices keep going up," complains Nataliya Bredikhina, owner of a TV shack.

It's not until six months later, when Lugovoi has been elected to Russia's state Duma, that I am granted a proper interview with him. The location is Lugovoi's upstairs office in Moscow's Radisson hotel. Despite his contempt for Britain's "establishment", Lugovoi turns out to be a fan of English literature. An English language edition of the complete works of Arthur Conan Doyle sits in a glass-fronted cabinet case. "I've read all of Sherlock Holmes. I'm also very fond of Conan Doyle's *The Lost World*," he explains. He mentions other things he likes about Britain – whisky and football. Our interview takes place just days before the 2008 Champions League final in Moscow, contested between Manchester United and Chelsea, the latter owned by Roman Abramovich, a close associate of Putin. "Two English teams playing in front of a Russian public. Marvellous! I must get a ticket," he enthuses, making a note in his diary, as Lugovoi's assistant Sophia brings us – fittingly – tea.

I ask Lugovoi what happened at the Millennium Hotel. According to British prosecutors, Lugovoi poisoned Litvinenko here. Lugovoi and Kovtun had met Litvinenko at the hotel around 4.30pm on 1 November 2006. It was while sitting in the Pine Bar that Lugovoi allegedly slipped radioactive polonium into Litvinenko's tea. Litvinenko died horribly three weeks later in the University College hospital in London. On his deathbed, he accused Putin of plotting his execution.

It was a setup, insists Lugovoi of his fateful encounter with Litvinenko on 1 November – Lugovoi, not Litvinenko, was the victim. He says they had originally agreed to meet the following day at the private security company Risk Management, but that Litvinenko called him "at least five times" and insisted the meeting be brought forward. This is Lugovoi's version of events: "We arrived at the Millennium Hotel. We sat down together. My family phoned and said they would be arriving in the hotel 15 minutes later. We took a seat in the bar. We ordered something. I've always said I can't remember whether we ordered tea at all. I remember that I drank some whisky or gin. Then Litvinenko arrived. He said next to nothing. He was very excited."

According to Lugovoi, the encounter was pointless, and blandly uneventful. He says: "The meeting was strange because the person who insisted upon it had nothing serious or important to say. Looking back, I had the impression someone wanted to see us together. After 20 minutes my daughter arrived and came to the table. We were already standing up. I introduced her and my son to Litvinenko and we all set off for the match [Lugovoi says he had flown to London to watch his team, CSKA Moscow, play Arsenal at the Emirates Stadium]. Litvinenko called me at 8.30am the next morning. He said he felt ill. He said he wouldn't be able to attend our meeting. I went for a walk down Oxford Street with my family and we did some shopping." The following day Lugovoi flew back to Moscow. He says he phoned Litvinenko in hospital on 7 November ("We had an excellent conversation") and again on 13 November – his last call before Litvinenko's agonising death from radiation poisoning on 23 November.

As Lugovoi tells his story – one of virtuous innocence and wrongful insinuation – I find it hard to dislike him. In person, he is disarming. He smiles, jokes, makes rueful expressions, creasing his face downwards so it resembles a flatfish; he lobs the odd word of English ("absolutely", he says with a cut-glass accent) into his Russian. He dresses, moreover, like an English gentleman – he's wearing a pink shirt, dandyish cuffs, and a grey business suit. On the wall is a photo of Putin shaking hands with Berezovsky, the Kremlin's arch-enemy; another montage shows Putin chopping the head off Mikhail Khodorkovsky, the jailed oligarch. But beneath the debonair media persona is he, I wonder, a killer and a liar? There's something disconcerting about Lugovoi. I find it hard to put my finger on it. But I come away with the impression that some vital moral part is empty and lacking, as if someone has hacked off his conscience with a pair of giant scissors.

Lugovoi has stuck to this blameless version of events ever since his name first surfaced in connection with Litvinenko. He gave an identical account to Scotland Yard detectives, who questioned him in Moscow in December 2006, and in countless interviews. After our meeting several aspects strike me as puzzling. Why is he unable to remember whether he ordered a pot of tea? And why the curious post-facto phrase, "I've always said I can't remember"?

UK investigators are firmly convinced of Lugovoi's guilt. Their case against him rests upon the billowing trail of polonium left behind by Lugovoi and Kovtun – not just in the teapot, but also in hotels, cafes, bars, aeroplanes, and even a chair at the British embassy in Moscow. Lugovoi visits the embassy immediately after the story breaks in November 2006. "He sat in a chair. We had to burn the chair," one British diplomat says. (He is using poetic licence. In fact embassy staff decide not to burn the chair. Instead, they lock the door to the conference room where Lugovoi sat. The room remains locked, the chair still in it.)

The full details of Scotland Yard's case against Lugovoi have yet to be revealed. But British officials believe that Litvinenko consumed only a tiny sip of poisoned tea. Had he drunk the whole cup he would have died within hours, his cause of death a mystery: in short, the perfect crime.

British detectives also point to two earlier polonium-carrying trips to London, by Lugovoi and Kovtun on 16 October 2006, and by Lugovoi on 25 October. They are uncertain whether these journeys were dress rehearsals for Litvinenko's eventual assassination, or assassination attempts that went wrong. British officials say that only a state could get hold of polonium. This is the most compelling proof of the FSB's role in the killing, they believe. "It's very difficult to obtain. There are very few sources. Our private judgement is you have to be a state or state organisation to get hold of it in the quantities it was used," one says.

Lugovoi's patriotic credentials go back a long way. Like many KGB recruits, he comes from a military family. One grandfather fought in the 1904-5 Russo-Japanese war and won a medal for his valour. Another took part in the Red Army's battle for Berlin. Lugovoi's father served 35 years as a colonel in the Soviet army. His brother worked on a nuclear submarine in Moscow's northern fleet. Born in 1966 in Baku, in Soviet Azerbaijan, Lugovoi attended the elite Soviet military command academy in Moscow. In 1987, together with his friend Kovtun, he joined the KGB. Both men served in the KGB's ninth directorate, which provided security to top communist party officials. During our interview I ask him why he joined the KGB. "They invited me," he answers. "Any normal Soviet officer would take it as an honour to be in the KGB. It means that you are the best."

Lugovoi denies that he was ever a spy. He says that his KGB job as head of a Kremlin platoon was mundane. Not for him glamorous counter-intelligence work; no, Lugovoi was busy training new recruits to stand guard outside the Kremlin's medieval red walls. "Just like your guards at Buckingham Palace," he says. "I taught people how to march – one, two, three. And yet people make me out to be some kind of KGB monster." In 1991, Lugovoi and other KGB "niners" – of the ninth directorate – became part of the new Federal Protection Service. They provided protection for top politicians including President Boris Yeltsin and Yegor Gaidar, who served as prime minister in the second half of 1992. Two photos of his trips to Washington with Gaidar hang on the wall; next to it is a photo of Lugovoi fishing.

Lugovoi left the presidential security service in 1996 and, like other ex-KGB employees, went into the security business. He joined Berezovsky, as director of security for his TV station ORT. He remained in contact with Berezovsky after the oligarch fell out with Putin and decamped to Britain. He and other KGB "niners" formed a security conglomerate, "Ninth Wave"; his trip to London was allegedly to discuss with Litvinenko a possible business deal.

Just before my interview with Lugovoi, I bump into Kovtun, his alleged accomplice. He is unshaven, and has the air of someone with little to do. When I emerge, I see him again – sitting outside Lugovoi's surprisingly cramped first-floor office next to the Moskva river and Kiyevsky railway station. Scotland Yard has not accused Kovtun of murder – one of the more puzzling aspects of the case. German authorities, however, charge him with bringing polonium-210 into the country. Eventually, they will drop the case. While Lugovoi flew directly to London from Moscow, Kovtun travelled to northern Germany on 28 October – leaving a trail of polonium: on a sofa in the apartment where he stayed, in a Hamburg government office, and elsewhere.

Kovtun tells me he is unhappy about the charges, which prevent him from travelling abroad. It was, he claims, merely "by chance" that he and Lugovoi met Litvinenko in the Millennium Hotel. "We sat down and waited for Andrei's family to turn up. They'd gone to Madame Tussauds but they got lost on the way back. If they hadn't got lost then Litvinenko wouldn't have sat with us in the bar." But what about the huge doses of radioactive polonium found in Lugovoi's hotel room? "By the time the polonium was found, 20 days had passed. There was plenty of time for the British intelligence services to organise lots of things," he says.

During my stint in Russia I and other journalists write dozens of stories about the Litvinenko case. But we make little progress in uncovering the truth behind the killing. When the whistle-blowing website WikiLeaks releases a trove of US diplomatic files, in the autumn of 2010, I'm hopeful they may reveal what really happened. The secret cables turn out to be something of a disappointment: US diplomats, it seems, don't know who killed Litvinenko either. But I do discover tantalising clues that point to high-level Kremlin involvement in the murder plot. The cables show the White House thinks Putin would have known about, and probably approved, the operation to murder Litvinenko.

The most striking cable comes not from Moscow but Paris. I find a secret message from the US embassy in Paris, sent on 12 December 2006, three weeks after Litvinenko's death. It details a discussion between the US assistant secretary of state Daniel Fried and his French counterpart Maurice Gourdault-Montagne, a presidential adviser to Jacques Chirac. The French prefer to attribute Litvinenko's poisoning to unspecified "rogue elements" rather than the Russian government. Fried, the top American diplomat in Europe, however, demurs. He thinks it more likely that Putin, given his "attention to detail", was aware of the Litvinenko mission. Gourdault-Montagne appears in the cable as MGM:

Fried commented that the short-term trend inside Russia was negative, noting increasing indications that the UK investigation into the murder of Litvinenko could well point to some sort of Russian involvement. MGM called attention to Chirac's statement encouraging the Russians to co-operate in the investigation. He wondered aloud who might have given the order, but speculated the murder probably involved a settling of accounts between services rather than occurring under direct orders from the Kremlin. Fried, noting Putin's attention to detail, questioned whether rogue security elements could operate in the UK no less, without Putin's knowledge. Describing the current atmosphere as strange, he described the Russians as increasingly self-confident, to the point of arrogance.

Fried's comments cast doubt on the version of events put forward by the journalist Martin Sixsmith in his 2007 book *The Litvinenko File*. Sixsmith concludes his investigation into Litvinenko's killing by stating that Putin isn't likely to have known about the assassination plot. Its instigators, Sixsmith thinks, are former or serving members of the FSB, acting on their own initiative to get rid of a troublesome traitor. Their goal is also to ingratiate themselves with their Kremlin superiors.

But the WikiLeaks cables show the strenuous efforts made by the Russian authorities to prevent the truth emerging. German investigators discover Kovtun has left a trail of positive traces of polonium-210 in Hamburg prior to his 1 November departure for London. They detect polonium at Erzberger Strasse 4, where he spent a night. The apartment belongs to Kovtun's Russian-German ex-wife Marina Wall. There are further traces in another house in Haselau, 20 miles from Hamburg, where Kovtun slept. They find it in his rented BMW. The cable – sent by the US consul general in Hamburg, Duane Butcher, and citing German investigators, says: "Kovtun left polonium traces on everything he touched – vehicles, objects, clothes and furniture."

The polonium wasn't on Kovtun's skin or clothes; instead, it was "coming out of his body". Germany had wanted to test the Aeroflot plane that flew Kovtun to Germany, and had prepared to ground it on its next arrival in Germany. Investigators' conclusion, the cable records, is that "the Russian authorities must have found out about German plans because 'at the last minute' Aeroflot swapped planes."

The German and the British investigations share the same key weakness. There is a clear evidential trail linking the three Russians to Litvinenko in London. But the trail dries up in Moscow. It remains unclear who ordered Litvinenko's assassination and why. US diplomats report back on the various theories swirling around the Russian capital. Two of these strike me as credible: that Kremlin hardliners arranged it to spark a crisis with the west and persuade Putin to stay on for a third term as president; or that past or present FSB officers did it out of revenge.

Litvinenko had done the one thing Russian spies should never do – broken the KGB's loyalty code. By decamping to Britain and even writing books about his former colleagues, he had defied the organisation's *omertà*, the Sicilian code of secrecy. Putin has talked contemptuously of Litvinenko, saying that he didn't know any secrets; other Kremlin officials have echoed this, intimating that he simply wasn't worth murdering. Lugovoi, meanwhile, has blamed MI6, Berezovsky, the Georgian mafia, Chechen terrorists and even Tony Blair.

Diplomats quoted in the WikiLeaks cables conclude that the truth about Litvinenko's killing "may never be known". In a confidential dispatch a week after the murder, the US ambassador in Moscow, William J Burns, examines some of the many conspiracy theories. He freely concedes that much of the speculation surrounding Litvinenko's radiation poisoning is probably inaccurate or "self-serving". One source has told Burns he believes the assassination is the work of "rogue or retired FSB or military intelligence agents controlled by forces either within or without the Kremlin". The same source – together with another source in the opposition – suggests that Lugovoi is the most likely culprit. "[They] find it suspicious that a Moscow-based businessman and former FSBer like Lugovoi would want to co-operate commercially with a man like Litvinenko who was on the Kremlin's – and the FSB's – enemy list. Lugovoi may have been dispatched to cultivate, and kill, Litvinenko, xxxxxxxxxxxxxx thought." A third source believes Putin wasn't involved – seeing him as a "pawn in a wider game". A fourth, however, disagrees. He sees Putin's fingerprints on the murder.

Burns also examines the killing of the journalist Anna Politkovskaya, the month before Litvinenko's death. He sums up like this:

> All the above putative versions of events are handicapped by a lack of evidence and by the existence of other motives for the killings and other potential perpetrators. Whatever the truth may ultimately be – and it may never be known – the tendency here to almost automatically assume that someone in or close to Putin's inner circle is the author of

these deaths speaks volumes about expectations of Kremlin behaviour as the high stakes succession struggle intensifies.

My own view remains that Lugovoi is guilty of Litvinenko's murder. The polonium trail leads not just back to Moscow but to the front door of the FSB. The Burns cable is telling. Why would a former FSB agent seek to collaborate on a business project with someone publicly identified as a Kremlin enemy abroad? Unless authorised from above, such an association would be commercially reckless, suicidal even. It could lead to severe repercussions – confiscation of business, tax raids, arrest. So Lugovoi, and the other two members of the ex-KGB troika, were acting under orders. The mystery is whose.

CHAPTER 4

Winners and Losers

Nashi youth camp, Lake Seliger, 200 miles northwest of Moscow
19 July 2008

*It is likely that Russian law enforcement authorities
will not disturb Luke Harding again.*

LETTER FROM THE FSB

Several weeks after my visit to Lefortovo prison, the FSB writes me another letter. The spy agency's investigation into the Berezovsky affair has apparently made good progress. The investigators have concluded that I don't have any information on Berezovsky's audacious "plot" to overthrow the Kremlin. The FSB says it is not planning to take action against the *Guardian*, or any of its correspondents. I read:

> As of today, it has been determined that Luke Harding was not directly involved in the interview. He did not contact B Berezovsky and does not possess any evidence. Therefore, he is not of interest to the law enforcement authorities.
>
> In connection, therewith, it is likely that Russian law enforcement authorities will not disturb Luke Harding again.

At first glance this is welcome news. And yet the letter, written in bureaucratic Russian prose, raises more questions than answers.

Why do Berezovsky's distant rantings produce such a virulent response from the Kremlin? And why am I under suspicion – though now, seemingly, exonerated? Do they think I'm on the oligarch's payroll? Or involved in espionage, using my job on the liberal *Guardian* as a sort of improbable deep cover?

It's hard to come to any sensible conclusions. But it appears the FSB is a strange organisation indeed: suspicious, deeply paranoid, unfamiliar with the non-Russian world, and prone to irrational or emotional acts.

Still, I take some relief from the agency's assurance that it won't bother me again. Unfortunately, it is shortlived. On Sunday 12 August 2007 I fly back to Moscow from London from our annual summer holiday. My family stay in the UK. They are there for two more weeks.

In my hand luggage I bring a video given me by an old family friend, the poet and actor Heathcote Williams. It is a tape of a BBC *Panorama* investigation into Litvinenko's death. There is also a film by Litvinenko's friend Andrei Nekrasov. The documentary is titled *My Friend Sasha: a Very Russian Murder*. It includes footage of Litvinenko in hospital after his poisoning. Heathcote has helpfully pasted on to the cassette TV programme notes cut from a newspaper. They include the famous photo of Litvinenko – bald, gaunt, and defiant – lying on his London deathbed.

I dump the tape under the TV at our flat. I forget about it. When I return from work on Thursday, I find both of the two locks to the front door locked. I'm almost certain that when I left that morning I only locked one of them. Nothing else is amiss, however. I'm out all day on Saturday. The following evening, Sunday 19 August, alone and without family distractions, I decide to have a look at the Litvinenko tape.

The first part is normal: it begins with the BBC's *Newsnight* programme, hosted by Jeremy Paxman. There is a piece on Northern Ireland followed by an interview with the actor Peter O'Toole. Just as the Litvinenko programme is about to start the picture disappears. The screen is completely distorted. It is still possible to hear the commentary – just – but it's playing faster than normal, and sounds a bit like Mickey Mouse. It looks to me as if the Nekrasov film has been carefully effaced. There are no images at all – just a screen of scrambled lines.

I check with Heathcote. I explain the weird situation. He emails back to say the tape had played without problem for him. I can't think of any explanation other than the obvious: that the FSB broke in again to my flat, took umbrage at the video and decided to erase the contentious parts. Or did the tape with its Litvinenko image somehow trigger this second break-in? Either way, it's clear my visitors have returned. I have a growing sense that we live in two different worlds, two opposing mental realities. In one, the Litvinenko tape is a harmless home recording from a friend. But in another, it's evidence of a dark conspiracy to defame the Russian state.

It is often forgotten that UK-Russian relations under Vladimir Putin were once positive. Indeed, one of Putin's biggest fans was none other than Tony Blair. After succeeding Yeltsin in 2000, Putin's first trip abroad was to Britain. Russia's new president – at this point an enigmatic figure, subject of the question "Who is Mr Putin?" – called into Downing Street for talks. He even met the Queen at Windsor Castle.

Blair robustly defended his guest from Moscow, in the face of criticism of the Kremlin's new war in Chechnya and human rights abuses. He hailed Putin as a fellow-moderniser, a strong partner who would bring order to the process of political and economic reform. After a successful bilateral meeting between the leaders in November 2000, one Russian official even remarked: "We cannot remember a time when Anglo-Russian relations were better, not even before the revolution."

But this Anglo-Russian smooch-in didn't have much of a honeymoon. Towards the end of Putin's first term it became clear that the relationship was heading for divorce. Several reasons drove this estrangement. Putin's increasingly authoritarian policies at home meant that many of his opponents fled the country. A large number settled in London, the new de facto capital – as in tsarist times, when Lenin pitched up here living in Pentonville and Bloomsbury – for Russian dissidents and disgruntled revolutionaries. The Kremlin and Downing Street disagreed over the war in Iraq. (Putin regarded it as another egregious example of Anglo-Saxon imperialism.) And from 2003 onwards, as pro-western reform movements shook Georgia and Ukraine, the mood of paranoia inside the Kremlin spiralled. Putin –

and the FSB – became convinced that Ukraine's "orange revolution" had been triggered not by popular street protests but by CIA spies carrying bagfuls of dollars.

But one of the most vexed areas of UK-Russian dispute is mutual legal assistance and extradition. Over a plate of beef carpaccio in one of Moscow's fancier Italian restaurants in summer 2007, I ask Dmitry Peskov, Putin's press spokesman, when the current problems between London and Moscow began. Peskov's answer is unequivocal: 2003. (Peskov also complains that while flying first class on British Airways from New York to London, a stewardess jokes: "I hope there's no polonium this time, Mr Peskov." "And you want me to encourage people to go to this country!" he says.)

Why 2003? The date corresponds with the decision to grant Berezovsky, Putin's biggest enemy, political asylum in the UK. A British court decision the same year had also denied the Kremlin its extradition request for Akhmed Zakayev, the Chechen rebel leader accused by Moscow of terrorism. By 2007, Russia has lodged 21 applications for the extradition of Russian citizens from the UK, many of them connected to Yukos, Khodorkovsky's bankrupt oil company. All are unsuccessful. Britain's courts refuse them on the basis that the individuals are unlikely to get a fair trial in Russia and, in many cases, are being persecuted for their political views.

This is true: the phrase "telephone justice" has been coined to describe Russia's politically biased judicial system – a reference to Kremlin officials' habit of handing down verdicts to judges. The repeated conviction of Khodorkovsky, following farcical trials, gives further proof of this.

But Putin viewed Britain's refusal to extradite Berezovsky as a personal betrayal. He was reportedly incensed that Blair failed to pick up the phone and inform him of the court's decision. For his part Blair, I am told, was growing disillusioned with his one-time Russian ally. Asked what he thought of Putin, Blair apparently told one Downing Street staffer: "He's a bad man." In a 2008 meeting with US Senator John McCain, Blair described Putin as "increasingly autocratic", saying he has "undone much of Russia's democratic progress". The west's strategy, Blair believed, should be to make Russia a "little desperate". He told McCain that Russia needed to be "shown firmness and sown with seeds of confusion".

The difference in values between the two countries – one democratic, the other authoritarian – are not so much a gap as an unbridgeable chasm. In Putin's system, it's inconceivable that a judge would defy the Kremlin's wishes. He is sure to have interpreted the British court's rulings not as a demonstration of judicial independence but as a deliberate anti-Russian snub, ordered up by Britain's arrogant political establishment. Putin never forgives Blair. His dislike of Britain transfers seamlessly to Blair's successor, Gordon Brown.

From these perceived slights flowed a series of hostile actions by the Russian government. In January 2006 Russian state television broadcasts footage supposedly showed British intelligence officers retrieving information from an artificial "rock" concealed in a Moscow park. The 30cm rock resembled a small, innocuous light brown boulder – the kind of boulder familiar to fans of *The Flintstones*. The FSB alleged that Moscow-based UK diplomats used the rock to communicate with Russian "agents". These "agents" worked inside Russian non-governmental organisations – a group regarded by the Kremlin as a disloyal fifth column, synonymous with spying and western meddling. Russian human rights activists dismissed the story as a crude smear. Its aim was to discredit legitimate NGOs and weaken Russia's already feeble civil society, they said. Worse was to follow.

In the febrile weeks after Lugovoi is charged with murder, bilateral relations take another sharp downward spin. The Russian government bluntly rejects British demands that Lugovoi should be extradited to the UK. Instead, it does everything it can to protect him, and to prevent him from standing trial in London. A furious Putin cites Russia's constitution, which – like other European legal systems derived from the Napoleonic code – forbids the extradition of nationals. He also dubs the request "arrogant" and indicative of Britain's "no brains" colonial mentality.

The row – likened by one Russian analyst I know to a mutual spitting competition – rages throughout the summer of 2007. I call Garry Kasparov. Putin, he says, is afraid that if the case goes to trial in London he might be called as a witness. Putin is baffled by London's refusal to cut a deal over Litvinenko, and to value a single human life above business, he says. "Putin believes that everything has a price. He is a very suspicious man. If something is not being negotiated it is a conspiracy. It is a normal thought process for him."

In July the new foreign secretary, David Miliband, expels four Russian diplomats in London in protest at Moscow's failure to hand over Lugovoi. Miliband makes clear he believes the FSB was involved in the operation to kill Litvinenko; he severs co-operation with the spy agency and introduces a new, tougher visa policy for Kremlin politicians travelling to London. In response Russia kicks out four British diplomats from Moscow. This tit-for-tat is, by FSB standards, restrained.

Secretly, however, the FSB is stepping up the pressure, using its favoured methods of intimidation. The British government is unable to fully staff its Moscow embassy because of visa restrictions, according to a subsequently leaked US cable. It adds that "local Russian hires have been harassed by the FSB". Some are victims of break-ins. British diplomats also suffer intrusions. The aim is to demoralise embassy staff, to "short tour" them, so they leave Russia early.

The mood among British diplomats in Moscow is embattled. Tony Brenton, the UK's ambassador, holds a series of breakfast briefings for British journalists. The venue is Brenton's residence, off Old Arbat in Bolshoi Nikolopeskovsky lane: a Russian haute bourgeois building, probably built for a merchant or senior official in the late 19th century. Russian staff in black uniform with white aprons present plates of sausages and scrambled egg; there is coffee and orange juice and toast. The atmosphere is convivial; 18th-century British maritime prints in fading greens adorn the walls. (They are a reminder of Peter the Great's visit to Deptford, London, in 1698, when he studied shipbuilding.)

The briefings are off the record. But the Litvinenko case is a major theme, as Britain's relations with Russia stumble from bad to worse. No one expects things to improve in a hurry.

During the same period the US ambassador William Burns writes that Russian officials show no interest in Lugovoi facing British justice. This isn't surprising, he tells Washington, "given the sensational nature of the murder and uncertainty over where the trial may lead beyond Lugovoi".

The Russian government has opened another flank in its attack, declaring war on the British Council, the cultural wing of the UK government abroad.

The Russian authorities had first accused the British Council in 2004 of illegal commercial activity and failing to pay taxes. Tax police wearing bala-clavas raided the council's rectangle-shaped main office, located with several other cultural outreach operations in Moscow's Foreign Literature Library, on the bank of the traffic-hemmed Yauza river.

The use of tax inspections is one of the Kremlin's favourite tools. They are deployed against political opponents and human rights organisations. After Litvinenko's murder, Russian officials intimate that the campaign against the British Council will stop if Britain agrees to drop its investigation into the killing. In December 2007, after the Brown government makes clear there can be no deal on Litvinenko, Russia's ministry of foreign affairs announces it is closing down the British Council's offices outside Moscow. The order is effective from 1 January 2008.

The British Council's Russia director, James Kennedy, is a personal friend. Over dinner at his Moscow flat, in a crumbling 19th-century block not far from the capital's Garden Ring, we exchange tips on how to cope with the FSB's pervasive electronic surveillance. James says that he suspects his flat is bugged, as well as the chauffeur-driven car in which he travels to work. Both of us agree the best strategy is to ignore the eavesdropping and to carry on as if it doesn't exist. During the British Council crisis, I find myself telephoning James most days. On 14 January 2008, the British Council defies the Russian order to close and reopens its branches in St Petersburg and the Urals city of Yekaterinburg. The Russian government is furious at this "provocation".

The FSB's response is swift, nasty and predictable. On 15 January, it calls on Russian British Council staff members (seven in Yekaterinburg and 16 in St Petersburg) and tells them to discontinue their work with the British. The agency's methods are never understated: police from the ministry of internal affairs arrive at six employees' homes after midnight. In one case, they warn that a much-loved family pet might meet with an unfortunate "accident"; they inquire about the health of frail elderly rela-tives. Tax officials warn other employees that they face criminal investigation. The same evening, traffic police in St Petersburg, with a camera crew in tow, stop the car of Stephen Kinnock, and accuse him of drink driving. Kinnock is the director of the British Council's St Petersburg office in the city and the son of Lord (Neil) Kinnock, the former leader of the British Labour party.

British officials are indignant at this bullying and entrapment. "It's classic KGB-style intimidation of our staff so they feel their position is untenable," one tells me. Another likens the FSB's methods to "punching a librarian". In London, Martin Davidson, the British Council's chief executive, reluctantly admits he has no choice but to suspend the regional offices. "We saw similar actions during the cold war, but frankly thought they had been put behind us," he sighs.

In private dispatches to Washington, William Burns expresses solidarity with his beleaguered British cousins. He remarks that the Brown government "hopes to shame the GOR [government of Russia] with the collateral damage that its actions against the Council will cause for the thousands of Russian students who use the facilities, both as a resource and a test-taking center for those seeking UK university admissions." The US ambassador observes that their numbers include "many of the nation's elite offspring". This shame strategy doesn't have any effect. Foreign minister Sergei Lavrov – whose own daughter studies at the London School of Economics – remarks that British behaviour is "evidence that the British side is nostalgic for colonial times". And Major General Yuri Drozdov, a retired KGB officer, tells the Russian press the work of the British Council is directly linked to the "activities of British intelligence whose agents are working, with the United States, to divide and control Russia".

British critics of Russia see the closures as ominous. Denis MacShane, the former Labour Europe minister, and an MP never short of a soundbite, dubs them examples of the "new and nasty Russia that is coming into being in the 21st century … It is sad that the nation of Tolstoy and Tchaikovsky should seek to victimise the British Council, which promotes culture and exchanges between artists, musicians and writers. But today's Russia is slowly reverting to an uncultured authoritarianism, which is deeply worrying."

I ask Fyodor Lukyanov, the editor of the magazine *Russia in Global Affairs* and my favourite Russian analyst, what he makes of it all. Surely such Soviet-style behaviour damages Russia's reputation? "My deep conviction is that Russia hasn't cared about its international image for a long time," he replies.

The Kremlin also sponsors an ugly, personal campaign of harassment against Tony Brenton. The British ambassador's "crime" is to appear at a civil society seminar in July 2006 together with Eduard Limonov – a Russian writer and the leader of the banned National Bolsheviks, a ferociously anti-Kremlin youth organisation, regularly persecuted by Russia's police and courts. (Limonov had also been incarcerated in Lefortovo, I later discover.)

Following the forum Kremlin youth activists stalk Brenton across the streets of Moscow and elsewhere. The activists are from the pro-Putin youth group Nashi – it means "Ours" in Russian – set up by Kremlin political technologists in the wake of the orange revolution. Nashi activists heckle Brenton during his public appearances. They harass his wife and jump in front of his official car, dumping leaflets on his windscreen. These actions are not spontaneous: as Burns points out, the activists are obviously being paid.

The British Foreign Office complains to the foreign ministry that these tactics breach the Vienna Convention.

After Russia's parliamentary elections on 2 December 2007, which see Putin's United Russia party win a crushing if manipulated victory, Nashi activists set up a picket again outside Britain's riverside Moscow embassy. It's a grey, frozen Wednesday; I decide to wander down there and take a look. The activists stand next to the murky Moskva river; they look miserably cold and damp. Around 20 demonstrators are armed with new placards. The placards show a blown-up photo of Brenton with the word *Loser* stamped unflatteringly in English in red ink across his forehead. It has been even worse – previous Nashi gatherings have compared Brenton to Hitler. British officials, believers in the power of reason and dialogue, invite Nashi's leader in for a chat. This merely prompts another demonstration, with banners shouting "We don't want your tea".

"Mr Brenton is a loser because the elections in Russia didn't give him the result he wanted. He wanted an orange revolution here. But he didn't get it," Konstantin Goloskokov, a 21-year-old student at Moscow University tells me outside the embassy. He adds: "We don't believe Mr Brenton should interfere in the internal affairs of our country. We have asked the foreign ministry to strip him of his accreditation." Another Nashi activist, Masha Drokova, tells me: "I'm waiting for him to say sorry."

Never mind that the election had been rigged – and that millions of public sector workers had been instructed to vote for Putin, told that if they didn't they might lose their jobs. Putin had won and Brenton had lost. In Putin's Manichean world it was that simple. Eventually, the Nashi activists discontinue their embassy sit-ins, as Burns puts it, "presumably under instruction".

Six months later, in summer 2008, I catch up with Nashi activists at their annual camp on the banks of Lake Seliger in Russia's picturesque north, near the town of Tver, three hours drive from Moscow. Hundreds of tents have been erected in a shiny pine forest. There are portable toilets, washing lines and cooking pots. Across the lake an orthodox church with three gold towers shimmers in the distance. It might almost be an ambitious summer camp for Boy Scouts – were it not for the giant portraits of Vladimir Putin strung between two trees in a central clearing.

I discover that the most hated nation in the Kremlin's pantheon of perceived evils is no longer Britain but tiny Estonia. Russia regularly lambasts Estonia and its post-Soviet Baltic neighbours Latvia and Lithuania for "fascism". The dispute is not over extradition but 20th-century history. The Estonians, understandably, disagree with the Kremlin over their "liberation" by the Red Army from the Nazis, seeing it as a second occupation. Estonia's decision to move a statue of a Red Army soldier ignites a furious Russian response; Nashi supporters lay siege that May to the country's embassy in Moscow, bringing along a large inflatable tank.

Next to a sandy beach I discover Nashi activists keep a pig. They have named the animal Ilves, after the Estonian president, Toomas Hendrik Ilves. The pig's minder, Dmitry Ivanov, is dressed in an American costume decorated with stuck-on fake dollar bills and a top hat. He tells me: "We're not fanatics. We merely support the course of Russia's ruling elite. We want people to live well. Only an idiot would be against this." The future is Russia's, he confidently predicts: "We will be not in the top five but in the top three economies. By 2020 people will be migrating to Russia from countries like yours."

The camp, I observe, blends Kremlin propaganda with the chance to have a free holiday and flirt with the opposite sex. There is a climbing wall, dance classes, mountain bikes, a gym and even a Segway; the forest air buzzes with the scent of pine resin and youthful hormones. On the sand a young woman in an orange bikini sunbathes while reading Russia's constitution. The Kremlin funds Nashi and Vladislav Surkov – Putin's chief ideologist – is its presiding spirit.

Some of the group's stunts are silly rather than pernicious. One of the stalls set up on a sandy through-track belongs to Antonia Shapovalova, a 20-year-old fashion designer. Shapovalova, like many Nashi supporters, comes from the provinces (in her case, the town of Kostroma in western Russia). In 2007 she caused a sensation by unveiling a pair of "Putin pants". These skimpy bikini bottoms sported the slogan *Vova, I'm with you,* with the word *Vova*, an affectionate diminutive for Vladimir, emblazoned alongside the crotch.

The camp also does it bit to overcome Russia's demographic problem: 20 young couples tie the knot in a mass ceremony on the main stage. Each couple sleeps in a heart-shaped tent decorated with red balloons; a baby conceived at the previous year's mass wedding, Vasya, is proudly shown off; there are couples from Dagestan in colourful costumes, the grooms wearing giant brown hats.

The reality, however, is that Nashi is an unpleasant organisation. The Russian government uses it to perform useful bits of demagoguery, and as a proxy to bully its enemies. During my stint in Moscow its targets, as well as Brenton and the Estonians, include the Putin critic Kasparov and the journalist and Soviet dissident Alexander Podrabinek.

Not far from the pig, I meet Nashi's leader, Nikita Borovikov. Borovikov defends the group's tactics. He says he sees nothing wrong with harassing Russia's enemies – and describes its stunts as "farce". Why pick on Tony Brenton? "He supports fascists and extremists," Borovikov replies. "It's awful for Russia's image to be insulted. If the government doesn't do anything, society is forced to act."

Russia, it turns out, has plenty of enemies – an endless supply of foreign and home-grown ones. Near the main stage there are several banners. One shows Estonia's president in the uniform of an SS officer; others feature Mikheil Saakashvili and Viktor Yushchenko, the pro-western presidents of Georgia and Ukraine, next to the slogan "An evil spirit has got into our Slavic brothers". At the far end of a sandy track I discover a Belarus theatre troupe performing a satire on The Other Russia, Kasparov's pro-democracy movement. The actors, wearing masks in the style of *Spitting Image*, perform a line dance waving American flags, accompanied by the theme tune from *The Benny Hill Show*. Boris Berezovsky conducts; Khodorkovsky appears in a pair of handcuffs and stripy blue prison pyjamas. The skit reminds me of Soviet propaganda about evil capitalists in cylinder hats. It strikes me as a further example of how the Kremlin has taken the Soviet model – in this case the communist Komsomol youth organisation – and repackaged it, made it shiny for the Facebook generation.

Back in Moscow, I ask Ilya Yashin, the youth leader of the liberal party Yabloko, what he thinks of Nashi. "It's a completely artificial movement dreamed up by the presidential administration," he says, adding that it brings shame to his generation of Russians. Its supporters are rewarded with free cinema tickets, membership of swimming clubs and prestigious internships in state corporations. They are not stupid but cynical, he suggests: "There is a depth in Russia of psychological and political apathy."

Yashin concedes it is wrong to compare Nashi to the Hitler Youth – they have been dubbed the *Putinjugend* – since they don't actually kill anybody. A better analogue, he thinks, is Chairman Mao's Red Guards. In a macabre footnote, Nashi also found themselves venerated, together with Putin, by Anders Behring Breivik, the 32-year-old Norwegian who confessed to mass murder in July 2011.

The small seaside town of Senigallia is situated off Italy's wind-swept Adriatic coast. It is a quiet sort of place. The town's seafront boasts a small marina and promenade. On the beach there are cafes with stripy deckchairs; black-headed gulls swoop above the waves. Senigallia has a castle of sorts, as well as an attractive park planted with monkey puzzles and firs. When I arrive I find the tourist office shut. But in the old town, under the arches of a thick-walled passageway, I discover a cafe selling excellent ice-cream.

Senigallia is the unlikely home of Walter Litvinenko, Alexander Litvinenko's 71-year-old father. Together with his wife, Lyuba, and several other Litvinenko relatives, he lives in exile here, on the coast of provincial Italy. In March 2010 I go to visit them in their cramped three-bedroom flat, tucked away in an anonymous cul-de-sac. The family fled Russia in the spring of 2008. But as Walter Litvinenko explains, his problems with the Russian state pre-date his son's murder, and go back to 1998 when Alexander – known by the family as Sasha – publicly denounced his employer, the FSB. The FSB's boss at the time was Putin. The family was living in Nalchik, a town in southern Russia in the foothills of the Caucasus mountains. Alexander was arrested. In Nalchik, Alexander's half-sister, Tatiana, and her husband – both employed by the local FSB – were sacked. A car mysteriously knocked over and killed Litvinenko's grandmother as she crossed the road.

The family's difficulties worsened following Litvinenko's radiation poisoning and death in London. There were threats and intimidation. The Russian media dubbed the Litvinenkos traitors. Relatives severed contact. According to Walter, hints were made that his teenage grandson – who was about to be conscripted into the Russian army – would be sent home in a body bag. Walter was informed that the location of his younger son Maxim – who had already moved to Italy – had been discovered. Reluctantly, the Litvinenkos concluded they had little choice but to leave Russia. "I wasn't afraid for myself, but for my children," Walter tells me, wearing the same flat-cap he took to his son's drizzly funeral in London's Highgate cemetery.

The Litvinenkos are reluctant exiles: on the wall is a map of Russia; next to it several orthodox icons; on the bookshelf an Italian-Russian dictionary. "At home I loved going mushroom-picking. But I grew afraid of going into the forest. It would be very easy for somebody to kill you there," Walter points out.

But life in Italy turned out to be disillusioning. After two years in the country, Italy's leader, Silvio Berlusconi, declined to grant the family asylum – a fact that Litvinenko attributes to Berlusconi's close personal friendship with Putin. He tells me the delay can be explained by Berlusconi's unwillingness to displease the Kremlin. "We have fallen victim to a political game," Litvineko says. "Berlusconi is no better than Putin. All European governments have been flirting with Putin. Berlusconi's dependence on him, and on Russian gas, means that we don't get asylum."

The claim strikes me as depressingly plausible. Paolo Guzzanti, a former senator in Berlusconi's Forza Italia party who fell out with the prime minister over his friendship with Putin, says it is likely Berlusconi blocked the applications. "I have no confirmation of this, but it seems obvious, given the brotherly relationship between Putin and Berlusconi, that all possible obstacles to granting asylum will be raised in order to slow down the procedure and make it impossible," he says. The Italian government denies this. It later gives them permission to remain in Italy, though this is not the same as asylum.

The Litvinenkos also allege they have suffered harassment from the Italian police, who raid the family's restaurant, La Terrazza, in the nearby resort town of Rimini. Tatiana says that one policeman grabbed her by the arm. When she struggled free, he pushed her to the ground; she blacked out and suffered concussion. The Litvinenkos say they don't know if this harassment is a local phenomenon by a police force ill-disposed towards all Russians who flock to the Adriatic coast or a personal campaign, cynically authorised from above. "I thought Europe had 100% rule of law. We discover in Italy this isn't true. It's connections and the mafia. It's as if we never arrived in Europe but ended up in some Russian province," Tatiana says.

Walter Litvinenko blames Putin for his son's death. He believes that the three-man hit squad of Lugovoi, Kovtun and Sokolenko, who met his son in the hotel bar, were acting under Kremlin orders. "I know it was Putin who killed him," he tells me. "He's a sick person. A normal person wouldn't have killed Sasha."

Litvinenko presents no proof for his allegation; his bitterness and harsh public accusations towards Putin are understandable. But he offers the following logic: "Russia is a vertical system. It's like in the Soviet Union. Only Putin can decide these questions, just like Stalin. Without Putin's approval it [Litvinenko's murder] could not have happened." Tatiana disagrees with her father. She refuses to finger Putin or anyone else. She does reproach Berezovsky – Litvinenko's fickle patron – for leaving the family in the lurch. "He's clearly not interested in us, and we wouldn't stoop to ask for anything."

I find the Litvinenkos in dire straits. They had been surviving on prawns salvaged from the freezer of their defunct restaurant; a few days before I arrive they spend their last euros on 10 eggs. A local church donates them bread and apples; otherwise they eat pancakes. When I visit they don't have enough money to pay the €540 for next month's rent. It is a sad postscript to the Litvinenko story – murder, flight, poverty and an uncertain future in an alien land. On top of that there is the anxiety that even here they might not be safe. "There is a certain subconscious fear," says Walter Litvinenko. "In Nalchik I wasn't afraid because I knew everybody's faces. Here it is different. At any moment a person could come up to you and that would be the end."

In May 2011 Tatiana calls me. She updates me on the family's news. It's not good. Lyuba – who brought up Alexander Litvinenko – has died. The Italian government is still refusing to give the Litvinenkos basic state support. Walter Litvinenko has moved out and is living alone in a one-bedroom apartment. He is too poor to pay his bills. The electricity on his flat has just been switched off, and he sits alone in the dark.

CHAPTER 5

Five Days in August

The frontline at Gori, Georgia
11 August 2008

*With sublimely perched old churches, watchtowers and
castles dotting its fantastic mountain scenery, Georgia has
to be one of the most beautiful places on Earth.*
LONELY PLANET GUIDE TO GEORGIA, 2008

When the shooting begins I'm sitting on a beach in Cornwall. It is every correspondent's worst nightmare – to be in the wrong place when a story breaks out on your patch. In this case, the news is of a war in Georgia, a small country of 4.5 million people on the doorstep of Russia.

After an agreeable afternoon bobbing in the waves with Phoebe and the children – Ruskin, 8, and Tilly, 10 – I stroll back to our rented cottage next to the beach. I glance at my mobile phone. There are 17 missed calls. Shit! I turn on the BBC news. I discover my friend Richard Galpin is already reporting from Georgia. He is standing next to a large hole in the road, apparently caused by a Russian bomb. The Georgians have made a doomed attempt to seize back the rebel province of South Ossetia; Russia has responded with a full-scale invasion.

The news isn't entirely a surprise. Six weeks earlier we had flown from Russia to Georgia for a family holiday. It turned out to be one of our best. Relations between Moscow and Tbilisi were already poor following the Georgians' arrest in 2006 of Russian "spies"; nonetheless, direct flights between the two capitals had just resumed. In Tbilisi we stay at Dodo's, a cheap guesthouse recommended by the *Lonely Planet* guidebook. From here we drive out to a series of ancient cave monasteries near the border with Azerbaijan, picnicking on sausage, flat bread and Georgian cheese under a medieval fresco of the Last Supper.

We also travel north up the Georgian Military Highway. There are few other tourists. The road, used as a military supply route in the 19th century, cuts through the Caucasus Mountains; we hike through alpine fields of lilies and pinks. In an abandoned stone watchtower Ruksin, Tilly and I discover a mountain goat. The border with Russia is closed; we clamber up a sheer vertical path to an old church above the frontier town of Kazbegi. We also motor through Gori. The town is the birthplace of an unpromising cobbler's son, Josif Stalin. After Gori we visit Borjomi, a faded imperial spa town known for its mineral water and set amid a semi-tropical forest. Here we splash in a sulphurous outdoor swimming pool.

Back in Tbilisi I find ominous signs of what is to come. I pick up a copy of Georgia's English-language *Messenger* newspaper. It reports that the US secretary of state, Condoleezza Rice, is in town for talks with Georgia's pro-western president, Mikheil Saakashvili. Saakashvili is an outspoken enemy of Putin, whom he derides as "Liliputin". The contempt is reciprocated. While the talks are going on Russian jets buzz Saakashvili's presidential palace.

Since sweeping to power in 2003 on the back of pro-democracy street protests, Saakashvili has made no secret of his ambition to join Nato and the wider Euro-Atlantic community. The Kremlin resents Saakashvili's attempts to escape Russia's geopolitical grip. It backs Abkhazia and South Ossetia, two separatist territories that broke from Georgia in the early 1990s. In Moscow, one commentator, Pavel Felgenhauer of *Novaya Gazeta*, predicts that the simmering political crisis between Georgia and Russia will explode into war by the summer. Few believe him.

And then, on 7 August, war does indeed erupt. Years on, its causes will remain bitterly contested. But after days of intense cross-border shelling, with the Russian-backed South Ossetians firing on Georgian-controlled villages, Saakashvili sends in his forces to recapture South Ossetia. The Georgians briefly seize the capital, Tskhinvali.

But Russian tanks are already rolling into South Ossetia, whose puppet administration, the US and others believe, is essentially under the control of Moscow and the FSB.

A resurgent Kremlin is suddenly embroiled in a proxy conflict with Nato and the west. After 24 hours, Saakashvili's US-trained forces withdraw chaotically from Tskhinvali under heavy Russian fire. Some soldiers simply abandon their Cobra vehicles – armoured Humvees with 40mm guns. Bodies lie on the streets. Saakashvili's military adventure turns swiftly into a rout.

The conflict seems to catch world leaders unawares. President George W Bush, Saakashvili's ally, is at the Beijing Olympics with Putin.

I take a train back to London. All flights to Tbilisi are cancelled – the Russians are bombarding the airport. I fly instead to Baku, the capital of neighbouring Azerbaijan, on the Caspian. From here I drive west through the night to the Georgian border. My destination is Gori, which we'd passed in June, and the frontline in this new confrontation. My *Guardian* colleague Tom Parfitt is walking across the Caucasus. He is, by chance, in Vladikavkaz, the capital of North Ossetia. He heads for Russian-controlled South Ossetia.

As I cross into Georgia, grey smoke plumes in the air; Russian bombers hit a disused communist-era aerodrome. I travel for several hours through eastern Georgia; we overtake horse-drawn carts transporting melons and pass fields of yellow sunflowers.

Russia casts its invasion of Georgia as a strictly peacekeeping operation. The aim, the Kremlin says, is to protect civilians. Any journalist who dissents from this narrative – as I discover later to my cost – is automatically dubbed a "spy". But when I arrive in Gori it is clear this doesn't apply to Georgian civilians, who have faced three days of Russian aerial attacks. Several Russian bombs land in residential areas. I peer inside one house hit by a Russian missile.

I meet its owner, Kostia Arsoshvili. There isn't much left of his living room; he sits in the middle of a glass-strewn carpet. The chandelier has fallen to the floor. The window frames of his children's bedroom are blown out. Kostia's neighbour fares worse. He has been killed after a bomb landed on his roof. "I was lucky. I got my children out 15 minutes before the bombs fell," Kostia tells me, showing off his wonky door lintels and broken windows. "I don't know who's to blame for this war. The only thing I know is that it isn't me."

Ostensibly the Russian Backfire bombers that hit Kostia's house are aiming for a Georgian tank base, two miles away. The bombs don't reach their target. The error may have been an accident – but, from the ground, it looks more like deliberate vengeance against Saakashvili, whose soldiers and tanks have already fled towards Tbilisi.

With Georgia's air defences flattened, the Russian air force flies insouciantly across Georgian airspace. Russian fighters hit a radar station in the capital, sending panic-stricken residents fleeing from their beds at dawn. In Gori, residents examine their wrecked homes. Across the road from Kostia's home, scorched and twisted metal lies in the courtyard, surrounded by clothes, pillow feathers and the smell of burned flesh. The upper levels of the five-storey block have disappeared; its neat vine trellis is staved in as if by some giant fist.

"We lived on the fifth floor. We fled just before the attack started," Nana Tetladze says. But her pregnant neighbour Marca, who lived on the second floor, wasn't quick enough. "She and her husband were both killed. I don't know what happened to their seven-year-old boy," she says. In the courtyard I find the mangled remains of Marca's white car.

That evening in Tbilisi, I chance across Irakli Bakhuashvili, the head of Georgia's military planning division, in my hotel lobby; he has just completed a meeting with western diplomats. He is gloomy about Georgia's prospects and says the Russians are advancing on all fronts. They are surging across the west of the country from Abkhazia, Georgia's second breakaway republic, he says, and have seized the key towns of Kutaisi and Senaki. The commander admits that "half of Georgia is under Russian control"; he says that the depleted remnants of Saakashvili's soldiery intend to form a defensive ring around Tbilisi. "This is a classical full-scale invasion. This is an occupation."

This Russian advance sparks panic – with some foreign observers scrambling to pull out, refugees fleeing and mobile phones jammed. It is not clear whether the Kremlin intends to march all the way to Tbilisi. I ask Batkuashvili if Russia's ultimate target is to capture Saakashvili – whom Putin accuses of war crimes. "The idea is to punish Georgia and the Georgian government," he replies. "And Misha [Saakashvili]. They hate Misha." Another Georgian official says Russia has intimated its demands for the withdrawal of its forces – a pledge that Georgia will abandon its aspirations to join Nato and commit itself formally to "neutrality". "It means shelving our Euro-Atlantic aspirations," he adds, sombrely.

WikiLeaks cables will subsequently reinforce this interpretation. A year before the war, US diplomats in Moscow and Tbilisi detailed the scale of covert Russian actions in Georgia. South Ossetia, they reported, was in effect controlled by the FSB – the agency's footprint spread across the region. The ambition? "No doubt the Russians would like to see Saakashvili removed," wrote the US ambassador in Tbilisi, John Tefft, on 20 August, "but the variety and extent of the active measures suggests the deeper goal is turning Georgia from its Euroatlantic orientation back into the Russian fold."

The next morning I set off again towards Gori, with my translator, Lika Peradze, a graduate of Tbilisi's state arts academy and our driver, Zura Kevlishvili. Zura had driven us into the mountains on our family holiday. He is increasingly nervous as we approach the front-line. Along the road are signs of the Georgian army's panicked and ignominious retreat. An incinerated Georgian tank lies in the verge. Its roof has been sliced off. Other Georgian military vehicles appear to have merely conked out during their hapless flight. One tank has two flat back tyres; its crew leave their apples behind next to the gun turret. A pair of military trucks had concertinaed head on. Nearby is a dumped artillery piece.

We press on to Natsreti, a roadside village eight miles outside Gori. And then from nowhere, a Russian helicopter gunship looms above us in the white sky. It is 200 metres away. The gunship looses off several orange-fizzing rockets. Zura panics and brakes; a car slaps and shunts us from behind. The rockets pass us and plunge into a line of tall electricity pylons, sending smoke billowing across the highway. We limp over to the village. Zura is concussed; his car a wreck.

The locals on the frontline appear bewildered as to why Georgia is at war with its mighty Russian neighbour. "I don't know which side to blame. I don't even know why this has happened," 73-year-old Olya Tvauria tells me. Olya says she and the other women and children spent the night in a neighbour's cellar; the men fled to the mountains, concealing themselves among the fir trees. The Russian bombers turned up at 2am, pounding Gori's post office and military hospital and killing its doctor.

We sit in Olya's vine-covered house. There are chickens, luscious plum trees and courgettes bursting into bright yellow flower. Many of her neighbours have already left. "I'm an Ossetian but I prefer to live here," she says. She offers olive oil for Zura's throbbing head and brings us flatbread and homemade Georgian cheese.

Now car-less, Lika and I hitch a ride into Gori's centre with two young Georgians; one has a revolver hidden in the dashboard. There are few other vehicles on the road. I'm impressed by Lika's courage. In Moscow, Medvedev announces that Russian forces are halting military operations. After five days their advance deep into Georgia's west and centre is over, he suggests.

This news comes too late for Gocha Sekhniashvili. He had been standing a few hours earlier in Gori's main square, next to the town's giant statue of Stalin. Survivors describe how a Russian bomb fell without warning. "The bomb came down suddenly. Our windows blew in. Everyone's windows shattered. People were screaming and dying. Others were hiding," says Gocha's friend Tamaz Beruashvili. "I grabbed our bags and ran. I saw Gocha lying face down in the rubble."

Gocha isn't the only victim: the strike kills at least five civilians. They include a 39-year-old Dutch TV journalist, Stan Storimans. He had been working near the square's grandiose Stalin museum, built next to the modest two-room wooden house where the dictator grew up. Stalin's statue is supernaturally undamaged. The Georgian flag hangs from the fine-columned municipal hall. A mangled red Golf car lies alongside a dead dog. It's hard to work out what the Russians had been trying to hit – more probably, the goal was simply death and mayhem.

The next day Lika and I return to Gori. We find a new driver, Koba Chkhirodze. An engaging, gangly figure with a scruffy three-day beard, Koba is a war zone natural: friendly, fearless and inquisitive. Now 41, he served in the Soviet army. At the frontline he instinctively points his car away from danger, in case we need to make a speedy getaway. He is also a patriot – and talks excitedly about how he plans to start a partisan war if the Russians fail to clear off.

As we reach Gori, there are no signs of a Russian withdrawal; instead we learn Russian tanks from South Ossetia have advanced into Gori's centre, parking up next to its sandstone church. Armoured vehicles are also encamped on the main E50 highway just outside town, severing Georgia's eastern and western halves. We leave our car next to a petrol station. We sit in the shade of a fir tree. Next to us is a new Russian checkpoint. The checkpoint's Russian officer, Major Nail, turns out to be both witty and philosophical. I ask why he has invaded Georgia. "There isn't any difference between Georgia and Russia," he replies. He adds: "The landscape is beautiful. But we also have big mountains in Dagestan."

A few hours later the Russian army is on the move: an armoured personnel carrier nudges past the top of the hill. It pauses, as if getting its bearings, and then sets off towards Tbilisi. Behind it, an endless column of Russian military vehicles appears on a shimmering horizon – trucks, tankers and a beaten-up Nissan. The Russian army is on the move.

What isn't clear is where it's going. For the next eight miles – past yellow fields and through a hazy mountain valley – we drive ahead of the column as it continues its sedate progress from Gori towards the capital. Nobody knows whether this is the beginning of a formal Russian occupation of Georgia or something else: a leisurely Sunday afternoon drive perhaps? The column continues deep inside Georgian territory. It gets to within 30 miles of Tbilisi. It turns left. A Russian soldier hops out of his vehicle. I ask him what he is doing. "We've been told to stay there," he tells me, pointing down a rough dirt track towards the rustic hamlet of Orchosani, just over a mile away. "The only reason we've come is because of a *provokatsia* [a provocation] by Saakashvili," he says.

It's a strange day. In theory the conflict between Russia and Georgia is over, as European negotiators led by the French president, Nicolas Sarkozy, hammer out a peace deal. In reality I find Russia's mighty war machine trundling serenely through the Georgian countryside. A couple of Russian trucks overshoot and miss their target. One breaks down. A soldier hops out with a long metal rod and gets the wheezing vehicle going again. Where is he from? "Chechnya," he replies. "We've come to help."

But for the terrified residents of Gori and surrounding villages this is flagrantly untrue. Fleeing villagers from the rustic border zone next to South

Ossetia speak of a militia army of Chechen and Ossetian volunteers. These irregulars arrive shortly after the Russian tanks and troops. They embark on an orgy of looting, burning, murdering and rape, witnesses say, adding that the irregulars had carried off young girls and men. "They killed my neighbour's 15-year-old son. Everyone was fleeing in panic," Larisa Lazarashvili tells me. "The Russian tanks arrived at our village at 11.20 am. We ran away. We left everything – our cattle, our house, and our possessions. We have nothing left."

"They were killing, burning and stealing," adds Achiko Khitarishvili, from Berbuki. "They took young people hostage and drove them away. These were Chechens, Ossetians and Cossacks." He continues: "My village isn't in a conflict zone. It's pure Georgia."

These claims of Russian atrocities are, at first, difficult to verify. But the mood of panic is real enough – with villagers escaping towards Tbilisi by all means possible. One family of eight piles into a tiny white Lada; others flee on tractors; an elderly group escapes on a horse-drawn cart. The sky is filled with white smoke. A string of villages between Gori and South Ossetia are on fire: Tkviavi, Karaleti, Rekha, Variani – burning. Across Georgia as many as 200,000 people are on the move. The irregulars are also stealing cars – turfing out the occupants, including several journalists, at gunpoint. Those who flee express a feeling of betrayal. They say Medvedev has duped them. "I believed Medvedev when he said there was peace. That's why we all stayed in our homes. But it isn't true," 62-year-old Lamzira Tushmali tells me. "There is no ceasefire."

The 2008 war between Russia and Georgia is an odd kind of conflict. Reporting from Afghanistan, during the US-led war against the Taliban in 2001, I sometimes found myself sleeping in my vehicle, out in the freezing desert next to the northern frontline. Often there was nothing to eat. In Georgia, I stay in the five-star Marriott hotel at the bottom of Rustaveli, Tbilisi's languid main avenue.

The hotel has a high-speed internet connection and basement swimming pool. In the mornings, Lika, Koba and I – together with the *Guardian* photographer Sean Smith, who has flown in from London – commute to the

Russian blockade at Gori. In the evenings, after writing up my articles, Sean and I stroll into Tbilisi's old town. It's a pleasant neighbourhood of wooden houses with latticework balconies and pretty gardens of dahlias and figs.

Often we go to Shemoikhede Genatsvale, a restaurant on the cobbled Leselidze street. It serves wonderful *khinkali* (meat dumplings) and *khacha-puri* (cheese bread). We drink excellent Georgian wine. Later, as the conflict begins to ebb, I browse in Prospero's Books, an English-language bookshop and cafe. Its owner is Peter Nasmyth, a charming Englishman and Geor-giaphile. He gives me a copy of *Timeless*, a 1949 novel by a Georgian aristocrat, Nicholas Tchkotoua. Nasmyth has republished it after it was redis-covered in a Camden bookshop. It is a love story between a Russian princess and a Georgian prince – set at the end of the 19th century in the remote Caucasus mountains, as well as Paris, Tbilisi and Davos.

The Russian military prevent journalists from visiting Gori – or from travelling to the Georgian border villages north of the town adjoining South Ossetia. But we find more and more refugees. One group cowers under a ditch as a Russian armoured convoy rolls past; once the convoy is gone they emerge, wailing and weeping. "There are bodies everywhere. I saw hundreds of dead. There are people lying in the streets," says Elene Maisuradze, an elderly lady of 73. "The villages of Kurta, Chala and Eredvi are full of corpses." Elene says she fled from the Georgian village of Tkviavi after two groups of gunmen arrived at her home.

"They say in Russian: 'Where are the boys and where is your car?'" Elene recounts. "I don't understand. One of them is Ossetian and he translates. I tell them I'd sold my car and they go away. But then some others turn up. They enter, ask me where my basement is, and shoot it up. I'm crying. They say: 'Kill her, kill her.'

"My neighbour is a Russian woman and she tells them: 'Don't do this.' They fire into the ground instead and say: 'Fuck Saakashvili.'"

It takes three days for news of the slaughter to emerge – the time it takes for Elene and other survivors to plod to Gori on foot. The group travels at night and survives by eating peaches, apples and plums; one old woman, Matika Elbakidze, 93, dies on the way.

Another refugee, Nugzari Yashavili, describes how he was walking back to his house in Tkviavi. He was in the fields. Some 50 metres away, he spotted several strange gunmen approach his neighbour, Gela Chikhladze. "They come up to Gela, grab him round the shoulder and slit his throat," Nugzari says. "There are five of them. They arrive from South Ossetia in a jeep. They go across the village from house to house." Nugzari, who is 65, says he hid in a cornfield. He watched as the Chechen and Ossetian irregulars helped themselves to his furniture and generator. Further down the road they shot his cousin. I ask Nugzari to draw me a map. He writes names, ages, addresses. Other refugees, independently, give the same grim accounts.

It's clear that this murderous militia has dropped in from Russian-controlled Tskhinvali, a few miles away. With the apparent support of the Russian army, the irregulars are carrying out a campaign of ethnic cleansing – killing teenage boys, stealing vehicles, looting, and then setting fire to Georgian houses. Despite the putative end of Moscow's war with Georgia, Russian-backed militias are enacting their own revenge on Georgians living on both sides of the South Ossetian border.

The Russian army – which controls this zone – is conniving in the slaughter. It prevents us from investigating. We are stuck outside Gori, obstructed by Russian tanks. We sit for some time. One tank nosily squashes several small fir trees; others leave a swirling pattern on the highway's grey tarmac. Up in the nearby mountains, black smoke pours from a burning Georgian military base. Every few minutes there is a percussive rumbling explosion; the air smells of cordite.

Despite the ceasefire, the situation is still volatile and dangerous. Without warning a white Niva jeep sweeps past the Russian checkpoint, from the direction of Tskhinvali. It pulls up in front of us. A South Ossetian commander jumps out; he is drunk, angry, wild-eyed, furious and evidently enraged at the sight of so many foreign TV crews. It is clear that we are the enemy. A soldier from the same car waves a pistol and shouts at us to leave. He starts shooting into the tarmac. The Russians do nothing. We run for the car.

It is two more days before we finally manage to reach Tkviavi. We take a looping mountain back-route to Gori, bypassing two Russian roadblocks. In Gori's main square we discover Alexander Lomaia, Georgia's national security secretary, who is leading a humanitarian convoy. We tag along. We head north out of town. Russian soldiers wave us through several new checkpoints. The scale of ethnic cleansing in the district 10 miles north of

Gori is soon apparent. Many villas along the road are burned and looted. In my notes I later discover a reference to "charred balustrading". A brown teddy bear lies in a verge. Only a few residents are left.

In the hamlet of Karbi, Jemal Saginashvili, a 72-year-old Georgian, shows me where a Russian cluster bomb landed in his apple and plum orchard. The trees are charred and blackened; bits of the bomb lie in a boggy puddle. The roof of his house is smashed in; shrapnel pockmarks the walls of the neighbouring house. "My relative Dodo got a large piece of metal in her lung. We summoned an ambulance to take her to hospital but she died," he explains.

In Tkviavi we see more destruction. The locals recount how "Chechens or Cossacks" – it's not clear who – killed one resident, Shamili Okropiridze, on 12 August. Shamili's house is on the corner of the main road through the village; he heard the rumble of approaching tanks and peered out into the street, just as the Russian war machine and its proxies came through. Someone shot him. "His body lies in the street for a week. It turns black. We want to bury it but the Russians won't allow us," his neighbour Rusvelt Metreveli tells me.

At his front gate I find dark bloodstains. There is a smell of death. I find Shamili's slippers on the porch. His house is unlocked. In the kitchen his plates are neatly stacked. On the table is a photo album; there are black and white snaps of Shamili, as a muscular young man, relaxing on holiday at the Soviet Black Sea coast. An armed intruder has broken into the bedroom – putting a neat single shot through the internal window.

I examine the photos of Shamili's parents, which hang in the living room. I find his bag, packed for departure. There is a photo of Stalin pasted on the wall next to the old Georgian flag. It's clear that Shamili lived alone; I discover later he has a daughter in Tbilisi. A day earlier Russian soldiers buried him in his garden, next to a biblical vine. Rusvelt says he survived the past two weeks by hiding in a field, dodging the South Ossetian and Chechen paramilitaries.

Other villages north of Gori suffer a similar fate. We drive further into what is still a pretty, fertile valley; wild peach trees grow by the roadside next to tall avenues of poplars. There are further signs of destruction – looted petrol stations, the upturned ribcage of a dead cow, dumped tractors.

At the crossroads in Tirdznisi are the calamitous remains of a minivan hijacked and shot by a South Ossetian gang. The minivan lies on its side; a corpse still sits in a grassy verge; nearby are shoes, broken glass and abandoned passports.

Medics in our convoy decide to recover the body, but the smell is unbearable; they change their minds. "The bus was going to Tbilisi. The Ossetians stopped it and took some people hostage. Others escaped," Tariel Gulisashvili tells me. "Five people from the bus are missing. We don't know what happened to them." Others say the Georgian village of Eredvi is completely destroyed by fire. This revenge is understandable – after all, South Ossetian civilians died in the attack by the Georgian military.

But this looks like something else: a systemic attempt to drive Georgians out from the land they have occupied for centuries and create a new mono-ethnic map. Over in Brussels, Sergei Lavrov, Russia's foreign minister, assures the world Moscow is withdrawing its forces from occupied Georgia. On the way home, however, I spy Russian soldiers laughing and skinny-dipping in the turquoise Patara Liakhvi stream; their khaki tents are pitched on a glittering willow-lined bank. They don't appear to be going anywhere.

The next day we avoid Gori and head up into the mountains and to the town of Akhalgori. This sleepy district is – or was – under the control of the Georgian government. Its mixed population of Georgians, Ossetians, Armenians and the odd Russian lived contentedly together. The previous evening, however, South Ossetian militias sweep into Akhalgori, on the coattails of the Russian military. When we arrive most of the Georgians have legged it. Akhalgori's Georgian administration has also fled to Tbilisi, just 25 miles away.

The commander tells us that the town is now under full South Ossetian control. It has been liberated, he declares. "It will be part of an independent country within the Russian Federation." Surrounded by fellow militiamen armed with Kalashnikovs, he explains the new map of Georgia. "This used to be our territory. This is our territory. And this will be our territory in future," the captain says, pointing to a large bulge of land around Akhalgori.

The captain's soldiers have taken over the town's two-storey police station, where the Ossetian flag now flies; one scuffs away the Georgian flag just removed from the roof. Russian soldiers perch on top of an armoured vehicle. They are relaxed and in good humour: they give Sean and me a ride. One jokes: "Let's go all the way to London! We don't need a visa."

The capture of Akhalgori seems significant. It appears part of a wider Kremlin plan to redraw the map of Georgia – reducing it to a small leftover rump and boosting the size of its separatist territories. Before the war, the South Ossetian rebels control one small town, Tskhinvali, and a handful of villages. Moscow is now re-imposing the old, much bigger borders that South Ossetia enjoyed when it was an autonomous area, or *oblast*, within the Georgian Soviet Socialist Republic. Back then Akhalgori was called Leningori.

In the centre of town I find armed teenage South Ossetians patrolling the dusty streets. Each has a white armband round their arm to indicate their new function: "peacekeeping duties". Most of Akhalgori – population 10,000 – is deserted. A few people, mostly ethnic Ossetians and the elderly, opt to stay.

I ask the commander why his militias have been ethnically cleansing Georgian villages between South Ossetia and Gori. "We did perform some cleaning operations, yes," he says – using the Russian verb *chistit*. "We were looking for fighters." He goes on: "Why are you journalists not reporting about the civilians killed in the [Georgian] attack on Tskhinvali? We have Georgian soldiers whose bodies have been lying there a week. Their government doesn't care about them."

The acrimonious war between Georgia and Russia spills from the battlefield into public discourse and from there into international inquiries: who is to blame and which side is telling the truth? The Russians accuse foreign journalists of pro-Georgian bias.

Back in Moscow, Russia's state-controlled media are presenting their own version of the war. It omits certain details. It fails to report on the Ossetian militias who kill and plunder their way across Georgian villages. Indeed, ordinary Russian TV viewers have no clue they are taking place. Instead, the focus is solely on the martyrdom of the South Ossetians. The Kremlin – embarrassingly slow to get its message across in the early days of the conflict and still reliant on crude Soviet methods – launches a furious attack on foreign journalists. It intimates that western reporters covering the conflict are, in reality, agents of the CIA.

The Kremlin certainly has a decent story to tell: there are human rights violations on both sides. Several dozen civilians died in Georgia's reckless military assault on Tskhinvali, together with 12 Russian soldiers, and a number of South Ossetian policemen. Much of the city, including the old Jewish quarter, is in ruins. But Moscow does itself no favours by inflating the number of victims– Putin claims 2,000 innocent civilians were killed. The real figure is much lower. (The European human rights commissioner Thomas Hammarberg records 133 South Ossetian victims; with 413 Georgians killed.)

The Kremlin also places Soviet-style restrictions on journalists. They are kept away from ethnic Georgian villages inside rebel-administered South Ossetia, burned down in the early days of the conflict. American and British reporters aren't allowed to travel independently inside South Ossetia; instead Kremlin minders ferry them every day from Vladikavkaz, inside Russian North Ossetia, to Tskhinvali, a grinding three-hour journey in a Hyundai minibus.

The Georgians lose the war on the ground, and – as one reporter jokes – cement their reputation as the "Italians of the Caucasus": more fond of poetry, pleasure and song than their vicious Chechen cousins. But they are the runaway winners of the media battle. Saakashvili is a permanent fixture on CNN. He hosts David Cameron, Condoleezza Rice, David Miliband and Angela Merkel, as well as the leaders of Poland and the Baltics.

The media-savvy Georgians send hourly text updates. Crucially, the Georgian government gives the foreign media free rein to roam around – and even allows them to risk getting shot. It helps with transport: flying groups of journalists by helicopter to the steamy port of Poti, briefly occupied and trashed by Russian forces.

I join one trip. We fly low over pasture and mountain to the subtropical Black Sea coast. Russian bombers destroyed the navel base here on 8 August, killing five. They also sank three Georgian coastguard cutters. The gun turret of one sunken vessel sticks out above the turquoise water; another white coastguard boat is listing and sunk. Russian soldiers also ransacked the port's main building, blowing apart doors and upturning filing cabinets.

One soldier has written on a whiteboard: "Georgian bitches. Die, pederast cocks." "They turned up in 23 armoured vehicles. They took whatever was valuable," Rezo Managadze, a port employee, tells me. In a smashed-up medical room I find a portrait of Mikheil Saakashvili. A Russian soldier has stamped on it. He added a single word: "Dick".

The Russians struggle to match this Georgian PR offensive. The Kremlin does lay on one trip for Tbilisi-based journalists into South Ossetia. The aim of the excursion is to hear a victory concert conducted by the Russian maestro and principal conductor of the London Symphony Orchestra, Valery Gergiev. Gergiev, born in North Ossetia, is a strong supporter of the Kremlin.

It seems a good opportunity to visit Tskhinvali. After piling on to an overcrowded Russian army truck, we bump past the scorched villagers north of Gori. We stop at Karaleti. Several houses along the main road are fire-bombed; an abandoned Lada lies in a ditch; the local school is pillaged. I interviewed locals here the previous day. They all gave the same graphic account: Ossetian militias swept into the villages on 12 August, burning, stealing and kidnapping.

Sasha, our English-speaking Kremlin minder, however, has a different explanation. "Georgian special commandos burned down these houses," he tells a large scrum of foreign reporters, some of whom are in the area for the first time.

I demur. "I was here yesterday. Everyone I spoke to said that gangs of South Ossetians had set light to these houses. Why would Georgian commandos set light to Georgian houses deep inside Georgia?"

Sasha's face falls. He's clearly not used to contradiction. "Those houses suffered from a gas or electricity leak," he answers, majestically. He then turns to a grizzled Russian colonel and – addressing him softly in Russian – orders him to dump me off the truck.

I protest. "You can't throw me off. We're in no man's land. I have no vehicle. The situation here isn't safe." Sasha breaks into a malevolent half-smile. "Of course we won't chuck you off." I can stay. But he refuses to answer further questions. We drive on.

In Tskhinvali, next to the broken statue of a now headless Ossetian poet, I meet my colleague Tom Parfitt. It's a brief encounter: we swap info on casualty figures claimed by both sides. Tom says on the drive from Vladikavkaz he counted 270 burning Georgian houses deep inside Moscow-backed South Ossetia.

Nearby, South Ossetia's rebel president Eduard Kokoity, a former wrestler, addresses a crowd. He calls on Russia to recognise South Ossetia's independence – something Medvedev, invoking the precedent of Kosovo, does soon afterwards. The concert takes place in South Ossetia's damaged parliament. Gergiev conducts Shostakovich's "Leningrad" Symphony No 7, a choice that evokes Russia's heroic resistance to Nazi Germany in the second world war.

Several Georgian prisoners – some kidnapped by South Ossetian para-militaries – watch the performance from inside a cage. I dictate my story through to London. My attempts to capture the surreal flavour of the occasion, and its triumphal military ambience, get mangled. I describe "soldiers sitting on armoured tanks surrounded by razor wire". The copytaker on the other end of the crackly line, far from the Caucasus mountains, mishears. When my article appears in the following day's *Guardian* the soldiers are indeed sitting on armoured tanks. But they are "surrounded by reservoirs".

When I get back to Moscow the official mood towards western journalists is angry and vengeful. The accusation that the foreign media misrepresented the war is everywhere. Russian TV depicts Saakashvili as a war criminal and tie-chewing madman. Russians are also told that the US gave a "green light" to Saakashvili's attack on South Ossetia.

This brainwashing is crude but effective. Most rally behind the Russian government's actions. My landlady, Olga, tells me that the Georgian leader is psychologically deranged. All but a handful of plucky liberal commentators parrot the Kremlin's narrative that the invasion of Georgia was a spontaneous humanitarian mission to save civilian lives and Russian citizens. The alternative view – that it was a punitive response designed to humiliate Saakashvili and to teach Georgia a brutal lesson in geopolitics – scarcely features.

On Tuesday 25 November 2008, I meet Boris A Shardakov, an official from the press department of the Russian foreign ministry. I have come to collect my 2009 press accreditation, which I need to stay and work in Russia. Shardakov is the "curator" in charge of visas and accreditation for the British press. He is a figure of medium height, in his late 50s, with steel-framed glasses and a grey moustache. During our encounter the year before I had detected no obvious charm.

Shardakov meets me downstairs in the press department's small lobby. He is evidently furious. He is holding a copy of an article I had written the previous day on Mikhail Beketov, a Russian journalist severely beaten and left for dead outside his house by unknown assailants. Beketov suffered brain damage, lost his right leg and four fingers. He is the editor of a local newspaper in the Moscow suburb of Khimki. The paper had published articles critical of a decision to build a highway between Moscow and St Petersburg directly through Khimki's forest. The main suspect in Beketov's beating is Khimki's mayor, a veteran of the Soviet war in Afghanistan. My article explains the background to the case and quotes another Khimki journalist – also beaten up – who remarks: "To be a journalist in Russia is suicide."

Shardakov flings my new accreditation card contemptuously down in front of me. He begins raging about the Beketov story. He addresses me in Russian using the "ty" form – usually reserved for friends, lovers, children and pets. It is a deliberate insult.

"Why do you stay in this country?" he begins.

"Is your family not afraid that if you remain here something unpleasant might happen to you also?"

Is this a threat? It looks like one. I suggest to Shardakov we sit down. We perch in the reception area on a leather sofa. "Boris, you know perfectly well I am simply reporting the situation regarding the conditions faced by some Russian journalists. Beketov isn't the first to be beaten up."

"There is a police investigation going on."

"I realise that. But investigations in Russia generally don't lead anywhere."

(This is true. Three years later Beketov's attackers have not been found; Khimki's mayor even sues the journalist, wheelchair-bound and unable to speak, for libel.)

Shardakov is not mollified. He tells me that the Russian government is unhappy with my reporting, the Russian embassy in London dislikes me intensely, and it would be best if I pack my bags and leave Moscow. He adds that my articles are "dividing" young Russians – in other words, causing them to doubt the state. "Is your wife not worried something might happen to you?" he repeats.

Shardakov then turns to the war in Georgia.

"You lied!" he shouts. "There were 200 British journalists in Georgia. All of you are liars."

I respond: "Boris, you weren't there. We have a range of opinions in the *Guardian* on the causes of the war. I reported from the Georgian side, my colleague Tom Parfitt reported from the South Ossetian side, and we endeavoured to give a balanced picture. I reported what I saw. This may not correspond to what you saw on Russian TV."

Shardakov concedes this last point. But the conversation is an unhappy one. Shardakov's manner is bullying; his tone sardonic. And the attempt to spook seems deliberate. Is this is a freelance initiative by Shardakov, I wonder, or is he following orders from above?

In the best traditions of the KGB, Shardakov – as we part – says one more time, just in case I've somehow missed the insinuation: "Are you not worried that something might happen to you?"

The incident with Shardakov is unpleasant. But a far worse fate is in store for other "enemies".

CHAPTER 6

Death in the Snow

White Chamber, 1 Prechistenka Street, central Moscow
19 January 2009

People sometimes pay with their lives for saying out loud what they think.
ANNA POLITKOVSKAYA

In the bitter aftermath of the Russia-Georgia war, the FSB resumes its campaign against us. In the autumn of 2008 there are further break-ins at our new *dacha* home in Sokol, in northwest Moscow. These intrusions show a new ferocity and malevolence.

In 2007 I had begun to log the FSB's activities: disrupted phone calls, missing emails, and at least two visits to our old Voikovskaya flat. I jot down an account of my interview with Major Kuzmin in Lefortovo. It includes a bad pencil drawing of the FSB building, with squiggly razor wire and a forlorn-looking tree in the courtyard. Leonardo da Vinci I am not. The notes are simply an *aide-memoire* for a piece I want to write on my Lefortovo experience. At some point they vanish from my office. It's no great loss. But to the FSB, presumably, the notes are further proof of my "espionage activity" and hostile intent. As is, I suppose, the fact I use shorthand, a skill I mastered as a cub reporter in the English seaside town of Hastings.

The FSB may be Russia's new, all-powerful nobility. But can it, I wonder, decipher my scruffy "Pitman 2000" shorthand swirls and strokes?

I begin a new log. This time I jot down incidents of FSB harassment on the back of my blue-covered medical record. Entries soon fill the back page.

The booklet is from the private Russian medical clinic just across from my Moscow office. It's here I go for treatment for double pneumonia. The pneumonia is my own fault; I contract it after swimming in January in a frozen lake off the Moscow island of Serebryany Bor.

Across Russia, orthodox believers take part in ice-swimming each Epiphany. I join them during each of my Moscow winters – even when the temperature sinks in 2010 to 20C below zero. It's an extreme experience; when you submerge yourself it feels like a nuclear explosion going off in your head. But then Moscow is an extreme place.

We are away in Berlin from Wednesday 29 October to Sunday 2 November 2008. The journey back from the airport by taxi is slow: it's raining and the roads are jammed. I chat to the driver; he's from Uzbekistan. As we pull up outside our cottage it's immediately obvious there is something odd: the upper right window to our upstairs bedroom is open. It's visible from the street – but no one else, glancing at our new creeper-covered home with its picket fence and purple roof, would realise anything is amiss. The window is a kind of personalised semaphore, I realise. Its message is just for me. It says: "We're back."

I had securely locked all the windows when we left for Germany. The upstairs windows can only be accessed from inside the property; to open the outer windows you first have to go upstairs and unbolt and open two inner windows, overlooking the street. Four bolts in all. So someone has broken in. Inside, I find the security system beeping. The following day we call in an engineer. He reports back with wonderment: the batteries have been removed from every single alarm point in the house – 14 batteries in all. "I've never seen anything like this!" he says. He goes to fetch more batteries. It's hard not to admire the thoroughness of our FSB intruders. These guys are professionals.

At some point on Monday 8 December, the intruders come back. I'm at work, the children at school, my wife out with her walking group, exploring the back streets of Moscow's old town. The first snow has fallen; temperatures have sunk below zero. This time, we find the gas-fired boiler which heats the cottage has been disconnected: a white wire has been pulled out; the house is freezing cold.

But the worst is to come: in the early hours of the morning a strange alarm sounds – an arpeggio of plinking and plunking. It wakes everyone up. I go and investigate. It is 2am. It appears to be coming from the cupboard under the stairs. I peer inside. I can't find anything. I go back to bed. Eventually, the mysterious "hurdy gurdy" noise ceases. At 4am, it lurches back into life. It goes off at 6am. We pass a troubled night.

My father, John Harding – a regular visitor to Russia – can't sleep either. After breakfast we talk on the way to the metro, threading our way through the backyards of Sokol's apartment blocks and children's playgrounds, our conversation urgent and serious. The FSB's tactics, we agree, are sinister. But, more than this, they are patient. The break-ins are cleverly attritional: designed to break us down, to disrupt and incrementally wreck our family life.

This isn't conventional torture. There are no thumbscrews or electric shocks. Instead, this is something more insidious and better suited to a regime conscious of its international reputation – a form of psychological terror that has the marvellous advantage of being invisible and completely deniable. Smart torture, if you like. Or soft torture.

The agency's aim, clearly, is to encourage me to leave Russia. But what if I refuse to take the hint? My father agrees to relay a message to the *Guardian*'s editor, Alan Rusbridger. He needs to know that this state harassment is getting steadily worse. Outwardly, we behave as though nothing is happening. (The FSB is likely to interpret any panic on our part as a sign of operational success.) Privately, however, I wonder how much longer we can put up with the FSB's mind games.

I spend increasing amounts of time working from home, now under siege. One morning I spot a young man lurking outside. On another occasion it's a BMW with tinted windows, discreetly parked just up the road. On 19 December 2008, the FSB breaks into the apartment of one of the *Guardian*'s Russian editorial assistants. She lives alone, is 41, and single. She returns home to her flat and discovers her beret lying in the middle of her living room floor. (When she set off for work that morning the beret is hanging on its peg.)

She tells her mother about the incident. Her mother refuses to believe her. I try to explain the situation and to assure her she isn't going mad. My assistant is frightened, worried, tearful. For some months afterwards she is depressed. She resigns her job. She severs all contact with the *Guardian*. I never see her again.

This pattern continues. Most days the FSB makes itself known in some trivial way. On 30 January 2009, I arrive at work to discover the double lock to the office front door stiffer than usual. I go into my room. The screensaver on my laptop shows Phoebe and the children pictured against the spectacular backdrop of the snowy Upper Caucasus Mountains; the photo was taken on our Georgia holiday, after a strenuous hike in the shadow of Mount Kazbek. The kids look sweaty and exuberant.

But someone has got rid of the screensaver. My family has disappeared. The screen is locked. Whoever deleted the photo has also wiped the keyboard of my laptop. The grime and dust are gone. For some time afterwards, the laptop gives me small electric shocks. On 3 February 2009, I send an email to the British embassy. The email doesn't arrive. It is returned to my inbox with the word "NULL" in ominous capitals. At 2.45am my phone rings. The caller hangs up.

By this point it appears that Russia's omnipresent security services are set on continuing their campaign until I finally get the message and leave Moscow. These bizarre break-ins are not without a certain crude humour. One day I find a cheap, second-hand paperback in Russian left by the side of my bed. The book isn't one of mine; nor does it belong to my wife. I pick the book up from my bedside table. I examine it curiously. The title: *Love, Freedom and Aloneness / A New Vision of Relating*.

The author is Osho, the late Indian mystic, sex guru and Rolls Royce enthusiast better known to his followers as Bhagwan Shree Rajneesh. I am not familiar with Osho's work. But someone has helpfully inserted a bookmark on page 110. The chapter offers tips for lovers. I read: "A real orgasm takes place when your inner man and woman come together."

The FSB, then, has left a sex manual by my bed.

The message is – what? That the agency is watching, and thinks I could perform better? I hang on to the book. It becomes a humorous talking point at dinner parties – made all the more piquant by the fact that our living room is bugged and the FSB, for all we know, is listening to us laugh about their bizarre, unwelcome gift.

I later discover that leaving pornographic material in the bedroom of a target was one of the KGB's more extraordinary tactics, used frequently earlier in the cold war. Putin's modern spies are still using – or have gone back to – the old KGB handbook. They've clearly been unable to think of anything original. But this isn't counter-intelligence. It's *Karma Sutra*.

On Monday 19 January 2009, the lawyer Stanislav Markelov sets off down Moscow's Prechistenka Street. Ahead is the gold-domed Cathedral of Christ the Saviour, knocked down by Stalin, rebuilt by Yeltsin and Mayor Yuri Luzhkov. A little further on is the Kremlin, with its ochre walls and towers.

Markelov is a human rights lawyer and friend of the murdered journalist Anna Politkovskaya. He is heading towards the metro. He's given a press conference protesting the early release of an army officer convicted of rape and murder. Walking alongside him is a journalist, Anastasia Baburova. She is 25 years old and a freelancer with the leading opposition newspaper *Novaya Gazeta*. On the sidewalk a soft snow has fallen.

Markelov never makes it. Unnoticed, a youth wearing a ski-mask trails the lawyer as he leaves Moscow's small independent press centre. Just outside a white-painted palace – one historic Moscow building that somehow survived the developers – the assassin comes up to Markelov from behind. He shoots him in the back of the head. Twice. According to one account, Baburova tries to grab the gunman as he jogs off. He shoots her in the head too. Baburova lies unconscious and gravely wounded; Markelov dies instantly. He is 34 years old.

By the time I arrive at the scene around 5pm Markelov's body has been removed; police have set up a makeshift cordon on the pavement. Vermilion splashes of blood are still visible in the snow. But otherwise there are few clues. Markelov was killed outside the White Chamber, a 17th-century *palaty*, or palace, with thick walls, small windows and vaulted chambers, done in early baroque style. The address is 1 Prechistenka. The building is shut. The security guards in the neighbouring office saw nothing. Neither did the women in the old chemist's shop opposite – she tells me a customer came in immediately after the shooting and that she called an ambulance. But of the killer there is no trace.

With little to go on I find myself noting down the irrelevant. Next to the murder scene snow has crusted the shoulders of a 1970s statue of Friedrich Engels. The upper-class anarchist Peter Kropotkin was born in an empire-style mansion in a side street. Markelov, I learn later, was attracted to the writings of Kropotkin and his fellow radical philosopher Mikhail Bakunin. I wonder what Kropotkin would have made of the posh boulangeries and cafes that have now sprung up to cater for Prechistenka's well-groomed citizens.

With no leads, I go to the office. Baburova, the only apparent witness, isn't able to give a description of the killer; she dies later that evening in hospital. And as ever when lawyers, opposition journalists and other critics of the Kremlin are gunned down in Russia, the police, who in normal circumstances keep a close eye on affairs, are mysteriously absent.

Writing my report for the *Guardian* that evening I count the human rights activists gunned down since Putin ascended to power. It's a long list. I begin with those linked to *Novaya Gazeta*, a source of continuous annoyance to Putin and his entourage.

Since 2000 four of its writers have been murdered. The most famous is Politkovskaya, *Novaya*'s special correspondent (gunned down by an assassin outside the lift of her Moscow flat in October 2006). There is also Yuri Shchekochikhin (mysteriously poisoned in July 2003) and Igor Domnikov (bludgeoned to death with a hammer outside his apartment in July 2000). Markelov and Baburova are victims number four and five. Then there is Litvinenko, poisoned in London in the month after Politkovskaya's death. Other victims include Magomed Yevloyev, the journalist-founder of an opposition website in the Caucasus republic of Ingushetia, shot dead in police custody in 2008. Others follow.

The murders of these Kremlin foes – journalists, lawyers and critics of Russia's security services – have a common dimension. In each case, these state irritants are murdered as a direct result of their professional activities. Friends and colleagues are in no doubt that these killings are politically motivated and carried out either by the Russian state itself, or by shadowy forces connected to it. Officials, however, blame the killings on the Kremlin's enemies. The officials argue that the murders are done to blacken Russia's international image. This argument looks increasingly ridiculous as the bodies pile up.

Shaken by the day's events, I telephone Markelov's friends. "We don't know who killed him. But we know he was killed for doing his job, without a shadow of a doubt," says Tanya Lokshina, from Human Rights Watch's Moscow office. She adds: "Stas [Markelov] was one of those people prepared to risk his life for the cause. He was funny, outrageous and sometimes quite obnoxious. He was a colleague and a friend. He was always telling jokes, including the most obscene ones. I can't believe he's gone."

Lyudmila Alexeyeva, a Soviet-era dissident and head of the Moscow Helsinki Group, says she finds it hard to speak: "The assassination of such a person brings shame to our country."

I check to see whether the Kremlin has put out a statement condemning Markelov's murder. But from Putin and Medvedev there is silence. State TV largely ignores his death. This snub is reminiscent of Putin's description of Politkovskaya, three days after her murder, as an "extremely insignificant figure well known only in the west".

Like other Russian human rights defenders, Markelov, I discover, was a strong character, known for his puckish personality. His life was full of paradoxes: he was fond of karaoke but sung appallingly; a devoted father of two, he was frequently away from home, travelling to anarchist summer camps held in Bakunin's country house; he was a vodka-drinking vegetarian. As a lawyer he took on a series of high-profile cases involving the Kremlin's enemies – defending anti-fascists, opposition journalists and victims of Moscow's two brutal wars in Chechnya.

In common with other members of Russia's close-knit bohemian circle of opposition journalists and human rights activists, Markelov received regular death threats. He dealt with them with grim black humour.

"A typical conversation would go: 'Have you written your will yet?'" Lokshina says. "The answer was always: 'No, neither have I.'"

In a long piece for the *Guardian* I write that Markelov's killing has a resonance that goes beyond his own country and is similar in its brazenness to the murder of Politkovskaya, another courageous Kremlin critic. It takes place against a backdrop of officially sanctioned harassment and persecution of Russian human rights organisations – against anyone, in fact, who challenges the Kremlin's monopoly on power.

The FSB, I later discover, accuses the US government of funding terrorism by supporting the activities of non-governmental organisations working in the Caucasus. It warns Washington that failure to halt its "incompetent" actions will lead to the refusal of visas for US citizens. The Kremlin's clampdown on NGOs is thought to be born of paranoia about an orange revolution in Russia. Alexeyeva tells me that the country's beleaguered rights defenders, however, aren't interested in overthrowing the regime. Nor are they US spies. They simply want the Russian government to uphold human rights and respect human dignity.

Over the next few days I examine possible leads in Markelov's killing. Markelov represented the family of an 18-year-old Chechen woman who was murdered and raped in 2000 by a drunken Russian army colonel. The case was one of the most notorious to arise out of the Chechen wars. Colonel Yuri Budanov snatched Elza Kungayeva from her father's house during a late-night raid in 2000, killed her inside his *vagonchik* – a hut or caravan – and then ordered his subordinates to secretly bury her body. He was convicted of murder in 2003, despite claiming he had gone temporarily insane and had mistaken her for a sniper.

In the wake of the conviction, "patriots" repeatedly targeted Markelov. In 2004 a group of five youths beat him up. Budanov was released from prison a week before Markelov's murder. In his last press conference, Markelov announced he was appealing the decision to give Budanov parole. (Budanov himself was shot dead in 2011.)

But this is only one avenue of suspicion. Markelov had also represented victims of police brutality, and helped stage anti-Kremlin protests. He had sought justice for one of the victims of the 2002 Nord-Ost siege, in which Special Forces used poisonous gas to storm a Moscow theatre seized by Chechen terrorists. One of his last clients was Mikhail Beketov, the journalist beaten to a pulp after defying the authorities in Moscow's Khimki suburb.

In 2005, Markelov acted for the prosecution against a federal soldier who had abducted a Chechen who subsequently disappeared. Markelov travelled repeatedly to Chechnya, often working closely with Politkovskaya.

He exposed a secret torture prison belonging to Ramzan Kadyrov. The only thing that everyone agrees on, I discover, is that he had lots of enemies.

Suspicion also falls on Russia's thriving neo-Nazi movement, for whom Markelov was a special hate figure. In 2006 he represented the family of Alexander Ryukhin, an anti-fascist activist murdered by skinheads. Several of those who took part in Ryukhin's killing received jail sentences. But the professional manner of Markelov's assassination doesn't fit with the pattern of other neo-Nazi attacks. Instead it speaks of someone with military experience. Pavel Felgenhauer – the columnist who correctly predicted war in Georgia – points the finger at the FSB.

He writes:

> In the opinion of the *Novaya Gazeta* staff, of which I am a member, the Russian security services or rogue elements within these services are the prime suspects. The boldness of the attack, by a single gunman in broad daylight in the centre of Moscow, required professional preliminary planning and surveillance that would necessitate the security services, which closely control that particular neighbourhood, turning a blind eye.

Novaya Gazeta prints a black-bordered edition. The front-page photo shows Markelov lying dead on the icy pavement. The headline pays tribute to his bravery. It reads: "No fear".

Three days after the murder, I attend Markelov's funeral. The cemetery sits under the shadow of the looming Ostankino TV tower in north Moscow; riot police ring the entrance. (The authorities are mindful that funeral processions can turn into protests.) Funeral workers wheel Markelov's body in on a gurney; a hole has already been dug; crows clatter among the silver birch trees overlooking the snowy grave. The day is raw and grey. Around 200 mourners have turned up. The lid is taken off his coffin.

As a young man Markelov sported a ponytail; he's buried in his lawyer's uniform of suit and tie. His brother Mikhail says: "This isn't the time to discuss what happened. It's a time to say goodbye." His relatives – he leaves a young widow, Galina, from Belarus, and two small children – kiss him on the forehead. Mourners throw red carnations into his coffin. The lid is banged shut. From somewhere I hear a deep, animal choke. Nobody from the Kremlin attends.

Afterwards, standing in the slush near the cemetery gates, I talk to some of the dead lawyer's friends. They say the question of who shot him is both unanswerable and more or less beside the point. What matters, they suggest, is that Russia is now a gangster state – formally a democracy but in reality nothing of the kind – where the murder of Kremlin critics can take place at any moment. Either the state is directly responsible for killing its enemies, or it condones the actions of shadowy external forces, they say. "Such a murder reflects the criminalized situation we have here. The Kremlin encourages extremist groups, and different reactionary forces see in its rhetoric a kind of support," says Alexey Gaskarov, an anti-fascist friend of Markelov. "In any European country when anyone important is killed the authorities immediately try and do something about it. Here they are silent."

One of those at Markelov's funeral is Natalia Estemirova. Estemirova, known as Natasha, is a friend of Politkovskaya and Markelov; she is the head of the human rights group Memorial's office in the Chechen capital, Grozny. "I think criminals are comfortable with the kind of government we have now. It's less comfortable for human rights advocates," she says. Estemirova dubs the authorities' recent behaviour strange, and says the Russian government deliberately mixes up human rights activists with traitors. Writing in *Novaya Gazeta*, she describes Markelov as "cheerful, charming, mischievous, and not recognising any obstacles". Her article ends: "Markelov's killing is a declaration of war. The question now is – on whose side is the state?"

On 4 November 2009, the FSB arrests two suspects in connection with Markelov's murder. Their names are Nikita Tikhonov and Yevgenia Khasis. Both are members of an ultranationalist group known as Unified Brigade-88. The group murdered Markelov, the FSB claims, in revenge for his efforts to put fellow ultranationalists behind bars after the murder of Ryukhin in 2006. Tikhonov was one of the suspects in that killing, but went into hiding and was never apprehended; he saw many of his friends jailed in the case. According to Alexander Bortnikov, the FSB's boss, Tikhonov was caught during a crackdown on extremist groups in Moscow and confessed to his crime. Several firearms are found in Tikhonov's flat: a 7.65mm Browning pistol, made in 1910 and allegedly the murder weapon, as well as cartridges and a silencer. Security cameras on Prechistenka capture Khasis, wearing dark clothes, acting as a lookout.

Most human rights activists find the FSB's explanation for the crime "plausible", US diplomats tell Washington in a classified dispatch. But the activists doubt that the two suspects were the only people involved in the crime, and hope for more investigation. One tells the Americans it is "unlikely the two suspects acted alone" and believes the mastermind of the killing is still at large. The Kremlin, however, is keen to close the case and enjoy the PR coup from solving a high-profile murder. The cable notes the "self-satisfied tone" of a meeting between Medvedev and Bortnikov to discuss the arrest of a couple dubbed "a patriotic Bonnie and Clyde". In May 2011 a Moscow jury convicts both accused, though it urges further investigation. Tikhonov is sentenced to imprisonment for life; Khasis gets 18 years.

One week before Markelov's murder, Umar Israilov pops out to buy some yoghurt. Israilov is a Chechen émigré. He is 27 years old and a former insurgent. In 2003, he was arrested in Chechnya; the Muslim republic was under the control of Ramzan Kadyrov's father Akhmad, an ex-separatist backed by Moscow, later blown up. Israilov claimed that during his time in detention he was tortured with electric shocks and said he witnessed fellow detainees beaten and kicked by Kadyrov and others. After being amnestied, he worked briefly as Kadyrov's bodyguard, before fleeing to Austria. In 2006 Israilov filed a complaint to the European Court of Human Rights alleging that Kadyrov personally tortured him in a secret prison. It's a brave move.

According to Chechen sources, emissaries from Kadyrov arrive in Vienna pressuring Israilov to withdraw his complaint. He refuses, and instead airs his grievances in an interview with the *New York Times*. Back in Chechnya, President Kadyrov imprisons Israilov's father Ali. Kadyrov's aim is clear: to pressure Umar to withdraw his deposition. Ali is tortured and held illegally for 10 months. After his release he submits his own complaint to the Strasbourg court. In Vienna, home to a large Chechen diaspora,

Israilov grows fearful for his safety. He complains to Austrian police he is being followed. They ignore him.

Then, on 13 January, three men ambush Israilov outside his local super-market in Vienna, where he lives with his pregnant wife and two small children. It is 1pm. Israilov knows what is happening and tries to escape – he zigzags across a crowded street, but is felled by four shots from his pursuers. Then they shoot him in the head. The assassins wear military-style trousers. Austrian police quickly arrest three suspects, and discover a trail leading back to Kadryov and his aide Shaa Turlayev. A mobile telephone belonging to Ramzan Edilov, the Chechen organiser of the killing, contains a photo showing Edilov and Kadyrov embracing.

Israilov's murder is merely one of a series of high-profile political assas-sinations abroad with links to Chechnya. One human rights activist tells me: "You can criticise Medvedev or even Putin. But it's very dangerous to crit-icise Kadyrov." She says the current climate of fear in Chechnya is reminiscent of the Stalinist period. True or not, critics of the president of the Chechen republic frequently meet a violent and unpleasant end, both inside Russia and abroad. Living in the European Union apparently offers no protection from Chechen death squads, dispatched to silence Kadyrov's critics. Another enemy of Chechnya's president, Magomed-Salakh Masaev, goes missing in August 2008 after giving an interview to *Novaya Gazeta*. He tells the paper he was repeatedly tortured at a secret prison in Kadyrov's home village of Tsentoroi. The Muslim preacher has not been seen since. Markelov had been working on Masaev's case. Both Markelov and Israilov were killed in professional-style executions – could the two murders, I wonder, have been related?

Chechen exile groups believe that only Kadyrov – already accused of involvement in Anna Politkovskaya's death – can authorise such assassina-tions in Europe. Kadyrov rejects the claim; his officials say Israilov was running an illegal refugee-smuggling racket and was killed as a result of a business feud. But the trail of bodies tells its own gory story. In February 2008, Musa Ataev, the former "foreign minister" of the separatist Caucasus Emirate is murdered in Turkey. At the end of March, Sulim Yamadayev, a warlord affiliated to Russian military intelligence, and one of Kadyrov's chief political competitors, is shot dead in Dubai. His assassination follows that of his brother, Ruslan, a member of the state Duma, who is gunned down while sitting in his luxury Mercedes outside the British embassy in Moscow. Sulim's assassins shoot him with a gold-plated pistol, allegedly smuggled into the emirate inside a Russian diplomatic bag. Dubai police accuse Adam Delimkhanov – Kadyrov's cousin and close associate – of ordering the assassination, and issue a warrant for his arrest.

Confidential US diplomatic cables disclose that the White House also considers Kadyrov to be behind this string of ice-cold killings. One cable, sent by US diplomats in Oslo on 24 June 2009, discusses the danger faced by Israilov's father Ali, now in hiding abroad following his son's murder. It says that "the FSB was probably consulted about this [Israilov's] killing, and gave its tacit approval". US diplomats add: "Ali's complaint at the European Court of Human Rights in Strasbourg stands as one of the few challenges to the system of impunity being set up in Kadyrov's Chechnya. Recently, two killings [those of Yamadayev and Ataev] confirm Kadyrov's willingness to use assassination as a tool." From Kadyrov's point of view, the assassinations are "pragmatic rather than vindictive", the diplomats conclude, adding that the Chechen leader is "quite savvy". They stress: "These human rights cases are an embarrassment for the Russian government and Kadyrov's logic may be that an assassination is preferable to the continuation of these cases in Strasbourg."

In February 2009 I bump into Natasha Estemirova again. We meet at the trial of four suspects charged with involvement in Anna Politkovskaya's murder. The venue is a small, overcrowded courtroom in Moscow's Military District Court, a yellow-painted neo-classical building on Old Arbat. The four suspects sit in a cage. Two of them are Chechens – Dzhabrail and Ibragim Makhmudov. The brothers are stocky, with dark, floppy hair and moronic expressions. A third defendant is Sergei Khadzhikurbanov, a former Moscow policeman. The fourth suspect is Lieutenant Colonel Pavel Ryaguzov, an FSB agent. Ryaguzov wears a black bomber jacket.

All four are accused of lending Politkovskaya's killer operational support, and are alleged to have carried out surveillance of her flat in Lesnaya Ulitsa. (Politkovskaya's home is two blocks from my office, not far from Moscow's busy Belorussky train station.) But the supposed hit-man – a third Makhmudov brother, Rustam, who allegedly shot Politkovskaya in the stairwell of her Moscow apartment – has disappeared. Investigators say he has gone abroad. In 2011 he is arrested in Chechnya. The person who ordered the journalist's killing, the mastermind behind the murder, is also missing. Police say they are unable to identify him.

Estemirova tells me the trial is a "farce", that there has been no serious attempt to investigate Politkovskaya's killing. "We don't have a killer. And we don't have the people who are really behind it," she says. "This isn't a real trial. It's simply meant to give the impression of justice." Much of the prosecution's case is odd, she adds. Listening to the evidence, I realise that Estemirova is right. It isn't just that the investigation is shoddy and inadequate – this is commonplace in Russian trials. In the Politkovskaya case, though, much of the physical evidence has disappeared.

According to her colleagues at *Novaya Gazeta*, Russia's "corrupted" security services have deliberately hindered the probe into her death. Simcards, computer discs and even a photo of Rustam Makhmudov, who is said to have fled to western Europe, all vanish. Footage showing the assassin emerging from the journalist's apartment block is also mislaid. The blurry video, shot from behind, shows her assassin: a dark-haired, narrow-shouldered man, his face largely concealed by a baseball cap. The time is shown to be 16:04. The Makhmudovs' lawyer, however, produces mobile phone footage of Rustam swimming in a Chechen river. He has broad shoulders.

During the break I lunch with Estemirova, together with Friederike Behr, a researcher for Amnesty International, and Christian Esch, Moscow correspondent for the *Berliner Zeitung*. We sit in the basement of a German beer cellar. Estemirova talks about England and Oxford – she spent part of the summer in the university town with her teenage daughter. We also chat about her human rights work in Grozny; she says she plans to go back to Chechnya after the trial.

She is 50, but appears younger; and strikingly elegant in a plain, unadorned black jumper. Estemirova is brave – to work in Chechnya as an opponent of Kadyrov requires immense pluck. But more than that, I think, she is possessed of an extraordinary, almost otherworldly courage and moral presence. She writes down her email address: estemirova@gmail.com. I promise to get in touch next time I'm in Grozny.

The Politkovskaya trial concludes with the acquittal of all four defendants. The jury is unconvinced by the prosecution's case. This is hardly surprising, given the bungled investigation and flawed trial. After the verdict, we stream out of court: the Makhmudovs' lawyer, Murad Masayev, praises the jury's unanimous decision. He says the Russian authorities should now try and catch Politkovskaya's "real killer". He adds that the three-month trial is a "fiasco" for Russia's investigative committee – tasked with solving the crime – and a "victory" for Russia. "Crimes like this take away the best people in our society. The only way to stop these crimes is to catch the real criminals," he says.

I ask him who, then, he thinks killed Anna Politkovskaya. "I really don't know. The investigators decided at some point to put these guys [the Makhmudovs] in jail and the real killers stay unpunished." Half an hour later the two Chechen brothers emerge into the street outside. They appear dazed; their families delighted. I ask Ibragim how he feels. "I feel free." What's he going to do now? "I'm going to pray."

Politkovskaya's family express disappointment with the verdict. At a press conference that evening, Anna's son Ilya says he respects the jury's conclusions but believes "the four people released today were involved in my mother's death". The family's lawyer, Karinna Moskalenko, is scathing about the investigators, saying it is extraordinary they failed to question Kadyrov in connection with the journalist's murder. She also criticises detectives for ignoring the fact the killing took place on Vladimir Putin's 54th birthday. (One theory says Politkovskaya was murdered as a macabre gift to the president. Two days earlier Kadyrov also celebrated a birthday, his 30th.) "This fact may or may not be linked to the crime. But you can't just ignore it," she says. In June, Russia's Supreme Court overturns the verdicts. It orders the suspects to be retried.

I'm sitting in my Moscow office. My mobile rings. It is 15 July 2009. On the line is Mark Rice-Oxley, a colleague in London on the *Guardian* foreign desk. Mark reported from Moscow in the 1990s; he speaks Russian and understands the country's murky workings well.

Mark says: "There's a story here you should probably take a look at. There's been another murder in Chechnya. It's a human rights activist."

My heart sinks. "Who is it?"

"Natasha Estemirova."

Three days later I'm on a plane to Grozny. I stay with a Chechen journalist in a quiet apartment block on the edge of town; he shares a flat with his elderly mother and 15-year-old son. In February 1944, his mother and her family – together with the entire Chechen population – were deported as traitors to Central Asia, on Stalin's orders. She returned to Grozny from Kazakhstan only in the late 1950s. I sleep on a mattress; it's warm here in southern Russia; the apartment echoes with snoring.

My friend and I set off the next morning to Natasha's apartment block. Chechen security men are parked outside. We wait. Eventually they leave; we go inside and talk to the neighbours.

The facts of her abduction and murder are these: Natasha leaves her flat in Grozny at 8.30am and sets off towards the bus stop. Usually it takes her 15-20 minutes to get to work – a bumpy ride in a shared minivan, down an avenue of green tower blocks. The route passes giant posters of Chechen warlord President Kadyrov, and several of Prime Minister Putin.

On this occasion, she never arrives. A hundred metres beyond the entrance of her 10th-floor flat – which overlooks a patch of grassy wasteland and a grove of shabby walnut trees – four gunmen are waiting. They grab Estemirova, bundle her into a white Russian-made Zhiguli car and drive off. A passer-by sees the abduction and hears her cry out, "I'm being kidnapped!" Her kidnappers head in the direction of Ingushetia, Chechnya's neighbouring republic. Probably they take the M-29 highway, though there is also a grassy back-route looping along a hillside. The road is a scenic one: it cuts through a dark tunnel of poplar trees; on the roadside women sell melons from the backs of trucks. The kidnappers breeze through several checkpoints.

Two hours later, Estemirova is dead. The men stop their vehicle soon after crossing into Ingushetia. Up ahead, a group of Islamist militants had just ambushed a government car, opening fire. Estemirova's kidnappers may at this point have panicked. They march her, hands tied, off the road. And then they shoot her five times in the head and chest – leaving behind her money, passport and ID card. This isn't a robbery. It is something else: a vile, cowardly, meticulous, state-sponsored execution, apparently designed to send a chilling warning to the small, dwindling number of activists working in Chechnya, Russia's rogue republic.

Estemirova's admirers had calculated that her international renown meant that she would transcend danger. But – as with Politkovskaya, another figure seemingly beyond the reach of a professional hitman – this wasn't enough. In retrospect her death seems both appalling and predictable. After Politkovskaya, who was a frequent guest at Estemirova's modest flat, came Markelov. And after Markelov came Estemirova – the obvious next target.

Sitting in a cafe next to Memorial's Grozny office, where Estemirova worked, I call Lokshina, her friend and colleague. "She was an amazing and inspiring person with an obsessive and unstoppable desire for justice," Lokshina says. "She was nice and funny, always smiling, always well-dressed despite her small salary and somewhat coquettish."

According to Lokshina, Estemirova knew the risks she was running. "After Stas was murdered she flew to Moscow for the funeral. She and I sat up late at night talking about the situation. We asked ourselves: 'Who is going to be next?' Natasha was next." She wouldn't have been surprised by her own kidnapping and violent death, Lokshina says. Estemirova had been working in Grozny for Memorial since 2000.

A historian by training, her job as Memorial's leading Grozny-based activist was to document and publicise abuses carried out by the Chechen law enforcement and security agencies, under Kadyrov's de facto control, as well as by jihadist militants.

By fixing, by recording, by naming, she sought to establish a higher truth in a region shattered by conflict and moral breakdown. Every day a queue of women would turn up at her office just off Grozny's main Putin Avenue. (After Kadyrov renamed the street in homage to Putin, Estemirova refused to even walk on it.) There, they would tell their stories – of relatives shot by Kadyrov's troops, missing sons who went to work and never came back, of houses torched by masked gunmen in uniforms. Estemirova would immediately fire off a letter to the local procurator, the official under the Russian legal system tasked with both investigating and prosecuting a crime.

At a time when the world stopped listening to Chechnya's woes, Estemirova had stayed on in Grozny. She continued to highlight extrajudicial killings, disappearances, torture and other crimes. She wrote reports for Memorial and articles for *Novaya Gazeta*. She co-operated with Amnesty International and Human Rights Watch. She believed in rule of law. She was an invaluable source of information for western journalists who – in Putin's second presidential term – visited Chechnya with embarrassing infrequency.

Inevitably, this led to confrontation with Kadyrov, Chechnya's thuggish tsar, and a man observed by US diplomats at a raucous Dagestan wedding dancing "clumsily with a gold-plated automatic stuck down in the back of his jeans". A former rebel turned pro-Moscow loyalist, Kadyrov has pioneered his own Kremlin-backed mini-Stalinist regime in the Muslim republic – the scene of Kremlin wars from 1994 to 1996 and 1999 to 2004.

As I drive though Chechnya it feels a bit like travelling through a giant version of Kadyrov's family photo album, so numerous are the portraits of Kadyrov *père et fils*. It's true that Kadyrov has presided over the republic's spectacular reconstruction, with much of war-smashed Grozny rebuilt. At the same time, he has turned Chechnya into a lawless personal fiefdom. His violent tactics – dressed up as anti-terrorist operations – are used not just against the unknown number of Islamist insurgents still holed up in Chechnya's forests and mountains, but also against the wider, terrified civilian population.

Researching her story, I learn that Estemirova received threats from senior aides of Kadyrov. In March 2008 Kadyrov summoned her to a meeting at which he expressed extreme dissatisfaction with her work and her opposition to his new edict forcing Chechen women to wear headscarves, a gender-specific rule against Chechen tradition. Estemirova told colleagues Kadyrov had threatened her. She quoted him as saying: "Yes, my hands are up to the elbows in blood. And I am not ashamed of that. I was killing and will kill bad people." A former school-teacher, she reproached him. But the encounter was clearly terrifying. Two weeks before her death Adam Delimkhanov – Kadyrov's alleged murderous enforcer – gave an interview to Chechen TV, saying that human rights activists were the same as terrorists; both, he said, needed to be "answered".

The front door to the Memorial office is shut; the organisation says it is too dangerous to carry on its work. I go round the back, and discover a side-door. I knock. Inside I find Shakman Akbulatov, Estemirova's co-worker. A colour photo of Estemirova is tacked to the wall. He says the Kremlin's decision in April 2009 to formally end Russia's war in Chechnya, which meant a number of security measures were lifted, saw a spike in human rights abuses across the republic. Suddenly, Natasha found herself deluged with new cases, as Kadyrov's forces abducted civilians – in some cases murdered them – and subsequently branded them as militants. Akbulatov is clear that her death was a punishment for her professional activities, which embarrassed the Kadyrov regime. "It was done to silence her," Akbulatov says. "She was as brave a person as you can imagine. She knew it was very dangerous."

What is unclear is why Estemirova's enemies chose this moment to kill her. At the time of her death she was investigating the case of Madina Yunusova, a 20-year-old woman whose husband was killed on 2 July 2009 in a special operation in the village of Staraya Sunzha, not far from Grozny. Officials claim, implausibly, she had fired a Kalashnikov and was involved in a plot to kill Kadyrov. Yunusova was injured in the shoot-out but survived. She then died in mysterious circumstances in hospital. What followed was a classic example of collective punishment. On 4 July, at 3am, men in camouflage fatigues arrived at Yunusova's parents' home in the town of Argun. According to neighbours, they set light to it, locking the family in a shed.

When I investigate I find the house deserted. Burned clothes lie in the garden, next to a plot of yellow dahlias. The Yunusovs have fled. Their flip-flops sit in the front porch, underneath a vine trellis; peering through a broken window I make out a blackened bedroom and charred mattress.

Speaking in Moscow, the head of Memorial, Oleg Orlov, directly accuses Kadyrov. "We know who is responsible. We know what position he occupies. His job is Chechen president," he says. "Ramzan personally hated Natasha. He insulted her and threatened her. We don't know whether it was Ramzan himself who gave the order to kill Natasha or his close associates. But President Medvedev seems satisfied to have a murderer as head of one of Russia's republics."

Kadyrov's response is characteristically wheedling. He denies involvement, calls her murder a "monstrous crime", and later blames the killing on Berezovsky. Medvedev describes her murder as an "outrage" but dismisses claims of Kadyrov's involvement as "primitive and unacceptable". The investigation into her death makes little progress – even though the identity of her killer is widely known.

I leave Grozny. I travel to Koshkeldy, in Chechnya's Gudermes district. The village is Estemirova's ancestral home; her aunt and other members of her family still live here. Several male relatives are sitting in the shade outside a rustic blue-painted house. They take me into the courtyard; we make ourselves comfortable in a bright side-room. On the table are plates of lamb and watermelon. Next door, a group of women sit on the carpet. From time to time they erupt in howls and sobs.

Estemirova's 15-year-old daughter Lana appears. She is remarkably composed. We sit for a while. She speaks English. She says her mother was aware of the danger she was in: "I know that she had threats. She didn't tell me about this but I knew it. I never told her to leave her job. I knew it was important for all the people. She didn't live for herself. She lived for those who needed her help." According to Lana, she never travelled with bodyguards and paid scant attention to her personal safety. "Her only concern was for me. If I missed her call or had my phone on vibrate she would say: 'Are you crazy? It breaks my heart when you don't pick up.'"

Estemirova's husband died during the first Chechen war – at around the time she decided to abandon her career as a history teacher and to embark on a career as an activist and journalist. She lived with Lana in a small Grozny flat filled with books, her international prizes, and a fluffy cat, Vanessa. Lana says she sees no future in Russia; she wants to study in England. "Even now I can't believe this has happened to me. I didn't look at her when she was dead. It was only when I saw her body [at the funeral] that I realised I would be alone."

I wander up to the village cemetery where Estemirova is buried. Her grave sits on a grassy hillside. It's a quiet spot. Her father is buried nearby. White butterflies flutter among the Islamic headstones; a light breeze blows.

Her headstone reads:

Natalia Estemirova
28.02.1958
15.07.2009

I stand for a moment, then go and say goodbye to Lana.

When Lana was a small girl growing up, Markelov and Politkovskaya were regular guests at Estemirova's modest Grozny flat. The three would stay up late, talking into the night – Politkovskaya focused and somewhat stern, Markelov clowning around and laughing. First Anna, then Stas then her mother – within three years all of the important adults in Lana's life have been murdered, I realise. Next door, the howling begins again. "My tears are finished," she says.

I had expected a throng of journalists at Estemirova's house. I am the only one. Where are the others?

CHAPTER 7

KGB! Give Me Your Papers!

Bistrot restaurant, Bolshoy Savinsky Street, Moscow
13 January 2009

News from Russia is a joke.
MALCOLM MUGGERIDGE, *WINTER IN MOSCOW*

I am the eighth staff correspondent to have reported from Russia for the *Guardian* since the Bolshevik revolution. My predecessors were a distinguished bunch. The first was Arthur Ransome, better known for his stories for children. Ransome shared a flat with a member of the Politburo, Karl Radek, played chess with Lenin, and had a passionate affair with Leon Trotsky's secretary, whom he married and carried off home to Britain. (This I learn from Martin Walker, another predecessor who covered Moscow in the 1980s.) The second *Guardian* correspondent – back then, of course, it was the *Manchester Guardian* – was Malcolm Muggeridge, who lived in Moscow in 1932 and 1933.

It is Muggeridge with whom I feel the greatest affinity. In his introduction to *Winter in Moscow*, Michael Aeschliman points out Muggeridge might have been expected to give a sympathetic account of the brave new world being constructed by the Soviets. He was, after all, the son of a socialist MP, a relation of the Fabian Webbs, and a writer for a respected liberal newspaper. Instead, Muggeridge was instantly appalled by what he found: tyranny, censorship, hypocrisy, brutality, poverty and what André

Gide – writing after the war in *The God that Failed*, a collection of essays by disillusioned ex-communists – called the "extent of the bluff".

Muggeridge reserved his especial scorn for the western journalists who colluded in the great deceit, sending propagandistic dispatches back from Russia, and ignoring or downplaying the horrors they know to be taking place under Stalin. In early 1933 Muggeridge managed to evade censorship and see the Stalin-made famines in the Ukraine and the north Caucasus. He documented the deliberate genocide against Soviet peasants, some 14.5 million of whom died as a result of what was, in effect, government-engineered murder.

Muggeridge smuggled his reports back to the *Guardian* via a British diplomatic bag. The newspaper published them, somewhat reluctantly, in March 1933. His articles prompted a furious response. In the west, Muggeridge's revelations were met with widespread incredulity; he was accused of being a liar. He found it impossible to get a job as a journalist – he had offended the liberal consensus, he wrote, which still looked indulgently at the communist experiment taking place under Stalin. He resigned from the *Guardian*. He was also unable to return to the Soviet Union.

Now long out of print, *Winter in Russia* was written 1934 on Muggeridge's return from the Soviet Union. It is a devastatingly satirical account of the western journalists who deliberately looked away from Stalin's famines – one of the greatest crimes in human history – and who deceived their readers about the true nature of the Soviet regime. He also attacked those leftwing intellectuals who allowed themselves to be duped.

Muggeridge is especially sardonic about Walter Duranty, the Pulitzer-winning correspondent for the *New York Times*. Duranty appears in the novel as a character called Jefferson. He is the quintessential "useful idiot". In his reports back to Washington, Duranty denied the existence of the famines, and was instrumental in persuading Roosevelt to recognise diplomatically Stalin's odious and tyrannical regime.

In his preface to the novel Muggeridge writes about the "position of foreign journalists in Russia and the manner in which news about Russia reaches outside."

He observes:

There is stiff censorship of course; but it is not generally known that foreign journalists in Moscow work under the perpetual threat of losing their visas and therefore their jobs. Unless they consent (which most of them do) to limit their news to what they know will not be displeasing to the Dictatorship of the Proletariat, they are subjected to continuous persecution.

That persecution, Muggeridge writes, can vary from "tiresome approaches" about visa status all the way through to "the imprisonment and exiling of any friends or relatives they may have who are unfortunate enough to be Soviet citizens".

He adds:

> The result is that news from Russia is a joke, either being provided by men whom long residence in Moscow has made completely docile … or by men who, while trying to say more than they can, are forced for interested or quite legitimate reasons, to be discreet. It is even not unusual for agents of the Soviet government to bring pressure to bear in editorial offices when the correspondent is not to its satisfaction."

Muggeridge also notes what he calls the "thorough" behaviour of the OGPU. The OGPU were Stalin's secret police – the forerunner of the KGB, and today's FSB, whose former boss Vladimir Putin now runs Russia. I know what Muggeridge means. Eight decades on, not much has changed.

The invitation is unexpected. It's January 2009. My mobile rings. On the line is Artyom Artyomov, aide to the Russian billionaire Alexander Lebedev. Would I like to have lunch with Alexander, Artyom wants to know. The previous week I had written a sympathetic profile for the *Observer* newspaper of Lebedev, a former deputy in the Duma and Russian newspaper tycoon. The *Guardian* had reported that Lebedev was holding talks with Lord Rothermere over the possible sale of London's loss-making *Evening Standard* newspaper. It appeared, though, that the talks had run into difficulties and that the *Standard* deal was now off.

I'd met Lebedev twice before. I'd been one of many guests at his 49th birthday party, held in the down-at-heel offices of his opposition newspaper *Novaya Gazeta*. Lebedev clearly wasn't your average oligarch: for a start, he wore sneakers, albeit posh ones. In appearance, he resembled a grey-haired member of a boy band on a dodgy comeback tour – he wore a painfully modish black suit and pencil-thin tie. Unless I was mistaken, he was also sporting a couple of Glastonbury-style wristbands.

The party had been frugal, in keeping with the sombre global mood following the 2008 economic crash. There were no girls dancing on tables, and no champagne. Instead guests munched on plates of bacon lard and sank shots of vodka. Friends and colleagues sang their congratulations; someone played the accordion. Revellers included journalists and spooks.

The offer of lunch is intriguing. As well as being a businessman with political ambitions, Lebedev is a former KGB agent. He served in the Soviet embassy in Britain in the late 1980s. We agree to meet in an upmarket bistro, not far from Lebedev's office, a three-storey yellow-painted contemporary townhouse, close to the Moskva river and Kievsky railway station. I order the New Zealand lamb; Lebedev has the pasta with octopus. The restaurant – done in overblown Middle Eastern style – is empty.

Lebedev says he liked my profile of him. I ask him why the negotiations to buy the *Evening Standard* have collapsed. What went wrong? Speaking in immaculate English, and leaning across the low glass table, Lebedev replies smoothly: "They haven't collapsed." He adds, casually: "I'm buying the *Evening Standard* on Thursday." I do my best to look nonchalant. But this is clearly a bombshell. It's also something that happens relatively rarely to any journalist in his or her career. I have a genuine old-fashioned scoop.

The story is so fantastic it might have sprung from an ingenious cold war thriller. As a junior spy in the Soviet Union's plush Kensington embassy, Lebedev had to read the British newspapers. Every morning he would plough through the *Financial Times*, the *Guardian* and the tabloids – looking for small hopeful signs of the downfall of capitalism. Generally there weren't any. He would write diplomatic telegrams, sent to his employer back in Moscow, the KGB's First Chief Directorate. The good ones might even reach the table of the Politburo. Lebedev's essayistic themes reflected the preoccupations of a bygone age: the campaign for nuclear disarmament, the Labour party – then as now in opposition – and the trade union movement.

When WikiLeaks releases thousands of secret US diplomatic cables Lebedev reads them with a professional eye, he later tells me – he'd written numerous similar dispatches himself. "Some cables were like Chekhov. Others were boring," he says of the US communiques. His own cables still sit somewhere in a dusty KGB archive.

Two decades after Lebedev's London posting, capitalism is still with us, though not exactly thriving. The Soviet Union has disappeared. But Lebedev's own fortunes have prospered. (In 2011, *Forbes* magazine estimates he is worth $2.1 billion, and is Russia's 45th richest man.) Sitting over lunch, I find myself smiling: the *Standard*'s new owner is a former enemy spy who first rifled through the newspaper while working as a lieutenant-colonel in the KGB's foreign intelligence directorate.

Lebedev's son Evgeny later recalls how as a child he used to walk past the building that now houses his family's *Standard* and *Independent* titles. The former Barkers store, in Kensington High Street, is located just a few hundred yards down the road from the Lebedevs' Soviet embassy accommodation. It's a post-modern twist that John le Carré, the great cold war ironist, might relish.

Lebedev is unwilling to discuss details of the historic deal, which sees him in January 2009 become the first Russian oligarch to buy a British newspaper. He refuses to divulge details of his tortuous negotiations with Lord Rothermere, heir to the *Daily Mail* empire, whom he simply calls Jonathan. "Jonathan is a very good man. He treats what he has inherited as his duty rather than something he enjoys," he says.

Lebedev is at pains to stress he is different from other Russian oligarchs who have snapped up British institutions. He has nothing in common with Roman Abramovich, the Anglophile owner of Chelsea FC, he tells me – or Alisher Usmanov, another billionaire compatriot who owns a quarter of Arsenal, Chelsea's London rival. "Chelsea is simply a money-making machine," he sniffs. He sees himself as a cut above other super-rich Russians, whom he dismisses as a bunch of greedy, uncultured, semi-literate oiks. They know nothing of early Italian painting, he complains. "They don't read books! They don't go to exhibitions! They think the only way to impress anybody is to buy a yacht."

Britain's newest press baron also insists he will be an enlightened and hands-off newspaper proprietor. He claims he won't play any editorial role in the *Standard*. "I will very meticulously state that it is not polite for a Russian to interfere in British politics. My influence will be zero," he says. He cautiously praises Gordon Brown, whom British voters will expel from Downing Street a year later.

The reaction in Britain to Lebedev's *Standard* takeover is unhysterical. But his purchase of the newspaper for £1 does spark amusing headlines. One says: "I'm from the KGB! Give me your papers!" When I mention this he observes: "This humour is one of the best things in the British media." Lebedev insists his motives are not opportunistic but idealistic. He is enthusiastic about Britain and its newspapers, and contrasts the media climate in the UK favourably with that of Russia, where most publications and all the main TV channels are under the Kremlin's thumb.

"This is something people in Britain do not understand," he tells me. "I have lots of friends in Britain at every echelon of society. All of them are saying: 'These bloody newspapers.' Try to imagine a society where you have no free newspapers. That's one of the messages I would like to bring with me. I think the press in Britain is one of the most important guarantees against bureaucracy becoming inefficient, ugly and corrupt."

During our lunch Lebedev says he has no plans to buy the *Independent*. Like the *Standard*, the *Independent* is in financial trouble. But it fits better with Lebedev's progressive views and his interest in unfashionable editorial themes like Darfur. It seems more up Lebedev's street than the sometimes parochial, often chauvinistic *Standard*; the *Standard* is part of the same newspaper group as the reactionary, show-business-obsessed *Daily Mail*.

But in March 2010, Lebedev acquires the *Independent* and *Independent on Sunday* from its Irish owners. The subsequent launch of *i* – a cut-price mini-version of the *Indy* – brings the number of Lebedev UK titles to four. Lebedev is no Rupert Murdoch, whose British newspaper empire begins to crumble in 2011 following *Guardian* revelations of phone-hacking and criminality. But Lebedev's influence on British public life is steadily increasing.

*

I get to like Lebedev. We have our disagreements: he is unhappy, for example, when I write an article for the *Guardian* about the fact that staff on *Novaya Gazeta* failed to receive their wages. (In 2006 Lebedev buys 49% of the paper, together with former Soviet Union president Mikhail Gorbachev, from the paper's staff. They are eventually paid; Lebedev blames the delay on problems with his now defunct German airline Blue Wings.)

In general, however, he becomes a trusted contact. We speak on the phone. I interview him again as his British media empire grows larger. I find Lebedev garrulous, clever and a source of marvellous gossip, much of it unprintable. He can be confusing – slaloming incomprehensibly between random themes: his perfidious business partners, global corruption, and British high society. He can also be prolix. But he is original, engaging and accessible. What's more he's the only billionaire I can call up any time.

One Christmas he sends me a bottle of Chianti. (I pass it on to a local charity.) The next Christmas it's a bespoke edition of *Lagoon*, the poem by Joseph Brodsky, illustrated with moody sepia photos of Venice. I read:

> By night, the Adriatic with its Easterly wind
> fills the canal, like a bath, to the brim,
> rocking the boats, like cradles; at night
> a fish not an ox at the bedhead keeps
> vigil, while in the window, as you sleep,
> the rays of a star out at sea stir the blinds.

The *Guardian* has strict rules about accepting hospitality. But I keep the poems.

Like the restlessly cosmopolitan Brodsky, Lebedev moves between two worlds, and two lexicons – the Russian and the Anglophone. In Moscow, Lebedev's position is of someone who is inside the political elite rather than outside it. He lives in Rublyovka, the Russian capital's exclusive *dacha*-colony and home to celebrities and politicians including Putin and Medvedev. Like other very rich men, he is evidently attractive to young women: his second wife is a glamorous former model. He is clearly a member of Russia's establishment, and enjoys its privileges.

But Lebedev also portrays himself as a semi-opposition figure. He describes himself on his blog as a "capitalist-idealist". (The blog includes his musings on the nature of global capitalism and on how the vulgar Russian rich behave on holiday in St Tropez.) But is he really an enemy of Mr Putin? The British magazine *Private Eye* suggests that Lebedev is closer to the Russian government and its power structures than he likes to make out.

It's certainly true that Lebedev is cautious not to make any direct criticism of Russia's ruling duo; he reserves his scorn for the country's greedy bureaucrats – in much the same way Russians of old would criticise the *boyars* – or nobles – rather than the tsar. He calls himself a "loyal oppositionist" – someone who wants to reform, rather than overthrow, the Russian government. When one of his titles, the *Moscow Korrespondent*, publishes a story about Putin's alleged affair with a lissom Olympic gymnast, Lebedev quickly shuts the newspaper down. From 2002 to 2007 he is a loyal member of the pro-Kremlin United Russia party and Duma deputy.

But, it seems to me, Lebedev's maverick support for *Novaya Gazeta* means that he's an unreliable figure for those in power. The paper is one of the few functioning media outlets critical of the Kremlin. It continues to report on themes the government-controlled media prefer to ignore – corruption; human rights; abuses in Chechnya and the neighbouring republics of Ingushetia and Dagestan; and the murky activities of the FSB. After Politkovskaya's murder Lebedev offers $1 million for information leading to the arrest of her killer. He calls me hours after Markelov's assassination; he says he is so worried about the risks faced by *Novaya Gazeta*'s staff that he thinks they should carry guns.

According to journalists on *Novaya Gazeta*, Lebedev is the genuine thing – a tycoon-intellectual with a social conscience. "Most Russian oligarchs seem to settle into, 'We can do nothing.' They spend their days in Courchevel, drinking wine, eating caviar and watching girls dance on the table," Yulia Latynina, a *Novaya Gazeta* columnist tells me. "There are also people who say everything is fine." She goes on: "Lebedev is trying to do something so the country will be better. But he knows that if he does anything to offend people in power there will be punishment."

(I meet Latynina at Lebedev's birthday bash. Latynina is a waspish critic of the Kremlin. She writes articles about corruption and the enigmatic oil trader Gunvor. She also suggests that Russia drew up its invasion plan for Georgia in advance of the conflict. I ask her how she is. "I'm fine," she replies, "apart from the fact that Mr Kokoity [the leader of South Ossetia] is trying to kill me." For several months, the paper assigns her bodyguards.)

Journalists on *Novaya Gazeta* say that Lebedev doesn't interfere on editorial matters – though he sometimes writes a column if he disagrees with someone, setting out his personal views. I get to know the paper's editor-in-chief, Dmitry Muratov. The paper's editors and Lebedev differ on the nature of Russian power, he says. "We believe the corrupt system in Russia is a vertically corrupt system personally created by Putin," says Muratov. "Lebedev and Gorbachev don't. They think it is bad Russian officials who are stopping Russia becoming a normal European country." Muratov says he respects Lebedev. But the tycoon isn't his friend: they use the formal "vy" form in Russian. When I bump into Muratov at a round table organised by *Novaya* I ask him why Lebedev isn't there. His reply: "How should I know?"

The survival of *Novaya Gazeta* is something of a mystery, given the Kremlin's vice-like control over most of the media, a situation that leads one US diplomat to remark that Russians all "feed from the same information trough". After Lebedev buys the *Standard* I spend a day at *Novaya*. I ask its journalists how the title manages to survive, given its knack for offending those in power.

Deputy editor Andrei Lipsky offers the most persuasive analysis. He says the paper plays a useful role for the Russian government. Firstly, he says, it allows the Kremlin to refute western criticism that there is no freedom of speech in Russia. Secondly, he adds, it provides real information for the country's nervous leaders, who are locked in a continuous and exhausting battle for position, money and influence. The paper is a more reliable source of what is really going on inside the country than the vast network of FSB agents, who generally tell their bosses what they want to hear. "*Novaya Gazeta* lies on the table of the presidential administration and all regional governors. Putin reads it, or people read it for him," Lipsky says, and laments: "They [Russia's leadership] have liquidated many real sources, starting with TV."

Lebedev has been more successful as a newspaper proprietor than as a politician. There was a long-standing feud with Yuri Luzhkov, Moscow's mayor until the Kremlin removed him from his post in 2010. In 2003, Lebedev ran against Luzhkov and lost. In September 2008, Lebedev and Gorbachev – who helped found *Novaya Gazeta* – announced their intention to form a new social democratic party. The project flopped, largely because political activity in Russia is impossible without Kremlin approval, but also because of the electorate's lack of interest.

A cable from the US embassy in Moscow, dated 10 October 2008, tells how Lebedev refused to participate in a new opposition movement, Solidarity, because of the presence of Kasparov. For reasons that are unclear, Lebedev decided to found his own party instead. "Polling indicates no popular support for Lebedev or Gorbachev," the cable notes dryly.

With his political ambitions thwarted, Lebedev appears to have turned to Britain. Here, at least, he can mingle with top politicians, as well as other members of Britain's top table. His friends include Geordie Greig, editor of *Tatler*, whom Lebedev installs as the *Standard*'s new editor. Other celebrities attend his glamorous annual charity fund-raiser held at Hampton Court – Hugh Grant and JK Rowling and Vanessa Redgrave are regulars; Elton John has performed. Lebedev's UK-based son Evgeny is a fixture on London's social scene. (At the 2009 Hampton Court party Lebedev Jr features in Russia's *Hello!* magazine; with his Romanov beard, shiny black shoes and lugubrious frock coat, he looks like a Ruritanian count.)

Evgeny, described as low-key and charming, runs his father's UK newspaper business. In the autumn of 2010 Evgeny acquires British citizenship. The Lebedevs charm offensive doesn't work with everybody, however. Following his purchase of the *Standard* and *Independent*, Evgeny meets the Prince of Wales – Britain's heir to the throne – at a reception. "I wondered if he might express a view on our papers as he has been covered in our pages. Or express a view about the morality or immorality of press behaviour ... But, no. Instead he asked me quite simply: 'Have you been interested in football all your life?'" Evgeny recalls. "And that was all. Maybe he thought I was Abramovich. Or maybe he thought that was simply all that Russians do."

In the months following his purchase of the *Standard*, Alexander Lebedev's diverse business empire comes under attack. In the summer of

2009, he summons me to his Moscow townhouse. The encounter has a whiff of James Bond about it. Inside, the furnishings and table-lamps exude a confident wealth. A pretty receptionist in a silk mini-dress meets me in the lobby; Renaissance drawings are stacked in a reception room. I am escorted upstairs to where Lebedev, now a British press baron, is waiting on the balcony. All that is missing is a fluffy white cat.

Lebedev says he's heard from "multiple sources" that he might soon be arrested and thrown into jail. He says it's not entirely clear who is behind the plot. But he says that "someone is coming up with $50 million" to have him locked up. He believes a group of shadowy investors is offering the money to corrupt law enforcement officers. Lebedev's own contacts inside Russia's power agencies inform him it would be prudent to leave Russia for six months, he says.

It's hard to know whether this plot is real, fictitious or exaggerated. Lebedev says he is ready for a spell in prison – but would rather avoid the fate of Khodorkovsky. I ask him if he is prepared to do time in Lefortovo, technically not a prison but a pre-trial detention and isolation centre. He replies gnomically: "Living here, you should always be prepared."

On 2 November 2010, Lebedev's gloomy forebodings appear to come true, when a group of masked, gun-toting officers stage a theatrical raid on his Moscow bank. The FSB organises the operation – specifically its K department, which specialises in economic crimes. The officers seize documents and files. (They claim the search is connected to a criminal investigation into another bank.)

When the SWAT team bursts in, Lebedev is ploughing up and down the bank's underground swimming pool. "I frankly thought they had come to arrest me," he tells me, adding: "I decided to keep swimming, thinking I would enjoy the pool for the last time." In the end, Lebedev isn't detained. He complains bitterly about the FSB's "*maski*-show" – a Russian word for the overdone police raids of the 1990s. The next day there is more bad news when dozens of tax officers in Ukraine raid Lebedev's luxury hotel complex on the Crimean coast.

It's hard to avoid the conclusion that the two raids are coordinated – Ukraine is, after all, now run by the pro-Moscow Viktor Yanukovych. Lebedev says he is determined to shrug off pressure to leave Russia. "I'm still here. I live here," he says. But he concedes: "In the worst case scenario the message from the raid is: Get out of Russia."

In conversation with me, Lebedev insists that Putin has nothing to do with what he says are increasingly well co-ordinated attempts to steal his business. Instead, he blames opportunistic elements inside Russia's shadowy bureaucracy. They are trying to grab a slice of his fortune, by exploiting his cool relations with the Kremlin as political cover, he says.

We touch briefly on the FSB's home intrusions and the security service's unsubtle attempts to make me exit Russia. "It's just typical harassment. They want to make things unpleasant for you," Lebedev counsels. He adds that even officers inside the FSB are exhausted by the political struggles going on behind the scenes, and by the country's depressing political system. "They don't see any future in Russia either," he says. The quality of FSB recruits is also extremely low, he says.

In May 2011 Lebedev announces that he's quitting business and joining a new political initiative. He says he is endorsing Putin's so-called "Popular Front", a movement whose sole goal appears to be to return Putin to the Kremlin in 2012. The decision looks like a tactical manoeuvre by Lebedev to fend off FSB attacks against his bank. Commentators sardonically compare the front, a supposedly non-partisan national coalition, to the "Bloc of Communists and Non-Party Members" founded by Stalin ahead of the Soviet "elections" of 1937.

To critics, the move is proof that Lebedev is in bed with the Kremlin. Lebedev rejects this. The Popular Front, meanwhile, decides that it doesn't want Lebedev as a member.

In December 2009 commuters on their way into London could have been forgiven for being nonplussed by a large poster featuring Barack Obama. The poster showed the US president's head next to that of Mahmoud Ahmadinejad, Iran's hardline leader. Next to the heads a slogan asked: "Who poses the greatest nuclear threat?" For most people the answer was surely a no-brainer – after all, so far Obama hasn't called for Israel to "vanish from the page of time". But for the Kremlin the Obama image was the latest step in an ambitious attempt to create a new, post-Soviet global propaganda empire.

Some two decades after the demise of the state newspaper *Pravda*, the Kremlin's 24-hour English language TV channel, Russia Today, was launching its first major advertising blitz across the UK. Dubbed North Korean TV by its detractors, the channel gives an unashamedly pro-Putin view of the world and says it seeks to correct the "biased" western view offered by the BBC and CNN.

When I visit its gleaming headquarters in Moscow, the station has renamed itself RT. The building is a short walk from Park Kultury metro station. It is also home to the RIA Novosti news agency and the *Moscow News*. I meet Margarita Simonyan, RT's 29-year-old editor-in-chief. "What we see as black and white might not be black and white. It's making people question their own stereotypes," she explains. "We offer an alternative to the mainstream view."

Certainly, RT's advertising campaign is provocatively contrarian – casting doubt, for example, on climate change in the week of the Copenhagen summit and comparing a British police constable to a tattooed football hooligan. But is anyone going to watch it? "I don't believe in unbiased views. Of course we take a pro-Russian position. The BBC says it openly promotes British values," she notes. A former member of President Putin's press pool, she got her job when the channel launched in 2005 aged just 25, fuelling rumours – possibly unfair – that she has admirers in high places.

The Kremlin has long been frustrated by what it regards as "bias" from the western media. And so it is now creating its own rival information reality. In 2011 the Russian government will spend $1.4 billion on international propaganda – more than on fighting unemployment. As well as its English channel, RT has a new Spanish service aimed at Latin America, a region of growing Kremlin geopolitical interest; it also broadcasts in Arabic. The government has trebled the budgets for its main state news agencies, RIA Novosti, and ITAR-TASS, despite Russia's economic crisis. (Both agencies can be relied on to give a pro-Kremlin view of the world; in Soviet times RIA Novosti was a virtual arm of the KGB.) There is also a paid-for monthly supplement in Britain's *Daily Telegraph*, *Russia Now*, and a revival of the

Soviet-era radio station Voice of Russia. Other Russian government-sponsored supplements have sprung up in the *Washington Post* and the *New York Times*, as well as in leading European papers.

The Kremlin, moreover, employs the public relations giant Ketchum and their sister company Gplus. They have offices around the world and in London use the services of Portland PR. And then there are the bloggers – a shadowy army of angry Russian patriots. The bloggers were initially active only on Russian websites, slapping down critics of the Russian regime. Now, however, these cyber-nationalists are also active on western newspaper websites, including the *Guardian*. Anyone who dares to criticise Russia's leaders, or point out some of the country's deficiencies, is immediately branded a CIA spy, or worse. (One disgruntled blogger calls me a "North Korean spy" and the "apotheosis of bastard western journalism". How, I wonder, can I be both?) In July 2011 a presumed Kremlin blogger sets up a clone Twitter account which mimics my own. Mine is @lukeharding1968. His looks the same but has a capital "i" at the beginning. He even uses my photo and bio. My clone tweets Dmitry Medvedev press releases.

Some observers believe that the bloggers are simply a spontaneous group of patriotic enthusiasts. More convincing, though, is the view that the Kremlin discreetly funds these anonymous pro-government commentators, in order to discredit opponents and to promote Moscow's authoritarian agenda.

"They [the Kremlin] are coming to realise that information matters, and that control of information internationally matters even more," says Evgeny Morozov, whose 2010 book *The Net Delusion* argues that authoritarian regimes are exploiting the internet and using it to crack down on dissent. The Belarus-born writer and academic says the Kremlin has taken a more "aggressive" approach following the war in Georgia.

The conflict was one of several PR disasters for Moscow, which also failed to get its message across after leaving European consumers shivering during two recent gas wars with Ukraine. "They have realised it's only by controlling what gets printed in the international media they can advance their hard policy agenda items," Morozov says.

Morozov takes a dim view of Russia Today – pointing out that it has a predilection for fringe guests and nutty conspiracy theorists. In communist times Russia's state-controlled media reported only bad news from the capitalist west, and good news from home, often with pictures of smiling factory workers and happy milkmaids. Russia Today operates on the same principle: with America generally portrayed as a dangerous, crime-ridden, lunatic-infested place, lurching from one catastrophe to another. During one 2011 broadcast RT even compared the Obama administration to Nazi Germany. "For me it's a comedy channel," says Morozov. "You watch it to see how badly mangled Russia's attempts at influencing foreign opinion are." That approach has now been replicated across a range of media, old and new. Russia, Morozov says, has gone from *Pravda* to Pravda 2.0.

During my stint at Moscow I get to know some of the channel's correspondents. Insiders pay tribute to the professionalism of the staff. It includes several British and American journalists and newsreaders. "Generally people there are pretty talented. But nobody is under any illusions what it's all about," one former employee tells me. "There is such a lack of objectivity."

I can't help thinking that the western journalists who toil for the channel amount to a new generation of "useful idiots", whom Muggeridge – were he alive today – would recognise immediately. RT even has its own Walter Duranty, a US anchor. His rabid pro-Kremlin views earn him the nickname Lord Haw Haw.

One of Putin's first acts as president was to shut down independent television. He started with the channel NTV. Writing in the English-language *Moscow Times*, NTV's former director Yevgeny Kiselyov marked the 10th anniversary of the station's demise by saying that today's journalism students would find it difficult to believe that Russia ever had independent channels. The FSB spearheaded the raid against the Moscow offices of NTV's owner Vladimir Gusinsky, with ownership transferred to state-connected Gazprom media. Gazprom also owns the influential *Izvestiya* and *Komsomolskaya Pravda* newspapers, both now cheerleaders for the regime.

A decade on, the state owns most Russian TV, either directly or indirectly. Kiselyov reels off the rules governing today's state-controlled broadcasters. They include no investigation of corruption and other abuses involving top officials; a "blacklist", stopping opposition politicians and critics from appearing on air; orders from the Kremlin on what to show or not to show; and the end of genuinely satirical programmes "lampooning the shortcomings and mistakes" of government figures. Self-censorship, as in Soviet times, is widespread. Editors know what topics to avoid, such as criticism of the government's human rights record and its policies in the north Caucasus.

In conversation, Kiseylov tells me that TV professionals have completely lost the production culture of going live on air – there are no live broadcasts in Russia any more. Government officials are absolutely unavailable for journalists, he adds. "Putin's regime, having set out to build its notorious 'power vertical', could not afford the luxury of independent television stations free from all state controls and broadcasting to the entire country," Kiselyov laments.

One Kremlin critic banned from state TV is Vladimir Ryzhkov, a former independent Duma deputy and historian. He says that 85% of social and political information in Russia comes from television – "under full control of the Kremlin". He contrasts this with the Gorbachev and Yeltsin period, when he says there was an attempt to build a more open, diverse and competitive political system, with different political forces, more or less independent courts, and in the 1990s a free media. "On state TV channels Boris Yeltsin could see himself as a drinker, an unhealthy person," Ryzhkov points out.

Under Putin these freedoms have disappeared, he says. "Newspapers are nothing in Russia. *Vedomosti* sells 60,000 copies a day. *Kommersant*, the most influential political newspaper, 100,000 copies. We have four independent political newspapers and [they sell] 1%. The internet has 20% usage. If we say [how many access] day-by-day political information it's not more than 5%. This means if you control TV you control everything. It's a classic authoritarian system." The internet is the only bright spot in Russia's pro-government media landscape. It is predominantly free but not a source of news for most Russians.

RT enjoys more freedom than Russia's domestic government-controlled channels. But while there is sometimes broad-based criticism of the regime, there is an unspoken understanding that you can't criticise Putin – or speculate about his alleged wealth – a former employee tells me. The same taboo exists at the *Moscow News*, a twice-weekly English language newspaper produced by RIA Novosti. "We have total freedom except in one respect," one editor admits. "You can criticise Medvedev. But not Putin." Other people familiar with the Kremlin's media strategy say there is a lingering misunderstanding among top Russian officials as to how the western world works. "They think it's enough to have good PR and that this is sufficient to act as a counterweight to the bad publicity caused by events in Russia. Obviously it's not," says Angus Roxburgh, a former BBC Moscow correspondent hired by the Kremlin as a PR adviser. I ask how the Kremlin could improve its image in the west. His tart reply: "They could stop beating up opposition demonstrators for a start."

In March 2009 I fly back to London to talk to my bosses about the worsening FSB situation. The *Guardian*'s editor, Alan Rusbridger, and the foreign editor, Harriet Sherwood, are supportive. We agree that harassment from the Russian security service has reached levels verging on intolerable. But what can we do about this secret war?

Rusbridger convenes a meeting with Michael Davenport. Davenport is the director for Russia, Central Asia and the south Caucasus at the Foreign and Commonwealth Office. He is, in effect, Britain's top diplomat on Russia.

We meet around the circular table in Rusbridger's office. The room is on the *Guardian*'s second floor, home to the newsroom. There is a view of Regent's Canal, with its houseboats and moorhens. Davenport is a bespectacled figure in his late 40s. He is sympathetic. He confirms that the Foreign Office is well aware of the FSB's modus operandi. He also explains that the Soviet Union exported these KGB techniques not just to other communist bloc countries, but to friendly secret services elsewhere – including in the Middle East.

Davenport recalls how he was himself the victim of a KGB-style break in – not in chilly Moscow but in sultry Cairo. The culprits were the Egyptian secret police, the thuggish *mukhabarat*, who received their training from the KGB.

Davenport has confirmed what we know: that the FSB is the author of my mysterious break-ins. But despite his reassurances, I find it difficult to convey the atmosphere of psychological pressure and cold war enmity that is now a part of our life in Moscow. Davenport admits that dialogue with Moscow has always been tricky. He offers the following memorable insight: "The problem with the Russians is that they don't think the way we think they should think." Later, I find Davenport's name among the WikiLeaks cables. In another inspired phrase he dubs Russia a "corrupt autocracy".

After this meeting British diplomats in Moscow raise my case with their Russian counterparts. In other words, they complain. Amazingly, this works. At least for a few months. The frequency of the intrusions reduces. Looking back at my notes I see the FSB ghosts return to the *Guardian* office on 4 or 5 June 2009. This time, they open the double-locked front window. When I arrive at work, white poplar blossom is billowing in from the snowy trees across the street. It is a strangely beautiful sight.

Western correspondents based in Moscow are understanding of my problems with the FSB. In particular Andrew Osborn of the *Daily Telegraph*, Shaun Walker of the *Independent* and Tony Halpin of the *Times* become close friends. Tony even shares with me a moment of humiliation. It takes place not in the Kremlin but on another theatre of battle – the football pitch.

CHAPTER 8

Political Football

Uefa Champions League final, Chelsea v Manchester United,
Luzhniki stadium, Moscow
21 May 2008

The World Cup will help us make a different people and a new nation.
ALEXANDER DJORDJADZE, RUSSIA 2018 WORLD CUP COMMITTEE

My personal fitness regime in Moscow could hardly be described as impressive. Jogging in winter on the capital's icy streets is inadvisable – too treacherous, and too cold for the vulnerable nether regions. It's only in April after many months of lethargy that I begin to exercise again, as the snow finally melts. Mostly, it's a perfunctory 15-minute lumber around our pastoral village.

Sometimes, I go across a road used by clanking trolleybuses to a nearby memorial park. It's dedicated to the Russian soldiers who fought in the tsar's army during the first world war; the sheer number of subsequent victims following the Bolshevik seizure of power in 1917 has blurred this sacrifice. There is a large cross and monument. Further on there is a cinema. On the route back a gigantic tower block looms over this urban district.

A couple of times the press corps manages a game of cricket played in the grounds of Moscow State University. We are not over-blessed with talent. More frequently we play five-a-side football. The pitch is a short stroll away from Luzhniki stadium, the venue for the 1980 Moscow Olympics and the capital's most prestigious football pitch. It is also the scene of my humiliating moment. On 17 October 2007, ahead of the England-Russia qualifying match for the following year's European Championships, I take part in a friendly game between English and Russian journalists.

Take part is, perhaps, an exaggeration. The game is played on Luzhniki's seventh pitch. I manage one pass to Jamie Redknapp, the former England international turned Sky TV commentator. I'm then mugged of the ball. The other side immediately score. It's my fault. Ten minutes later I'm substituted. The Russian "journalists" – who look to me suspiciously like professional footballers rather than flabby members of the fourth estate – win 9-3. I limp back to the metro station, Vorobyovy Gory, built on an impressive bridge across the Moskva river and with fine views of the university and the wooded Sparrow Hills.

The friendly is an augur of what happens later that evening, when England takes on Russia. Officially, the 80,000-seater stadium is sold out. But 48 hours before the game I buy two tickets from *spekulanty* – dodgy-looking youths lurking outside Luzhniki's *kassa*, or ticket office. The office is next to the stadium car park and a large statue of Lenin. The tickets are for the Russian fan zone. I buy them from Seryoga, a helpful tout who turns out to be a West Ham fan.

The October match takes place against a backdrop of smouldering Anglo-Russian tensions. Politically, in the wake of Litvinenko's murder less than a year earlier, relations are the worst for decades. Over the summer Putin had accused Britain of arrogance and "colonial thinking"; days before the match he claimed Russian democracy was superior to Britain's. He justified this by pointing out that he – unlike Gordon Brown, the British prime minister who succeeded Tony Blair unopposed – was democratically elected. This is technically true. But it is also, given the Kremlin's systemic elimination of all political competition in Russia, more than a little rich.

Among ordinary fans on both sides I find no hostility whatsoever. "Sport isn't politics. Besides our players are better than yours," Seryoga says, as I hand over 5,000 roubles (£100) in shiny green notes for two match tickets. Mark Perryman, the convenor of the London England Fans supporters' group, also takes a pragmatic attitude. He tells me: "I'm not going to go round Moscow draped in an England flag. But most countries we have played we have been at war with, or they have been part of our empire, or we have occupied them at some stage."

I call Vasily Utkin, Russia's most thoughtful football pundit. He says that Moscow is currently experiencing a wave of Anglophilia, following the release of a Russian translation of the latest *Harry Potter* book. "Who cares about politics? Everyone's spent the past two days reading *Harry Potter*. This is the best reflection of our relationship," Utkin says.

I take my father to the England-Russia match. When we arrive at Luzhniki the stadium is packed, the atmosphere raucous and good-natured. Before kick-off the Russian fans unveil a giant, 120-metre-wide banner; it fills an entire section of the ground. The banner shows a terrifying Russian bear, with yellow fangs. Its slogan is patriotic: *Rossiya vperyod!* – literally, "Forward Russia!"

When Wayne Rooney scores towards the end of the first half I jump up and cheer. This elicits a thousand murderous looks: no matter how cordial generally, going into the bear pit of opposing supporters is risky. At half-time it's 1-0 to England. To my relief, England concede two second-half goals – one an Andrey Arshavin tap-in, the other a penalty. England's 2-1 defeat will be decisive in the team's failure to qualify for the 2008 Euros, and contributes to Steve McClaren's sacking soon afterwards as England manager. Several factors explain England's poor performance, I reflect – the wintry weather, Luzhniki's plastic pitch and McClaren's blokeish incompetence. Russia played better and were the more disciplined side.

But the defeat also means my father and I can leave Luzhniki with all our limbs. The Russian supporters are in good spirits after their triumph over England, the motherland of football; they are generous, teasing and inquisitive.

"How did you end up in this part of the ground?" one bewildered Russian fan asks me. "Why weren't you with the other England supporters?"

"I work here in Moscow," I reply. "Congratulations to Russia. Your team played very well."

The game was an object lesson. First, I learn that there are moments when it is good to keep your mouth shut. But second, and more importantly, I start to appreciate that sport is an essential part of Putin's maximal vision of Russia as a resurgent great power. Sport was one of the Soviet

Union's strengths. But after the country's collapse, its network of sport youth clubs fell apart, with trainers in athletics, skiing, or figure skating drifting off into private business or other jobs.

By the time I arrive in Russia, Russian football is gradually recovering from the trough of the 1990s, though the Russian league still struggles to attract major international players, and suffers from embarrassing episodes of fan racism.

One of Russian football's most important supporters is Roman Abramovich. Other billionaires who fund the sport include aluminium tycoon Oleg Deripaska and oil magnate Vagit Alekperov. The Russian Football Union, meanwhile, emulates Peter the Great, who looked to Holland for boat-builders who could make him a navy. The RFU sends for Dutch coach Guus Hiddink. He becomes the manager of Russia's national team. It is Hiddink who gifts the Russian squad a sense of coherence and purpose it previously lacked. After vanquishing England, Russia under Hiddink reach the semi-final of the 2008 European championships, playing some inspiring football.

In May 2009, Luzhniki hosts another invasion of English fans, this time for the Champions League final between Manchester United and Chelsea. It is the first time that two English teams have reached the final. The game – it will turn out – is a foretaste of the 2018 World Cup, to be hosted by Russia. Thousands of English fans arrive in Moscow ahead of the game. The *Moskovsky Komsomolets* newspaper claims this is the biggest invasion since the Germans attacked the city in 1941-2. Only Napoleon turned up with a larger force in 1812, the paper notes.

I wander down to Red Square. The area has already been converted into an informal football festival; hundreds of fans are milling around its cobbles. Most, I discover, have come on charter flights from the UK. But others have arrived via the Baltic States; a few have even flown in from Sydney. "We've paid £4,000 on a package," Paul Southgate, a Manchester United fan, explains. "We came via Dubai and Singapore. At every stop of the way more United fans got on." What, then, did he think of Manchester United's opponents? "Chelsea is just a Russian play-thing. They are not a real team," he replies scathingly. "They haven't got any fans. The ground will be 90% United."

Next to Lenin's pyramid-shaped mausoleum is a five-a-side football pitch. Nearby, fans – Russians, mostly – queue to have their photo taken with the Champions League trophy. Others mob the Manchester United and Chelsea stalls, or buy official Uefa T-shirts costing 1,000 roubles (£20). I meet some enterprising supporters who have dropped in to see Lenin. "He looks a bit waxed, like something out of Madame Tussauds," John Hart, a Manchester United fan from Belfast, tells me. He adds: "It's eerie down there. It's pitch black and cold. You look at his face and see he's got hair." Hart says he and his friends booked early and flew to Moscow via Riga: "We are staying in a cheap hotel. We're doing the whole trip for £200."

The conditions for the players are a bit more luxurious. Chelsea's squad stay in the five-star Ritz Carlton hotel, the capital's most exclusive address. Rooms here start at £750 for the night of the final. Breakfast is extra. The hotel is next to Red Square. I spot Chelsea's goalkeeper Petr Čech sight-seeing outside St Basil's cathedral. "It's great to see people enjoying football here," he tells me, as tourists snap him on their mobile phones. Manchester United put up at the equally sumptuous Crowne Plaza, close to the White House where Yeltsin stood on a tank. Ordinary fans, meanwhile, are sleeping wherever they can: in Moscow's suburbs; in hostels; or in boats moored up on the mud-brown Moskva river.

The political climate between Russia and the UK is marginally improved. Ahead of the game, the Kremlin waives visa restrictions for fans with match tickets. Those I talk to say they encounter few obstacles while passing through Russian immigration. Russia's foreign minister, Sergei Lavrov, meanwhile, says the visa policy shows that Russia is a "civilised country". The full-blown row between London and Moscow seems temporarily forgotten; I find ordinary Russians welcome their British guests. "The British are not monsters," Olga Podyganova, a political science student, says. "Relations are terrible on an official level, but among ordinary people they are good." Who is going to win? "I guess Chelsea," she says.

Ahead of the game, I also pay a visit to Moscow's school number 232. The school in Trubnaya Street is where Abramovich – Chelsea FC's billion-aire owner – once studied. Three decades later, he is on the brink of Champions League success. The Luzhniki stadium is a 30-minute metro ride from his old classroom. Abramovich's former teachers describe the young Roman as a pleasant, kind but essentially ordinary boy – who exhibited few signs of future greatness. "He was a normal Soviet boy," Nadezhda Ivanovna, his old history teacher, recalls. "He used to sit at the back of the class. He made friends easily. He was better off than some of the kids, but this wasn't reflected in his behaviour."

Abramovich, I discover, usually got 3s: a decent but unspectacular grade. (The Russian scale runs from 1-5.) I examine black and white photos from the school's archive. They show a group of Soviet teenagers on a class trip, posing by a war memorial in the city of Volgograd – the former Stalingrad. One of them is holding a flower. He looks rather shy. This is Abramovich.

At the time, he lived with his uncle in the central Moscow district of Tsvetnoy Boulevard, close to school 232. His parents had both died. He graduated in 1983. I sense that his old teachers wish Abramovich well. At the same time there is bafflement that this innocuous and well turned out schoolboy should accumulate a multi-billion fortune – and a prestigious English football team. "I think it was down to luck, and to his family," Ivanovna says. "He was a lovely boy and he was in a very good class, one of my best. But at the end of the day I don't think I'm any less clever than Roman."

Abramovich, evidently, has played an important part in Russia's footballing revival. At his old school, he has funded a high-walled five a side pitch, where a new generation of schoolboys play football under lime and sycamore trees. He has also renovated the biology lab and computer room, both of which bear plaques carrying his name. Similarly, Abramovich bankrolls Russia's Football Union and national squad, paying Hiddink's wages until the Dutch trainer's acrimonious departure in 2010. Abramovich has funded all-weather pitches across the Russian Federation. Undoubtedly, he wants to give something back. But the Kremlin also insists upon gestures of patriotic philanthropy from its wealthier citizens. They know better than to refuse.

The Champions League final doesn't begin until 10.45pm Moscow time. By this point, most fans are exhausted, drunk, or nursing the beginnings of a hangover; and somewhat cold. I have a seat with a good view in the central section of the ground. The match goes to extra time. There is a penalty shoot-out. It starts raining. Chelsea's captain John Terry slips over and scuffs his kick, gifting Manchester United victory. It is 2am.

Watched by Moscow police wearing greatcoats, United fans stream out of the stadium. Many seem too knackered to celebrate, though a few burst into a desultory chorus of "Que sera sera, now it's three, it's three" – the number of United's European Cup triumphs. Others stop to pose for photos next to the Lenin statue. Several use plastic bags to fend off the pouring rain.

United fans commiserate fraternally with Chelsea supporters on the train back into the centre of Moscow. On the floor of the last carriage somebody has been sick. A supporter had covered the damage with a Russian tabloid.

The following morning I pay a visit to Manchester United's team hotel. After their victory, 350 Manchester United guests – players, manager Sir Alec Ferguson, wives, girlfriends, hangers-on – have partied until the early hours. I get there too late to see the players leave in a bus for the airport. The silver trophy – red ribbons still attached – goes with them in a customised flight case. But I do find the first-floor reception room where the players celebrated – a sea of champagne corks, empty bottles of Veuve Clicquot Ponsardin Brut, and an abandoned stick of magenta Chanel lipstick.

A clean-up is under way; workmen are busy removing the dance floor where the United players strutted their stuff. Among the debris, I spot a sheet of lyrics to one of their party songs. Someone had trodden on it. Given the nerve-jangling nature of United's victory, the words strike me as appropriate. They read: "I don't wanna work today/Maybe I just wanna stay / Just take it easy cause there is no stress." Yes, it is the most traditional of post-match celebrations: a team singalong to French tribal house DJ Laurent Wolf's hit "No Stress". It is difficult to imagine what Sir Bobby Charlton – a former United player and member of England's 1966 World Cup-winning team – would have made of it.

Downstairs, I spot 17-year-old Danny Welbeck, a member of United's reserve squad, as he wanders somewhat forlornly around the hotel lobby. The coach had apparently left without him half an hour earlier, whisking away a winking Cristiano Ronaldo and a mute Wayne Rooney. "It was just a little party," Welbeck says. Why did he miss the bus? "I just woke up five minutes ago." And what were the celebrations like? "Obviously, we were really happy," he says, before going off in search of a driver.

"It was a great party," one of the waiters, Sergei, tells me. "There was a live three piece-band. We had a disco, with a mixture of 80s and modern songs. I was pouring the wine. The players danced and sang. We also laid on a buffet." Others recount how Rio Ferdinand – the United defender – appeared on the balcony; he started clapping and cheering the fans gathered outside, chanting: "Manchester la la la."

But as another waiter, Vyacheslav, points out, Russians are used to partying and excessive behaviour. Next to him, bin liners are filled to the brim with empty beer bottles. Nearby workers remove wilting floral decorations in Manchester United red. "You Brits drink a lot," Vyacheslav suggests. "But we Russians drink more. You should have seen what it was like here after New Year."

The sea is a picture postcard blue. Down on a beach of black pebbles, tourists stroll along a wide promenade. In the outdoor pool of my hotel swimmers breaststroke their way up and down. From where I sit on a bench in a sub-tropical garden, they are tiny figures on an azure oblong. My hotel is the Zhemchuzhina – the Pearl. The name sounds beautiful in Russian. Its architecture, though, is spectacularly ugly: it is one of several hulking Soviet-era edifices along the seafront in the Black Sea resort of Sochi.

Sochi is Putin's favourite holiday destination. It is a place to which he is emotionally attached. If Peter the Great had St Petersburg as his northern capital, then Putin has Sochi, a balmy southern playground. Sochi is the venue for the 2014 Winter Olympic and Paralympic Games. This will be Russia's biggest and most important sporting event since the 1980 Moscow Olympic Games. Behind Sochi are the snow-capped Caucasus mountains, Europe's highest. It is here in the resort of Krasnaya Polyana that the skiing and other Olympic events will take place, with competitors and spectators shuttling between alpine peaks and the seaside.

With its sanatoria and spa cures, Sochi has been a popular resort since Soviet times. It was the place where Kremlin chiefs came to let their hair down. Stalin had several *dachas* here, including one down the road in the dreamy Riviera backwater of Abkhazia. Putin has palaces too – one official, and another unofficial, photos of which surface in 2010 on a whistle-blowing Russian website.

Following the International Olympic Committee's decision in 2007 to award the Winter Olympics to Russia, Sochi undergoes an orgy of construction. Much of this is controversial. Ecologists accuse the authorities of a disregard for environmental norms. Leaders from national minorities, meanwhile, also raise protests. Ethnic Circassians call on Moscow to recognise the "genocide" carried out against them by the imperial Russian army in 1864. Some of the victims are buried in graves near the site of the planned Olympic mountain-sports complex at Krasnaya Polyana, they complain, without success.

I fly to Sochi in April 2009. It is the month before the Champions League final. The reason for my assignment is Sochi's forthcoming mayoral election. For a brief moment, it looks like this might be a genuinely competitive contest, unlike the rigged elections to which Russian voters have grown accustomed. Contrary to expectations, the opposition leader Boris Nemtsov – the author of a dissenting pamphlet, *Putin: A Reckoning* – successfully registers himself as a candidate.

The remaining 20-plus mayoral hopefuls are a colourful lot. They include Alexander Lebedev, newspaper proprietor and unsuccessful candidate for the job of mayor of Moscow; ballerina and gossip-column favourite, Anastasiya Volochkova; pornstar Yelena Berkova; and local pensioners. Andrei Lugovoi, Litvinenko's alleged assassin, announces he will take part, but then pulls out. The Kremlin's contestant and United Russia candidate is Anatoly Pakhomov. Pakhomov is Sochi's acting mayor. He is also a former tractor driver.

It doesn't take long, however, for me to figure out that this is all a democratic paint-job. In reality, the Kremlin is up to its usual electoral malfeasance. I meet up with Nemtsov, a former deputy prime minister, in a sanatorium where he is addressing a group of local workers. Tanned, good-looking, confident, and wearing a pair of tight-fitting blue jeans and black jacket, Nemtsov has an obvious and easy rapport with his mainly female audience. (I later discover he has four children by four different women.)

He also grew up in Sochi. Independent polls suggest that in a fair contest he would win a significant chunk of the vote.

Terrified their candidate might lose, the authorities ban Nemtsov from appearing on local TV, and from local newspapers. National channels, meanwhile, scuttle reports on the Sochi election featuring Nemtsov. He and other opposition candidates face intimidation, fraud allegations and other bizarre tactics; the week before I arrive on the Black Sea coast a supporter of the Kremlin youth group Nashi hurls ammonia-laced cola into Nemtsov's face, forcing him to receive hospital treatment.

I interview Nemtsov on his way to a campaign engagement. We sit together in the back of a rusty yellow minivan as it rattles up Sochi's steep hills. Nemtsov says the Olympics is of dubious benefit to local residents, that its events should be shared out among other Russian cities – especially ones where there is more snow.

Some 2,600 locals are being turfed out of their homes to make way for an Olympic village. The games will cost Russia $6 billion. This is three times the cost of previous successful Winter Olympics. The huge additional cost can be explained by corruption and "banditism", Nemtsov tells me. The election has also been marred by blatant provocations, he says – someone paid $5,000 into his bank account in a deliberate breach of electoral rules. "It was criminal money or FSB money," he says.

Nemtsov notes that several oligarchs who promised to finance the Sochi Olympics have not yet put in the cash as a result of the financial crisis. Deripaska, for example, had pledged to build a new terminal for the city's airport. So far, though, this is an empty shell. When an inspection team from the International Olympic Committee flies in, panicked local bureaucrats hire teachers to dress up as fake passengers. They are instructed to mill around the half-finished terminal and pretend to be tourists. One "tourist" tells the delegates that she is en route to Bangkok – unlikely, since there are no flights from Sochi to Thailand. When the IOC departs, maintenance workers switch off the lights. It is a stunt of which Potemkin – the prince whose eponymous fake villages fooled Catherine the Great – would have been proud.

Nemtsov's future attempts to take part in Russian politics meet with a similar lack of success. In 2011 election officials refuse to register his Popular

Freedom party – co-founded with former prime minister turned opposi-tionist Mikhail Kasyanov. Despite polls indicating the party would win seats, it is banned from contesting elections in December 2011 to the federal Duma. Other opposition groups trying to register meet a similar fate. In the summer of 2011 Guennadi Timtchenko, whom Nemtsov had accused of profiting from his alleged links with Putin, got in touch with the Federal Bailiff Service. Timtchenko asked it to ban Nemtsov from leaving the country. The service issued an order. Since Nemtsov was already in Stras-bourg the idea was to stop him from returning to Russia. He flew back anyway, following international scandal at the decision, which echoes the tactics used in the 1970s against troublesome anti-communists.

Later that evening I meet up with Dmitry Kapsov. Kapsov is an activist with the organisation Environmental Watch on North Caucasus. We go for a drink in Tinkoffs, a seafront micro-brewery, and one of many cafes and overpriced al fresco restaurants along Sochi's crowded promenade. Kapsov is politically passionate and articulate – a rarity among Russia's apathetic youth. The previous month Russia's ecology minister Yuri Trutnev had inadvertently boosted Kapsov's campaign when he admitted that some Olympic building sites up in the mountains "looked ghastly".

According to Kapsov, construction work has been a disaster – with trees felled, national park regulations flouted, and a decrease in Sochi's bear popu-lation by a third. Builders have excavated so much sand from the city's Mzymta river that the whole ecosystem has been wrecked. "We can clearly state there is already a decrease in bio-diversity," he tells me. "The project is stupid, especially at a time of growing prices and rising unemployment." Kapsov says he has written in protest to the IOC's president, Jacques Rogge. Rogge, however, fails to reply, and passes the letter on to Russia's organising Olympic committee.

The following afternoon I interview Lebedev, who flies to Sochi to begin his mayoral election campaign. Lebedev shrugs off accusations of dilettantism, and says he is confident he can "win" the race. "The Kremlin is unhappy with the regional authorities and the way the Olympics are going. The corruption is disgusting," he tells me.

Lebedev's campaign, though, lasts just long enough for him to shake a few hands and for the Moscow tabloids to dub him "an English spy in sneakers". (*Izvestiya*, for its part, calls the billionaire "a freak".) Soon after that a judge disqualifies Lebedev from the poll – a decision Lebedev brands "insane". Writing on his blog, Lebedev compares the Sochi election to polls in Zimbabwe. A film on Sochi TV, meanwhile, describes Nemtsov as an agent of foreign influence.

The regional administration does its bit, too – bussing in thousands of teachers, doctors, soldiers and sanatorium workers to vote early, a tactic the opposition says is conducive to ballot stuffing. "These aren't real elections. It's the appointment of a Kremlin candidate with a little bit of local voting," the Communist party candidate, Yuri Dzaganiya, complains to me. "Our billboards get taken down in the dead of night. We can't distribute materials. I don't appear on TV. I've never been to Zimbabwe but the comparison isn't far from the truth."

Russia's federal elites seem indifferent to the damage the use of "administrative resources" in the poll – a euphemism for fraud – is doing to the country's reputation. In the Duma elections of 2011 it is similar mass-scale fraud that triggers major street protests. Moscow's only concern, I realise, is to ensure that a proven loyalist gets the job. To a large extent, this is about power. But it is also about money. A lot of money. "Putin's supporters have serious financial interests in Sochi," Nemtsov's campaign manager, Ilya Yashin, tells me. "It's important to find someone who can be controlled and who will turn a blind eye to corruption."

The poll is interesting in one other respect: residents of next-door Abkhazia are allowed to vote. Medvedev's decision to recognise Abkhazia in 2008 is a major boost to the territory, and to its separatist leadership based in the charming seaside town of Sukhumi. Abkhazia is a beneficiary of the Olympic billions pouring into its frontyard. At the same time, however, Moscow's support for the tiny Abkhaz nation could hardly be called altruistic. The micro-territory is of strategic value to Russia. It has a deep-sea port, 900 million barrels of oil onshore, and potentially even more offshore. Moscow construction firms building Sochi's Olympic facilities, moreover, use Abkhaz resources.

This, of course, incenses the Georgians. They call for a global boycott of the 2014 Sochi Winter Olympics similar to the US-led boycott of the 1980 Moscow Games, following the Soviet invasion of Afghanistan. Despite

EU sympathy for Georgia, there's little prospect the ban will gain much traction. Georgian parliamentarians say that it's immoral for a country occupying its neighbour's territory to host an event like the Olympics less than 10 miles from the occupied territory. But they also point to another, more realistic threat to the games – the spectre of jihadist violence from the north Caucasus spilling into Sochi.

I travel to Abkhazia in 2008. The trip is four months before the war with Georgia and amid ominous tensions on the unofficial border between Georgia and its breakaway province. Abkhazia is a revelation. Some 150 miles long, it seems a somnolent seaside paradise. It has mandarin groves, eucalyptus trees, and pebbly beaches. Like Sochi, Russian workers holidayed here in communist times, relaxing in purpose-built sanatoria built along the vertiginous coast.

The Abkhaz border is just a 45-minute drive from the centre of Sochi. I walk across the border. I pick up a taxi. The car is a ubiquitous Zhiguli – the Russian name for a Lada. Within 30 seconds of setting off along a potholed road an Abkhaz traffic cop flags us down and demands a backhander. Reluctantly, I hand over a couple of notes. Economic isolation has left Abkhazia cut off from the outside world. There are no cash-points – you have to bring Russian roubles. And there is barely any transport: a single train threads its way erratically along a narrow red-orange rusted coastal track, past crumbling neo-classical stations and palm trees.

At the Inguri river – the crossing point between Abkhazia and Georgian-government controlled territory – I discover bored Russian soldiers. They sit in a camouflaged bunker and watch locals cross a bridge. Down on the riverbank, fishermen using homemade willow rods dip in the swirling turquoise waters for trout. There is no gunfire when I visit – only the noisy croaking of frogs.

Up the road from the river is the pastoral border village of Dikhazurga. Here, cows wander among the walnut groves. But many of the attractive wisteria-covered villas are roofless and empty – abandoned when their owners fled across the river during Georgia's 1992-3 civil war, fought between ethnic Georgians and Russian-backed Abkhaz rebels. Some still have daffodils growing in the front garden. It's as if the owners had just popped out.

Almost half of Abkhazia's population – mostly ethnic Georgians – fled during the war two decades ago. Tbilisi wants the refugees to go back. Some have. Abkhazia, meanwhile, claims that it was itself the victim of migration politics when Stalin – a Georgian – settled Georgians here, following previous invasions by the Ottomans and the Greeks. Locals seem largely unbothered by the row and by the fact that their bucolic neighbourhood is a disputed territory, semi-annexed by Moscow but shunned by the west.

"We just eat *fasol* [a delicious bean dish], do our work and sleep," Khvicha Kobalia tells me. "We leave the politics to Putin."

Vitaly Mutko is in confident mood. I meet Russia's sports minister in Moscow in September 2010. It is three months before Fifa's executive committee will gather in Zurich to decide who will host the 2018 World Cup. I am one of a small group of journalists invited to meet Mutko at Luzhniki stadium. Mutko takes me to the VIP box; we gaze together at the cavernous ground and its luridly green artificial pitch. The minister was sitting here when Russia beat England in their 2007 European qualifier. It had seemed like England's night, he remembers. "Everyone was in a miserable mood at half-time. We were losing 1-0. I predicted we would score twice. And we did."

Ahead of the vote at Fifa's Swiss headquarters the bids from England and Russia are the two favourites. The others –a joint bid from Belgium and the Netherlands, and another from Portugal and Spain – are not seen as likely winners. Mutko, however, is careful to avoid any hubristic pronouncements. "Self-confidence sometimes leads to tragedies in sport," he says.

The Russians, nonetheless, strike me as quietly certain that they and not England will emerge victorious from Fifa's opaque secret ballot. From where do they draw this self-belief? Mutko says his optimism stems from an idea – a powerful idea – that a Russian World Cup will be a more dynamic, more compelling, and more nation-transforming event than a "safe" – and possibly dull – English one. It will be a moment in Russian history.

What is more, the tournament has never previously been held in the former communist bloc. Russia's bid, therefore, fits neatly with the stated desire by Fifa's president, Sepp Blatter, to bring football to new parts of the world (and, presumably, to lucrative new markets). I ask Mutko whether he thinks Russia's bid is more exciting than England's. He gives a little jump, then sweeps his fist through the air and utters a triumphant and affirmative *Da*. "I would just grab this country, Russia, and say there will be so much done for football," he tells me.

Mutko says he is irritated by stories in the British press flagging up Russia's problem with racist fans. (Lokomotiv Moscow supporters celebrate Peter Odemwingie's sale to West Bromwich Albion with a banner showing a banana and the message: "Thanks West Brom.") The minister is also rattled by reports of widespread corruption in Russia. He thinks these themes have been maliciously overblown in an effort to undermine Russia's bid.

That evening I watch Russia's Euro 2012 qualifying match against Slovakia. The venue is Moscow's Lokomotiv stadium. According to Russia's World Cup bid book, the 2018 final, a semi-final and the opening match will take place at Luzhniki. Other matches will be staged in a northern cluster centred on St Petersburg, a Volga cluster along Europe's longest river, and a southern cluster that includes Sochi. Putin is closely associated with Russia's bid. He has promised new stadiums, high-speed rail links between host cities, and new airports.

Russia loses the qualifier against Slovakia 0-1, courtesy of an abysmal goal-keeping blunder. Afterwards, I talk to Sergei Fursenko, the president of the Russian Football Union. Fursenko is wearing a suit and Russia fan scarf; he is gracious about Slovakia's victory. I ask him about the 2018 World Cup bid. He replies in quasi-mystical terms. Many football fans have only a vague idea of what Russia is like, he says. Hosting the tournament will enable visitors who come to Russia to experience the "Russian soul". He says: "You have not to be scared of Russians. People are very open. The soul is all embracing, including of foreigners."

After the match I'm invited to a dinner with members of Russia's 2018 World Cup bid committee. The venue is an Italian restaurant on the penthouse floor of the newly refurbished Hotel Ukraina, a Stalinist landmark overlooking the White House and Kutuzovsky Prospekt. The view is panoramic; the hors d'oeuvres delicious. Fifa's inspection team has just visited Moscow. I wonder whether the Fifa delegates ate the same luxurious parmesan.

I sit opposite Alexei Sorokin. Sorokin is the Russian bid committee chairman. An ex-diplomat in his late 30s, he speaks English perfectly, as well as French. Sorokin is a persuasive exponent of the Kremlin's patriotic philosophy – that the World Cup will transform the way Russia is perceived by the rest of the world, and allow Russia to take its "deserved seat" at the international top table. Sorokin strikes me as the model apparatchik. He is clever and articulate – but also capable of making nasty remarks about London, which he says has a "high crime rate".

Sorokin thinks the influx of fans will overcome the negative and unjust image of Russia internationally, an image concocted, he feels, by a hostile western media. "We would be perceived the way we merit to be perceived. It would eliminate this prejudice against us," he tells me. The tournament would also showcase what Russia has achieved "in a record period of time" since the end of communism.

Other bid committee members talk about Russia's ambitions in equally sweeping terms. Sitting to Sorokin's left is Alexander Djordjadze, the director of bid planning and operations. Djordjadze says the World Cup will be an event of historic proportions for Russia, on a par with the second world war and the defeat of the Nazis.

He addresses me: "England had everything. You ruled the world. You invented football. You have the richest league. You are solid and strong as a cultural entity. For us, the entire 20th century was an immense sacrifice. The World Cup will help us make a different people and a new nation. For Fifa to give it to Russia would be a bold political gesture."

One of Sorokin's jobs involved working at Moscow City Hall, run by Moscow's mayor, Yuri Luzhkov. Luzhkov was widely thought by ordinary Russians to be involved in spectacular corruption and organised crime. (A sentiment echoed in a US embassy WikiLeaks cable, which claimed the mayor sat atop of a "pyramid of corruption"; "total rubbish", Luzhkov insisted.) Wasn't it embarrassing that the mayor of the potential World Cup host city was known for dodgy deals, I ask. My question goes down badly. Sorokin intimates that Luzhkov may not be around for much longer – indeed, he is sacked three months later. But he is silent about corruption. Djordjadze is visibly annoyed. "Are you part of the Nemtsov crowd?" he asks me.

Over the next few weeks I forget about the Fifa vote. Elsewhere, however, there are mounting allegations of corruption involving Fifa members. In early November I receive a mysterious email. Its sender, "Alex", says he is in possession of confidential documents concerning Russia's World Cup bid. The documents are marked "strictly for internal use". Alex claims they describe "how Russian officials can work with members of Fifa's executive committee, through which channels the Fifa members can be influenced, and what might induce them to support Russia's bid during December's election."

The email could be genuine. Or fake. Or misinformation. Or a set up. Alex also intimates he wants money for his dossier. We exchange further emails. But I never get to see the documents. I resolve to make my own independent inquiries about Russia's World Cup bid, a vow I'm unable to fulfil.

Fifa awards the 2018 World Cup to Russia. The England bid receives just two votes. On the same day, and extraordinarily, Fifa gives the 2022 tournament to the parched desert emirate of Qatar. Allegations of Fifa corruption multiply until they resemble a large avalanche. (Fifa has robustly denied the claims.)

Later, I ask Stanislav Belkovsky whether Russia bought the World Cup.

Belkovsky answers like this. He says the Kremlin, the Russia 2018 bid committee and senior football officials all knew a week before Fifa's secret ballot that Russia had already won. Only England – represented in Zurich by the hapless trio of David Beckham, David Cameron and Prince William – were unaware that Fifa had already decided to give the competition to Moscow.

Russia, in my view, are more plausible winners than Qatar. And I have no doubt the 2018 tournament will be a success. But it seems possible that Russia and Fifa – both secretive oligarchies – may also have found a mutual language.

CHAPTER 9

The New Bourgeoisie

Agalarov Estate, Istra region, 30 miles west of Moscow
8 October 2007

*I see a new bourgeoisie developing in the Soviet Union from those
untried masses, with exactly the same faults and vices as ours.*
ANDRÉ GIDE, *THE GOD THAT FAILED*

Our cottage home is a haven amid the madness of Moscow. The *dacha* is
located in the artists' village of Sokol. Lily of the valley grows near the front
gate. Virginia creeper covers much of the wooden house, turning scarlet in
autumn. We even have our own birch tree. The window from our living
room looks out on shimmering greenery – a view out of the 19th century.
Well, almost: a hideous orange tower block edges into the picture.

The village was founded in the mid-1920s as an early Bolshevik experiment in collective living. Its denizens were sculptors, painters and scientists.
Many of the original cottages have been torn down. But our road, Bryullova
– named after the Russian painter Karl Bryullov – survives. Neighbouring
streets preserve the names of Levitan, Repin, Vereshchagin: 19th-century
artists whose limpid paintings hang in Moscow's Tretyakov gallery. In
Russian they are known as *Peredvizhniki*. I fall in love with their work.

Our neighbours seem themselves to have stepped from a Russian canvas:
an elderly man, with a Solzhenitsyn beard, lives next door in a crumbling
wooden pile. Behind us is a reclusive old lady. I spot her only once. We have
a small private garden. This is an almost unheard of luxury in Moscow.

Ruskin and I boot a football up and down the lawn; we hang a bird feeder in our plum tree; sometimes a great spotted woodpecker comes to visit.

One day a storm clefts the red sugar maple that grows next to our purple-roofed garage. Ruskin shins up the cracked trunk and rescues a lost Frisbee. Spring in Moscow arrives late. Our garden explodes into red tulips.

We are fortunate. Most Muscovites live in pokey Soviet-era flats. For rich Russians, however, there are grander – far grander – places to live.

With birds twittering gently in the background, Aras Agalarov explains why he has decided to build a housing estate for Russia's super-rich. Next to him work has almost finished on a vast classical villa; down the muddy track a Scottish baronial mansion rises magnificently above a line of newly planted birch trees. "The people who will live here are of normal social status," Agalarov tells me. "But there are certain rules. One potential buyer had an Afghan shepherd dog. We don't allow big dogs on this estate. So I wouldn't sell him a house." He chuckles. "Can you imagine? I lost $30 million because of a dog!"

Agalarov is a billionaire property developer. He is also a man with a vision: to build the most exclusive housing community in Russia, if not the world. The idea is for Russia's new billionaire elite to live here happily together. Agalarov describes his project as a kind of utopian social experiment – one without poor people. "I've planted all those trees to hide the village over there," he shows me, pointing beyond a fence to a row of dilapidated *dachas*. The estate is being fashioned on an 850-acre meadow in the Istra region outside Moscow, dotted with fir trees and white camomile flowers. When I visit several houses have already been completed.

Some, with fluted columns and acanthus capitals, owe a debt to the ancient Greeks; others have been done in doughty Gothic, with turrets and thick stone walls. I spot one magnificent trompe l'oeil ceiling, done by a budding Michelangelo; there are pillars and balustrades. No two houses are the same. The estate boasts an 18-hole golf course and an exclusive private school. There are 14 artificial lakes, waterfalls and a spa and beach resort with imported white sand.

Agalarov tells me he plans to build between 150 and 200 mansions. Each will cost about £10m to £15m. For this you get 2,000 square metres, a saltwater swimming pool, and the guarantee your neighbours will be the right kind of people. You also get the right kind of boulder: as well as hiring an American landscape designer, Agalarov has spent about £2.5 million on stones. Next to one of the lakes an army of migrant labourers are hard at work. They aren't Russian, I establish, but come from the impoverished fringes of the former Soviet empire – Tajikistan and Belarus – as well as neighbouring China.

But simply having a load of cash isn't enough to purchase a home here. Potential buyers must have a personal interview with Agalarov. They also have to sign a 30-page document agreeing to abide by Agalarov's own, at times eccentric, rules. Residents are forbidden from hanging out washing, carrying out home improvements, letting off fireworks and shooting birds from the windows. Additionally, all bodyguards are banished to small houses with pool tables on the edge of the community. "Most families have five or six bodyguards. Two hundred families means 1,000 bodyguards," Agalarov says, explaining his thinking.

Agalarov was born in Baku, the capital of Azerbaijan. *Forbes* ranks him as the 962nd richest person in the world. In 2011 Russia has 101 dollar billionaires – more than any other country apart from America. The magazine estimates Agalarov's fortune at $1.2 billion. He tells me his real wealth is more like £10bn – many of Russia's oligarchs, he says, are considerably wealthier than official estimates.

Many of those who buy property here have grown rich from the commodities boom that began soon after Putin became president in 2000. Their wealth is associated with the rise in oil and gas prices. Some, Agalarov hints, are well connected Kremlin bureaucrats, with homes in Kensington or the south of France, and sources of income that can only be guessed at. Agalarov says his own wife and daughter live in the US. He finds the pull of Russia too strong to decamp abroad, however. "My work is here. My life is here. My circle is here."

Agalarov drives me round his new billionaire's row in a British Land Rover. We reach the hamlet of Voronino, which abuts the watery edge of the estate. It is the only obstacle obscuring Agalarov's vision of a proletarian-free paradise. He has managed to buy 14 of its 28 houses, with a view to demolishing them. But the man at No 54 – a decrepit redbrick cottage – is refusing to sell, despite being offered $1m. Agalarov is confident that he will prevail. After all, in the brash world of Russian capitalism money usually does. "He'll sell in the end."

As well as his exclusive estate, Agalarov is the owner of Russia's largest exhibition centre, situated in northwest Moscow next to the city's thunderous outer ring-road. Crocus Expo is the venue for one of Moscow's most shameless annual events – its millionaire's fair. A Dutch entrepreneur, Yves Gijrath, founded the fair, which also takes place in Amsterdam and Shanghai, and is in its eighth year in Moscow.

The logic of a giant shopping mall for rich Russians is irresistible: "Russian customers like to buy, like to live and like to spend," Gijrath tells me, when I visit in 2008. Russians have a different, more prodigal, attitude towards consumption than Europeans, he says. "It's the same historical situation in any new economy. It was the same in the US in the 1950s, Saudi Arabia in the 1970s and Japan in the 1990s."

The fair offers goods for sale that would make Karl Marx's beard fall off – Gulfstream jets, beachside villas, designer skies and a $4,000 lawnmower. Near Crocus Expo's entrance a young woman pours Laurent-Perrier champagne while hanging upside down in a hoop. I learn that Russia's 103,000 millionaires can get into the event for free. Non-millionaires are allowed in, too, provided they stump up $64 for an entry ticket and put on a suitable frock or tuxedo.

Many of those who attend are young, pretty, female and wearing cocktail dresses. Though not millionaires themselves, I sense they are quite keen to meet one. "I'm not looking for a rich husband. I'm looking for someone with a big personality," says 26-year-old Irina, while clicking photos of her friend Olga in the back seat of an Aston Martin. (The Aston is priced at 11,637,795 roubles – about £260,000.) After a few seconds of reflection Irina adds: "Obviously if he was an oligarch with a big personality that would be OK."

Further inside the cavernous hall I find an exclusive German dental clinic, a sculptor exhibiting female nudes and a boutique selling Iranian silk carpets. There is also a 12 million Euro helicopter, complete with Versace interior. More congenial, to my eye, is a company flogging luxury *banyas*. For $300,000 you can get a Russian *banya* or steam-house built in a cosy log cabin in your garden.

I go to the *banya* frequently in Moscow with my friends, British and Russian. It's an addictive and stimulating experience. Once or twice, I try beating myself Russian-style, with birch twigs known as *veniki*. My favourite *banya* is close to the 1905 metro station. It's much less expensive than the celebrated Sanduny bathhouse, favoured by the capital's rich – though on one occasion someone swipes my sauna hat here. Rumour has it that the FSB used to send an agent to infiltrate a *banya* group made up of American correspondents. Of course, in the steam it's hard to tell who is listening.

A large part of the millionaire's fair is given over to luxury yachts. The oligarchic love affair with yachts is the stuff of tabloid headlines; I clamber on board one of the bigger ones – a sleek, white-painted Princess. The boat is made in Plymouth and is fitted out like a dinky London penthouse – complete with plasma TVs, comfy double beds and a kitchenette. (The only thing missing, I reflect, is a British politician.)

The Princess's Russian salesman, Yevgeny Kochman, says that business is remarkably good – and that there's a waiting list for the model I'm standing on, priced £1m. Given the dreadful state of relations between Britain and Russia, wouldn't Russians be afraid of buying British products, I wonder? "The politics is bad, yes. But among normal people it's fine. We buy your yachts, and you buy our gas," Kochman reasons. One of the firm's customers was the Chelsea FC owner Roman Abramovich, he says. He is quick to clarify: "That was a long time ago. He's got a bigger boat now."

It is a truism that successful politicians create their own luck. But after a disastrous decade in the 1990s, which saw Russia's economy default, Putin had the good fortune to arrive in power just as oil prices began to pick up. Soon, the Kremlin was enjoying a period of astonishing prosperity. During Putin's presidency, economic growth recovered strongly, averaging 7% a year. There was economic stability, fiscal discipline, and the appointment of liberals to key posts. Moscow paid off its foreign debts – which had stood as a symbol, according to the Putin view, of the country's humiliating weakness during the Yeltsin era, when Moscow was forced to go cap in hand to the International Monetary Fund.

As commodity prices skyrocketed, Russia's finance ministry found itself sitting on an enormous heap of cash. This money was put in a "stabilisation fund"; by 2008 it contained $157 billion. Ordinary Russians got a chunk of this sudden wealth: living standards rose, and average incomes doubled under Putin from the meagre figure of just under $400 a month.

This increase is crucial to understanding Putin's popularity during his first two presidencies. By 2008 and the global economic crash Putin's opinion poll ratings – while still impressively high – began to drop. State budgets found themselves squeezed as the oil price sank from $147 to below $50 a barrel. Inflation – fuelled by massive corruption and monopoly practices – grew.

Average workers, then, saw a small increase in their living standards. Well-connected bureaucrats and other insiders, on the other hand, grew dizzyingly rich, affording them the kind of lifestyles that predecessors could only have gasped at. "It's the dream of an old communist apparatchik come true," Yevgeny Kiselyov, the former head of NTV, tells me. "They [Russia's bureaucrats] can earn all the money they can, travel abroad and buy property in the Mediterranean, in western Europe or on Greek islands. Nobody expects them to behave well in their private life. They can divorce their wife and marry a younger woman. The only price they have to pay is loyalty to the boss. If you live by these rules nobody interferes in your financial affairs."

According to Kiselyov, the privileges of today's bureaucrats are part of a wider social compact between the rulers and the ruled: "Putinism is a practice in modern politics based on a kind of new deal between power and people. We allow you to do what you like. You allow us to rule as we like. It's based on corruption, complete disrespect for certain human and democratic values, on hypocrisy and double standards. It's about the redistribution of wealth and power." He cites a famous authoritarian declamation: "For my friends, everything! For my enemies, the law!"

For the opposition politician Vladimir Ryzhkov, the most conspicuous sign of corruption is the billions spent by Russians every year on property in London – £20 billion, for example, in 2006. Russians now form one of London's biggest communities; their numbers are estimated at between 200,000 to 400,000. He says that 60% of those who purchase homes in the capital are "bureaucrats from Moscow". Despite official salaries of $1,000 a month they are able to buy flats in Belgravia and send their children to expensive private schools. "Russian bureaucrats have their houses and families in London, and their children are going to Cambridge and Oxford. They keep their money outside Russia because none of them believes in Russia and none of them believes in official stability. All of them know that this stability could be finished any day. So it's a very strange political class."

Ryzhkov classifies this class as an "offshore aristocracy". Its thousands of members make their money inside Russia but prefer to live outside it, treating the motherland as a kind of colony. This wealth isn't earned through entrepreneurship, but is the fruit of opaque kickback schemes, Ryzhkov says. "They make money not in Bill Gates style by producing something but by taking bribes from oil and gas money."

In theory, senior government officials believe in the restoration of Russia's superpower status and spreading "sovereign democracy", the Kremlin's official ideological touchstone. In practice, Ryzhkov says, these officials have a much more primitive mission: to stay in power, get bribes, take this money outside Russia, buy houses outside Russia, and give their children a future abroad. "Today's political class is cynical and corrupted. But maybe it's good news for the world because Russia doesn't have global ambitions any more, as it did in the past."

Ryzhkov's background is as a historian. He tells me there is a direct connection between Russia's political system and the price of oil. When the price is low, he says, the Kremlin is keen to reform. But when the price is high it's time to restore the country's traditional autocratic model of government. He compares the Putin years with that of Leonid Brezhnev in the mid-1970s – another halcyon autocratic period sustained by a commodities boom, but which went on too long and eventually ended in political and economic stagnation: "It was the golden age of Brezhnev's Soviet Union. Now it's the golden age of traditional authoritarianism again because it's high oil and gas prices, and there is a lot of money. That's the main reason for stability, prosperity and restoration [of Russian authoritarianism]."

Under Putin, graft has increased dramatically – especially during Putin's second presidential term. Corruption, of course, didn't begin with Putin. It also flourished in the final two decades of the Soviet Union, when there was a sophisticated black market in anything from Aeroflot tickets to having your plumbing repaired. And the Soviet system of calling in favours, using connections, and exploiting acquaintances – known as *blat* – is as pervasive as ever.

Nonetheless, according to the Russian NGO Indem corruption has increased sixfold under Putin's rule. At the same time, as the *Moscow Times*'s Michael Bohm notes, the number of state employees has risen significantly under Putin, from 485,566 in 1999 to 846,307 in 2008, according to state statistics. Bohm draws the obvious conclusion: "The link is clear and direct. The more bureaucrats, the more corruption." He points out that Putin has allowed corruption to thrive since it is one of the foundations of his vertical power structure: "Putin's system of loyalty is highly dependent on the ability of his army of bureaucrats to embezzle and take bribes. Those who become wealthy under Putin obviously want to keep the current system in place for as long as possible."

When Vladimir Putin drives to work every morning, he doesn't pass the poor or the desperate. Instead, his prime minister's convoy streaks through the dreamy pine forests and fragrant birch groves of Rublyovka. The enchanting villages and hamlets either side of the Rublyovo-Uspenskoye Road have been home to Russia's elite since imperial times. Ivan the Terrible used to hunt here amid the sandy tracks and clearings. Centuries later the members of the Politburo and Central Committee were allocated country-side homes. Brezhnev's *dacha* was near the village of Zhukovka; the composer Dmitry Shostakovich and the cellist Mstislav Rostropovich had country homes in a nearby academic settlement. Solzhenitsyn lived for a while in a cottage at the bottom of Rostropovich's garden.

The *New York Times* correspondent Hedrick Smith, whose classic demystifying study of the Soviet Union, *The Russians*, was a 1970s best-seller, evokes Zhukovka's charms well. He writes:

It is a lovely, tranquil, timeless place, less than 20 miles from the throbbing city of Moscow and yet a world away. At sunset, one can sit high on the riverbank and look for miles and centuries at changeless Russia. The fields and shrubs and undergrowth here are wild and untidy, free of man's intrusion. The sky has a soft tint, not the bright orange or red of Florida or California sunsets, but a light, whitish glow because the region is so far north. The breeze carries the rich smell of pines. Muffled noises reach the ears – a dog's bark, a fish jumping, children far off laughing in the woods.

The artists, atomic scientists and intellectuals who once lived here are largely dead and gone. But the area is still home to Russia's elite. Putin's own country *dacha*, Novo-Ogaryovo, is near the hamlet of Usovo. His estate includes an avenue of pines that leads to a tasteful 19th-century-style manor house with a classical facade.

Journalists are ferried here from time to time in a bus that departs from Red Square. At Putin's mansion they are kept in a charmless side-room overlooking the courtyard. The room has a billiards table. Otherwise there isn't much to do other than to drink tea served in a colourful Chinese teapot and eat biscuits. After a long wait they are allowed to watch Putin deliver, more often than not, a public scolding to a government minister. Medvedev also has his own state residence, Meiendorff. It is a large brick castle, complete with fountain, and done in the kind of overblown baronial style popular with fans of Walt Disney.

Andrei Soldatov and Irina Borogan, journalists who monitor Russia's secretive security services, reveal that several high-ranking FSB officials have also been given land in Rublyovka. In Soviet times, KGB generals were allocated properties in the area – but had to vacate them when they retired from the service. The FSB generals, by contrast, received the land free from the state in 2003 and 2004.

Most of the original old clapboard *dachas* – already disappearing in Hedrick Smith's day – have been knocked down. Huge fortified brick mansions known as *kottezhi* have taken their place. Old paths have largely vanished. Rublyovka is the only part of Moscow where Phoebe – who runs her own walking group, braving wild dogs and squatter encampments – is unable to find a pedestrian route. Real estate here is some of the most expensive in the world. One of my Russian friends spends his time trying to defend his elderly father's crumbling Zhukovka *dacha* from raiders, who are attempting to steal his land, worth millions. The *dacha* also has treasures: plates with Nazi swastikas on them seized when my friend's father took part in the battle for Berlin.

Just down the road from Putin's *dacha* is an elite shopping complex, Barvikha Luxury Village. When I visit, there are few customers around – it's an overcast February day, still cold, and with snow on the ground. But all of the elite's favourite brands are represented: Gucci, Versace, Prada and Dolce & Gabbana, which has a special, mink-lined VIP room. Lamborghini and Ferrari have a showroom. "We thought New Year would be quiet. But we were extremely busy," Alexander Reebok, the manager of the private company that manages the village, explains. "We sell a Bentley a day. We don't sell quite as many Ferraris but they are rather low cars which are harder to drive in the snow."

I ask Reebok where his customers get their money. "Oil and gas definitely contributes to the overall situation in Russia," he replies. "The economy is developing. We are absolutely happy about that." The cheapest properties here cost $5 million, while the most expensive go for $100 million plus, he says.

The economic crash of 2008 gives a severe jolt to the fortunes of Russia's richest businessmen. According to the financial news agency Bloomberg, Russia's wealthiest 25 individuals collectively lose some $230 billion. Tycoons like Oleg Deripaska see their assets vaporised, while Abramovich – on paper at least – suffers a $20 billion wipeout. Alisher Usmanov, the football-loving tycoon, drops another $11 billion. Russia's RTS stock market loses 75% of its value.

By the end of the decade the fortunes of Russia's billionaires have bounced triumphantly back, however – in part thanks to a generous $50 billion state bail-out from Putin.

The big losers from the crisis, of course, aren't the rich. They are blue-collar workers, the elderly and the unemployed – in other words, Russia's multitudinous poor.

*

Fifty years ago the village of Slyozy ("Tears" in English) in western Russia was a bustling place. There were men, women, children, cows and pigs. Just down the road was a busy collective farm. Locals kept bees and looked after chickens. In the late 1950s they got their first combine harvester. With the collapse of the Soviet Union, however, and the end of communism, Slyozy has been slowly transformed – from a thriving agricultural community into a village of ghosts. After the second world war, and the departure of the invading Germans, it had a population of around 100.

These days, though, the population is rather smaller. When I arrive I find just four inhabitants. There is Olga, an 83-year-old widow, who walks with a limp and has an over-excitable dog, Verny. She lives in a crumbling *dacha* alongside the main road. Olga is a bit deaf. Her husband Boris died in 2004. Then there is Tamara – the village's youngest resident at a relatively sprightly 79. Tamara lives with her friend Alexandra, or Sasha, in a tidy cottage at the bottom of a snowy track. She has two chickens, two cats and a dog. Both women are also widows. Finally, there is another Olga. Olga number two is also 83, infirm, and unable to receive guests.

The village's last male inhabitant died in 2007, shortly before my visit. The scene is being repeated across Russia, the world's biggest country, where there are at least 34,000 villages inhabited by 10 people or fewer, almost all of them old women. "Last winter our TV aerial blew off. There are no men left in the village to fix it. We are hoping one of the visiting *dacha* owners will fix it over the summer," Tamara tells me, when I visit the village on a cold February afternoon. She stands outside her green-painted wooden *dacha* dressed – like all the women here – in a colourful headscarf and *valenki*, traditional felt boots.

The village is about 25 miles from Latvia and the border with the European Union and an hour's drive south from the historic town of Pskov, with its Kremlin and riverside cathedral. It has 12 houses. Five of them are falling down; only three are inhabited; two are summer *dachas*. The outhouses, greenhouses and fields are abandoned and silent. The village has an air of ghostly decay. In an abandoned shed I find numerous empty bottles of cheap vodka.

The only regular visitor to Slyozy is the social worker – who cycles in every day to deliver the ladies water from a well. There is the occasional grandchild who drops in from town. A bus brings groceries once a week; Tamara usually delivers milk and bread for infirm Olga, who can't really walk. "There used to be a few more of us. But eight people have died over the past three years. I buried my husband. Three men died last year. Now there are just women," Tamara says, clutching an apple bough snipped from her fruit garden. "I used to have bees," she says, pointing to a heap of abandoned box-like beehives. "I used to have cows, pigs and sheep. Now the men have died I don't have the ability to do it any more."

In fact, Slyozy's lack of men typifies the extraordinary demographic problem facing Russia, especially in the country's European north and west. Average male life expectancy in Russia when I visit is just 59 – well below the average in western Europe and many developing countries. For women it is 70. The 2010 census confirms that Russia's population is shrinking. It puts the total at 142.9 million, down 1.6% from 2002. There are 76.7 million women, but only 66.2 million men. (In 2010 male life expectancy rises to 63, and female to 74, according to official figures.) Most European countries are also facing smaller populations. But in Russia the decline is faster and lopsided.

Despite the natural resources boom, many of Russia's 30-million-plus pensioners live in poverty. Average pensions are 3,000 roubles (£65) a month. At a time when their western European counterparts are enjoying the good life, Russian pensioners can be seen on the streets of Moscow and St Petersburg trying to supplement their incomes selling gherkins, ladies' pullovers or woolly socks. Most of the sellers are women; in the cities, as in the countryside, there is a perplexing absence of old men. Russians are adept at dealing with crises – many grow vegetables in small kitchen gardens to survive, and others rely on a network of close relatives and friends. Inevitably, though, some, fall through the net.

In Slyozy, nobody is in any doubt as to why the men have disappeared. The problem is alcoholism – a ubiquitous rural phenomenon. Other social factors have certainly contributed: bad health care, smoking, unemployment and the poor health of many Russian pensioners who battled the Germans. (Olga tells me her late husband was wounded in the leg.) But ultimately the men of Slyozy drank themselves to death. "My husband drank throughout our marriage," Olga says, standing outside her *dacha*. "All the men in the village were drunkards. Now they've all died there is no one left around to drink." Olga lives on her husband's war pension – 5,000 roubles, or just over £100 a month. "I'm so lonely," she tells me.

In the neighbouring village of Velye, a short drive past Slyozy's derelict Soviet collective farm, locals paint the same picture. "Drink is a huge problem around here. It's a terrible problem in the village. It's a nightmare," says 79-year-old Zinaida Ivanovna. "The men here drink their pensions as soon as they get them. They sell whatever they possess to get more booze. They drink anything – moonshine and even window-cleaning fluids." Velye has a church, a school, and a village shop where the woman assistant tots up the cost of my lunch – a carton of fruit juice and a bread roll – using an abacus. There is a small museum documenting the village's agricultural history and a model of a vanished monastery. Pushkin lived 20 miles down the road; in summer tourists from St Petersburg drive past a serpentine road on the way to his country estate, sometimes stopping to pick flowers.

The men of Slyozy, meanwhile, all lie in the village graveyard. It is a picturesque spot, up a track to a birch forest and overlooking a frozen lake. Here, I discover Tamara's husband, Alexander Stepanovich. He died in 2004.

In the village square I do eventually manage to find a male – a pensioner in a large black furry Russian hat. At 79, he is Velye's oldest male inhabitant, he tells me. How come he's still alive? "I drink only milk," he jokes. "The others drink vodka." He adds: "Look at me. I look the same age as him," pointing to a man in his 40s, who has just turned up at the shop and who – it's late afternoon – is already reeling unsteadily.

During the late 1980s, life expectancy went up after Gorbachev launched a successful campaign against excessive drinking. In the 1990s, under the less than teetotal Yeltsin, the figure sank dramatically. Despite a marginal improvement, Russian men continue to die before old age. On average they consume a bottle of vodka a day. Some 30% of all male deaths in Russia are alcohol related.

"It's a really serious problem for our country. Low prices for vodka make the alcohol rate higher. In Sweden the government has dealt with this by putting up prices. But here you can buy homemade vodka for 15 or 20 roubles," says Dr Tatyana Nefedova, a senior researcher in the Institute of Geography, at Russia's Academy of Sciences in Moscow.

Other experts point to the fact that life in Russia is simply tougher than elsewhere. "Male life expectancy fell dramatically in the 1990s. Over the past 10 years it has been more or less stable. Many tropical islands have a higher life expectancy than Russia. On an island you have a good environment, plenty of fish and a quiet life," says Andrey Treyvish, a senior lecturer in geography at Moscow State University.

The phenomenon of women-only villages is of course linked to the depopulation of the Russian countryside. The trend increased during the late Soviet period, and accelerated in the 1990s, when many collective farms went bust. In 1926, 77 million Russians lived in rural areas; today the figure is less than 38 million. The young or ambitious fled to the towns, leaving behind the elderly, the incapable and the drunk. Russia is now an overwhelmingly urbanised society, with almost three-quarters of the population living in towns and cities. The country, by contrast, now has 13,000 villages where nobody lives any more – after the last Olgas and Tamaras died off.

Periodically the Kremlin promises large sums to revive rural Russia – pledging £2 billion, for example, in 2008. But human geographers doubt that subsidies will reverse the tide of migration from the countryside to the cities, which is turning huge chunks of Russia into an empty wasteland. Russian government officials acknowledge the scale of the problem – despite official attempts to increase life expectancy to 75 by 2020. For the moment, the number of Russian citizens shrinks every year.

As I leave Slyozy I'm struck that the women seem content with their modest lives. Their pensions are small but they are enough, they say. Tamara and Alexandra both voted for Putin's United Russia party during parliamentary elections in 2007. They say they are grateful for his reforms – which include providing them with 1,000 roubles a year in firewood – although Olga confesses she's not entirely sure she knows who Putin is. In these pockets of isolation, it seems, not even the most urgent and ubiquitous Kremlin TV propaganda can penetrate.

The women remember the Soviet era as a golden age. "We had so many people here after the war. There were three or four kids in each household. The work was difficult. We had to plant and harvest the fields manually. Things were bad. But gradually they got better," Tamara says. "The 70s and early 80s were best. We didn't have to pay for anything. There was free education and free hospitals. But after this things fell apart. At some point all the people left."

Tamara gives me some apples from her garden and shows us the outhouse where she keeps her chickens. She gestures across the sear and wintry fields and decaying outhouses. "We are the only ones left. There is no way more people will come here, so this village is doomed. Now all we are doing is sitting here waiting to die."

During my four years in Moscow I spend less time than I would wish reporting on the country's social problems, and the stark divisions between the haves and the have-nots. The disparities are bigger than in any other country I have worked as a foreign correspondent, including India, where I lived from 2000-2003, and other poor nations of south Asia.

In 2009 Russia overtakes Saudi Arabia as the world's biggest oil exporter; it is already the largest exporter of natural gas, and supplies a quarter of the EU's gas needs. In the same year official figures show six million Russian families sliding into poverty again – defined at an adult income of less than 5,497 roubles or £115 a month – with the gains in fighting poverty during the period 2000-2008 utterly wiped out. There are wide regional differences in income. The elite, living in Moscow and St Petersburg, and those in crumbling villages and single-factory industrial towns, inhabit vastly different worlds.

There are also plenty of ironies, in a rich country full of poor people. During a visit to the provincial town of Oryol, 220 miles southwest of Moscow, I meet Tatiana Shcherbakova, a 68-year-old pensioner. When I visit her tiny flat, Tatiana is sitting in the living room. It is incongruously decorated with a giant photo of a sun-kissed tropical beach. It shows shimmering palm trees, islands and a yacht. She tells me the picture pasted to her wall is of the Canaries, one of many exotic destinations Shcherbakova would like to visit but can't. "I don't have the money to travel," she explains. "It's my great passion. I've always wanted to see Vladivostok. But the train ticket is too expensive."

This is one of the strangest aspects of Russia's post-Soviet journey. Thirty years ago, when the world was divided into two rival camps, Shcherbakova wasn't allowed to travel to the west. But she took advantage of cheap internal fares to roam across the vast Soviet Union – holidaying in Moldavia, swimming in the Black Sea, dipping in the Danube and hiking in the mountains of Kazakhstan. Now Shcherbakova is free to travel anywhere. But on a meagre state pension of just 5,600 roubles a month she can't afford to. Even a trip to her local spa looks unlikely. Most of her pensioner friends survive on even less. (Shcherbakova is entitled to a top-up because, back in 1943, the Germans seized her and her family when they overran Oryol, the scene of a famous second world war tank battle. They spent five months as slave labourers before the Red Army arrived.) "It's enough to buy food. I'm not hungry," she says. "But I don't ever think I'm going to make it to the Canaries."

The week before my trip to Oryol, Russia's orthodox church had taken the highly unusual step of warning that the gulf between rich and poor was growing wider than ever. Some 20% of Russians lived below the poverty line, the church said. The richest 10% were now at least 25 times wealthier than the poorest 10%. Precise estimates were difficult, the church added, because the rich in Russia – like the rich everywhere – tended to conceal their real wealth.

And there was a serious gap between urban and rural life, the church confirmed, warning: "Russia possesses between 30 and 40 per cent of the earth's resources. Revenues from exports of natural resources built the stabilisation fund. But only a very small part of society is getting richer. It is doing so at a pace that amazes even some of the richest people in the world. On the other hand, the majority of the population lives in destitution."

In the rustic villages just outside Oryol, I discern few signs of any wealth. Instead, hunched *babushkas* tend to a few chickens and geese or harvest potatoes and onions from earthy plots. As in Slyozy, the young people have all left, while most of the older men appear to have died. "It was much better during Soviet times," says 79-year-old Tonya Fominykh, chaining up her guard dog and inviting me into her one-room wooden cottage. "Pensions were small but they were equal. We lived well. Now our pensions are nothing."

Every month, Fominykh receives a paltry 1540 roubles – less than £35 – from the state. When her house burned down in 2004 she was forced to sell her only cow. She spent three decades working for the Soviet police force but now survives on handouts from neighbours and her son. "We can survive but we can't live," she says.

Elsewhere in the village of Lavrov other residents seem in even worse shape. With some difficulty I call on Sasha Ivanovich, who lives in what can only be described as a hovel – a fetid wooden shack, strewn with dirty rags and unwashed plates. Ivanovich – asleep or drunk – takes several minutes to open the door. He shows me a bucket of potatoes from his garden. They are his main source of food. He can't afford anything else, he says. "Everything has got more expensive. Bread has gone up. Cigarettes have gone up. My sister pays my gas bill. I can't afford vodka." He looks up. "Can you give me 100 roubles?" I dig into my pocket and hand him a note.

In the process of writing about the trip for the *Guardian*, I recognise that Kremlin economists face a dilemma – if they raise pensions they risk stoking inflation, already in double digits. But plainly very few of Russia's billions have trickled down to the poorest groups – pensioners, the unemployed, low-level government employees or Shcherbakova, a former local TV editor, whose mathematician husband hobbles around on a pair of wobbly crutches.

It strikes me that in the quest for fiscal discipline, the cash-rich Kremlin has failed to notice that it now presides over the most unequal society in Russia's history. "I don't believe this [argument about inflation] to be true," says Natalia Rimashevskaya, a poverty expert at the Russian Academy of Sciences. "At the moment, 30% of all salaries are below the minimum needed to live," she tells me. "Pensions are very low. The average is 2,500 roubles [£55]. This leaves pensioners on the edge. If prices go up, they fall into poverty."

Although average wage levels have gone up significantly under Putin, the statistics conceal the fact that for millions of poor Russians wage levels have hardly changed at all, Rimashevskaya says. One of the biggest problems, she adds, is Russia's regressive tax system, which sees both oligarchs and humble road sweepers paying an identical flat tax rate of 13%.

Back in Oryol, Shcherbakova says that despite her current impecuniousness she doesn't want a return to the old Soviet Union. "I can't say it was better. It was like a dream or something out of a novel," she reflects. "There was nothing to buy. But it was OK." There is, however, no going back: "I'm not nostalgic about those times because I'm a democrat."

CHAPTER 10

The Once and Future War

Lubyanka metro station, opposite FSB headquarters, Moscow
29 March 2010

I remembered a Caucasian episode of years ago, which I had partly seen myself, partly heard from eyewitnesses, and in part imagined.
LEO TOLSTOY, *HADJI MURAD*

When we arrive in Moscow we make a conscious decision not to buy a car – the traffic jams are too terrible, driving too dangerous, verging on suicidal. Instead, like less wealthy Muscovites, we use public transport. This quixotic decision makes the morning school run – my favourite part of the day – a convoluted process.

First, a walk round the corner from our cottage to a temporary bus stop. Then a short ride to Volokolamskoye Shosse, a hideous multi-lane highway, and our tram stop. Our tram is No 23. It's usually packed; we cling on at the rear. On public holidays the tram plays patriotic music. Often, it moves faster than the backed-up cars – sweeping past grey apartment buildings and an embankment, flashing green. The tram rattles under Victory Bridge, then accelerates over a railway bridge and down towards the crowded suburb of Voikovskaya.

The last stretch involves a stroll through a small urban park. There are poplar trees, a modern high-rise apartment, dogs, a postal sorting office, and finally the British school, an inconspicuous two-storey building set behind high railings. That final leg is the best. We talk about maths problems, cosmology, whether there is a God (we agree there isn't), Russia's fiendish grammatical cases and *The Simpsons.*

At some point the local municipality installs a flashing green man at our treacherous pedestrian crossing. We joke that it is a rare example of President Medvedev's "modernisation" programme. Tilly walks the last 100 metres on her own – at the age of 12, she already finds her father *embarrassing.* I accompany Ruskin to the school gate; a small, preoccupied figure in a blue overcoat. He pushes open a heavy metal door and disappears. I take a shared minivan back to Voikovskaya and then the metro to work.

It's Monday morning, 29 March 2010. Another typical school day. We've almost completed the walk to school when my mobile phone rings. It's the *Guardian* foreign desk – there are two explosions on the Moscow metro, and many dead. The news is breaking. There are few details. I farewell the children, and dash to Voikovskaya metro station. Moscow is panicked and gridlocked but, to my surprise, the metro is still functioning normally, and is the only way to reach the centre of the city. I take the first train.

Within 20 minutes I arrive at Teatralnaya station, next to the Bolshoi Theatre, which is still being restored and in scaffolding. From here it's a short walk past a bust of Karl Marx and the Metropole hotel to the scene of the first bombing. Someone, it seems, has blown up Lubyanka metro station. The explosion takes place almost directly beneath the Moscow headquarters of the FSB. The choice of Lubyanka – a place synonymous with Russia's secret police, and with repression and terror in the Stalin era, when victims were shot in its basement – is clearly no coincidence.

This is the first major terrorist attack in the Russian capital for six years. The giant square next to the metro station is cordoned off. There are firemen and emergency service workers at the station. A helicopter buzzes overhead. But there are few signs of casualties. One man tells me he is looking for his wife. There are rumours – they turn out to be unfounded – of a third explosion.

The Lubyanka itself is undamaged – a forbidding, enormous building, radiating a kind of gloomy, anonymous power from behind its severe classical-style facade. Lights burn at its windows. But from outside it's impossible to discern any human shapes. Who is in there?

I stand in the middle of Lubyanka Square, next to a traffic island. It was here a giant statue of Felix Dzerzhinsky used to stand, until exuberant pro-democracy crowds removed it on 27 August 1991, in the wake of the KGB's failed coup against President Gorbachev. It was the KGB's lowest moment. Within a few years, however, the service – now re-branded the FSB – was back, and by the end of the decade its former chief was in the Kremlin. Periodically, calls are made to restore Dzerzhinsky. But so far he hasn't got his old spot back. He now stands in the sculpture garden behind the New Tretyakov gallery, an atmospheric graveyard of fallen Soviet idols.

The FSB has shown itself skilled at breaking up opposition political rallies, demanding money from big businesses and chasing after foreign spies, real or imagined. But it has shown less competence in stopping terrorist attacks. The service failed in 2002 to stop Chechen terrorists seizing a Moscow theatre. Two years later it proved unable to prevent the massacre at a school in Beslan, in which 334 hostages were killed, including 186 children. The service enjoys enormous resources, the support of the Kremlin, official prestige. But it is seemingly incapable of keeping Moscow safe from a small group of determined religious fanatics.

In its obsession with foreign enemies the FSB had missed the point: that the biggest threat to Russia's stability comes from homegrown extremists. Within a couple of hours of the bombings, it is clear that two female suicide bombers from the north Caucasus were responsible for the explosions on Moscow's packed metro. They had detonated their bombs at the start of the morning rush hour. At least 40 people are killed and 100 injured. The bombers boarded the metro early in the morning, apparently undetected. One blew herself up at Lubyanka metro, a short walk from Red Square, at 7.56am. The second bomber set off an explosive belt at 8.37am at Park Kultury station, close to the famous Gorky Park.

In my report that evening for the *Guardian* I reflect that the blasts represent a serious blow to Putin, and to the Kremlin's floundering efforts to pacify the troubled Muslim republics of Chechnya, Ingushetia and Dagestan. The targets appear to have been carefully chosen, a symbolic strike at the heart of Russian government. The first bomb is clearly aimed at the FSB, the agency responsible for brutal counter-insurgency operations across the north Caucasus. The second bomb, some believe, may have been intended for Oktyabrskaya metro station, next to Russia's interior ministry.

Putin cuts short a visit to Siberia. He flies back to Moscow. He declares that the "terrorists will be destroyed." But the bombings are a direct affront to Putin, and a sign that his strategy for the region isn't working.

For hard-up Chechens, it's a tradition born of necessity. In early spring locals set off into the snow-covered forests in search of wild garlic. (The garlic – like English wild leeks or ramsons – has broad green leaves and a pale bulb-like stem.) On 11 February 2010, about 200 residents from the Chechen town of Achkoi-Martan travel in a convoy of battered buses to the neighbouring republic of Ingushetia. The party includes four teenage boys. They are Adlan Mutaev, 16, his brother Arbi, 19, and their two friends Shamil Kataev, 19, and Movsar Tataev, 19.

By 3pm the boys have stuffed their canvas sacks full of garlic, which they plan to sell in the local market. They are on their way out of the forest to get the bus home. Suddenly, and without warning, Russian commandos concealed behind a hillock open fire. Shamil and Movsar are both wounded. Adlan is shot in the leg, but manages to hobble into a ditch. He hides. His brother Arbi also attempts to flee but men in camouflage fatigues catch up with him.

According to the Memorial human rights group, whose investigators interviewed relatives and survivors, Arbi is forced to drag his two wounded and bleeding friends across the snow. Shamil begs for his life. But the Russian soldiers are impervious. They place a blindfold over Arbi's eyes. They open fire – executing Shamil and Movsar on the spot. At least two other wild garlic-pickers suffer the same fate: Ramzan Susaev, 40, and Movsar Dakaev, 17. Their corpses are found 48 hours later.

The boys had unwittingly strayed into a "counter-insurgency operation", conducted by Russian forces in the densely wooded border zone between Chechnya and Ingushetia. The soldiers are apparently looking for militant Islamist rebels who are waging their own violent campaign against the Russian state. Instead they come across a group of unarmed teenage boys. They kill them anyway. The murders take place amid a picturesque massif of low hills and snow.

In a video three days after the metro attacks in Moscow, Chechnya's chief insurgent leader, Doku Umarov, claims responsibility. He says that the suicide bombings are in revenge for the deaths of the civilians shot dead while picking garlic. Umarov identifies the spot where the boys were gunned down: near the Ingush village of Arshaty. He also alleges that FSB commandos used knives to mutilate their bodies, mocking their victims in death. "As you all know, two special operations were carried out to destroy the infidels and to send a greeting to the FSB in Moscow," Umarov says. There are doubts over the credibility of his statement. But the video appears on KavkazCenter.com, the main source of news from the rebels' self-proclaimed Caucasus "emirate".

Umarov's explanation looks like a piece of opportunism. After all, any suicide attack in Moscow is likely to have been planned well in advance. The Moscow police are also hunting several accomplices. But at the same time the claim illustrates a bigger truth about the conflict: that both sides are locked into an endless cycle of bloodletting and revenge. As one political scientist, Andrei Piontkovsky, points out, violence in Russia's north Caucasus is becoming less a serious regional conflict and more an existential threat to the entire country.

It seems undeniable that the brutal actions of security forces have fuelled the insurgency that now rages across Russia's southern reaches, the mountainous ethnic republics of Dagestan, Ingushetia, Chechnya and Kabardino-Balkaria. Since 1992, and the emergence of a Chechen nationalist movement, the Kremlin has repeatedly used force to try and defeat the insurgents. This strategy has been counter-productive. But Moscow seems unable to think of another one.

Three days after the bombing I fly to Vladikavkaz, the capital of North Ossetia. From here I intend to travel to Nazran, Ingushetia's chief town. My goal is to discover what drove two women to blow themselves and others up on the metro, and to uncover the underlying causes – social and political, tribal? – of this spiralling civil war.

At Vladikavkaz I take a taxi to the border with Ingushetia – a 15-minute drive that passes a roadside memorial cemetery for the victims of Beslan. At the border, I get out. I cross on foot. I take with me a small case containing a couple of T-shirts and a change of underwear. It's warm – 25C – with a glaring white sky. The crossing is unusual, but tensions still smoulder between the Ingush and Ossetians following an ethnic conflict in 1992. Drivers are reluctant to cross between the republics. The conflict – over land – was one of several that broke out in the former Soviet Union at the time of its collapse. Others, dubbed "frozen conflicts", included Chechnya, South Ossetia, Abkhazia, Tajikistan, Nagorno-Karabakh and Transnistria.

A border guard examines my passport. He waves me through. Just inside Ingushetia, I hook up with a local Ingush journalist, Vakha Cherepanov, who is waiting for me on the grassy roadside with a vehicle. We drive on together to Nazran – a small, dusty town of low, redbrick buildings – and the office of Memorial.

Inside Memorial I meet Magomed Mutsolgov, a human rights activist whose brother "disappeared" four years ago. He is a friend of Politkovskaya, Markelov and Estemirova – all of them now murdered. I ask him about Ingushetia. The picture he sketches is grim: "People are abducted. People are killed. There are no guarantees of security." We sit in an upstairs study overlooking Nazran's ruined and windowless police station; the previous summer a suicide bomber driving a truck packed with explosives blew up the station.

Mutsolgov tells me that the situation has dramatically worsened over the past two years, with law enforcement and federal security agencies in Ingushetia out of control. These federal troops are responsible for dozens of summary and arbitrary detentions, as well as acts of torture and inhuman and degrading treatment. Russian security forces carry out extra-judicial executions, he says.

Typically, armed personnel wearing masks encircle a village or district in a so-called "sweep operation", similar to the one carried out in Arshaty. They force their way into homes, beat residents and damage their property. Suspected militants are taken away. Many never return. Others are simply shot, with weapons and uniforms planted on them. They are then charged posthumously with membership of an illegal organisation.

According to Mutsolgov and other human rights workers I talk to, the Kremlin's brutish counter-terrorism methods in the north Caucasus have made the insurgency worse. "Violence produces more violence. It drives people to the militant underground. The security forces behave with complete impunity, and people are humiliated, tortured or see their relatives disappear. They join the rebels out of a desire for revenge," he says. "This impunity is the biggest factor in recruitment for the underground." The Kremlin frequently boasts about having "wiped out" rebel leaders. But the strategy is ineffective, Mutsolgov suggests. "Someone else always takes their place."

After 16 years, two wars in Chechnya, and the loss of hundreds of thousands of civilian lives, the conflict in Russia's southern backyard is worse than ever, he says. The nature of the armed insurgency in the north Caucasus has changed, however. From 1994 to 1996 Boris Yeltsin fought a war against mainly secular Chechen separatists who wanted – like the newly independent Georgians over the mountains – their own constitution and nationalist state. In the period 1999–2004 president Vladimir Putin fought a second Chechen war. The aim was to definitively crush Chechen separatism.

Now, however, the Kremlin is battling another kind of enemy. The new generation of insurgents has an explicitly Islamist goal: to create a radical pan-Caucasian emirate ruled by sharia law, a bit like Afghanistan under the Taliban. These jihadist rebels are not lacking in ambition. A month before I visit Ingushetia, Umarov vows to "liberate" not only the north Caucasus and Krasnodar Krai territories but Astrakhan – on the Caspian Sea – and the Volga region as well; in other words a large chunk of European Russia.

The rebels' tactics have also grown more fanatical. Umarov has revived the suicide squads used by his predecessor Shamil Basayev, whom the FSB assassinated in 2006. As well as the attack on Nazran's police station, another suicide bomber succeeds in ramming the car of Ingushetia's president, Yunus-Bek Yevkurov. (He survives, but his driver does not.) There have been numerous other attacks in Chechnya and Dagestan – almost 20 suicide bombings in 2009 and 2010, Mutsolgov says. With the Moscow metro bombings, the rebels have demonstrated a new tactical capability to bring the war to Russian cities.

Increasingly, the rebels are also exploiting a powerful new virtual weapon: the internet. On 2 March 2010, Russian Special Forces launch a massive operation in Ekazhevo, a suburb of modern redbrick houses on the outskirts of Nazran. There they exterminate Said Buryatsky, a Siberian-born Islamic convert whose jihadist messages, posted on YouTube, have attracted a large global following among disaffected Muslims. Under fire from Russian artillery, and moments from death, Buryatsky records a final message for his disciples.

I want to visit the scene of the battle, a short drive from Nazran. But Vakha, my Ingush journalistic fixer, advises me that travel to Ekazhevo is too risky. Instead, Memorial workers play me video footage they have obtained from the village. It shows a picture of devastation: pulverised houses, wrecked cars and alleyways strewn with bricks. After the battle, Russian forces displayed a haul of weapons seized from the rebels – together with a blown-off human hand.

"The government's methods have led to a radicalisation of the underground. The rebels have only one goal: to beat Russia at any price," Timur Akiev, the head of Memorial's Nazran office tells me. Akiev is critical of both sides. He accuses them of failing to respect human life: "The rebels and the security forces behave in the same way towards each other. The civilian population is caught in the middle." Rights groups simply want the state to uphold human rights. Instead, he says, the authorities increasingly lump human rights workers and the rebels together.

Like its imperial tsarist predecessors, who subdued the Caucasus in a sustained and savage campaign of tree-felling and village burning, today's Russian leadership has little understanding of the region or its nuances, Akiev says. He also condemns the metro bombings. "I don't understand how you can kill Russian civilians in revenge for the killing of Chechen civilians. It's absurd. The people who died in the metro had nothing to do with the conflict. They could have been relatives of the people shot picking garlic in the woods."

My plan is to stay the night in Nazran's Assa hotel, which overlooks a small municipal lake popular with fishermen. But Vakha informs me that a few hours earlier local security forces have detained three journalists from Agence France-Presse. I decide to change my plan and return to

Vladikavkaz. During the first Chechen war journalists were allowed to roam around freely – with images of the Russian army's humiliation at the hands of the rebels screened around the world. During the second war, Putin, having learned from Yeltsin's mistakes, kept a tight grip on media coverage.

The Kremlin is keen to discourage foreign journalists from travelling independently in the north Caucasus. It prefers them to remain in Moscow or take part in organised press tours where their activities can be closely monitored. Parts of the region are off limits, owing to "counter-terrorism operations". These rules, however, are arbitrary and subject to unannounced changes. Before leaving Moscow I phone the local FSB. They are unable to give me any information. I also try Kaloy Akhilgov. He is press secretary to Ingushetia's President Yevkurov. Akhilgov invites me to Nazran. He promises to arrange an interview with his boss.

My passage out of Ingushetia is smooth – until I reach the crossing-point with North Ossetia. At the border an official, in plainclothes and armed with a Kalashnikov, taps on the window. He asks for my documents. I give him my passport. He is immediately excited. "We've got another one!" he enthuses into his radio.

Minutes later, I'm in a minivan driving back into Nazran. The guard – young, floppy-haired, arrogant and stupid – says he's taking me to the office of the federal migration service. Here, the service's Russian boss says I've committed an administrative "violation". A few days earlier, I am told, a decision was taken to ban foreigners from Nazran.

It's obvious that the plainclothes officers aren't border officials at all: they are FSB. Their office is unremarkable – four tables, a couple of chairs and a photocopier; on the wall is a framed portrait of Dmitry Medvedev. One of the FSB officers points at Russia's president. He jokes: "Putin's deputy!" He uses the Russian word *zam*, an abbreviation for *zamestitel* (deputy). The Russian in charge says that, like the Frenchmen who were in the same office a few hours earlier, I will have to pay a fine. The sum payable is 2,060 roubles – £45.

I protest. I have an invitation to meet Ingushetia's president, I explain. I point out that it's quite hard to interview him without visiting Ingushetia. The FSB boss is unimpressed. He intimates that Yevkurov is, for him and his powerful agency, a person of little significance.

A third, older man approaches. He asks me to roll up my shirtsleeves. He takes a pad of ink. He applies it not to just to my fingers and palm but all the way up to my elbows. He is apologetic. He presses my hands and arms down on a new criminal file. When the boss is out of the room he turns to me.

He whispers: "They're all FSB, you know. Personally, I think it's embarrassing to treat foreigners in this way. We should be showing you hospitality."

The man escorts me across a courtyard to a washbasin. He produces a new bar of cheap white soap, unwraps it, and hands it to me. I start washing off the ink. This takes some time. I feel angry. I realise my ordeal is a minor one. But I wonder at the fate of local Ingush boys, suspected of links to the rebels and brought in for "interrogation". What happens to them?

When I re-enter the room the FSB boss is back at his desk. I can't stop myself and ask him if he thinks harassing foreign journalists is perhaps counter-productive – might not other techniques lead to more sympathetic treatment? I point out that the Kremlin is spending more than $1.4 billion in 2010 on international propaganda. It would be better value for money to treat journalists a little better, I say.

The FSB guy is furious.

"How do you know this figure? I think you are a British spy. Are you a spy?"

I tell him the figure isn't exactly a state secret – it's published in the Russian budget.

The exchange over, I ask the FSB officials whether any of them have travelled abroad. None of them, it transpires, has left Russia. The FSB can be commended in one respect: its recruits are psychologically homogenous. All of them share an institutional phobia of the west, a place as remote for them as Europe must have been for medieval Japan.

After an hour I'm free to leave again for North Ossetia. The fingerprint guy shakes my hand. He is friendly, again muttering apologies. "Come back and visit us," he says.

Back at the border crossing, a regular soldier in uniform stops me. He wants a payoff. "Do you have euros or sterling?" he asks. He calls me into his sentry booth. I tell him it's been a long day. Eventually he lets me go –

Family
My wife, Phoebe, and children, Tilly and Ruskin, after a sweaty hike in the Georgian mountains. I had this image as my screensaver. The FSB deleted it from my laptop during a break-in in January 2009.

Putin and Medvedev
Vladimir Putin and Dmitry Medvedev, Russia's prime minister and president respectively. During four years in the Kremlin, Medvedev failed to escape from Putin's shadow, leading US diplomats to dub him Robin to Putin's Batman.

LUKE HARDING

VLADIMIR RODIONOV, EPA

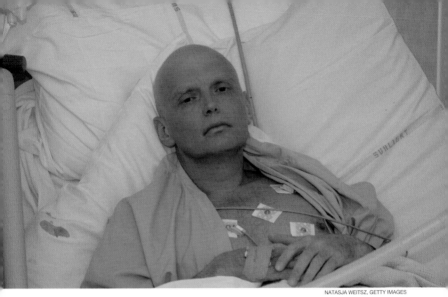

NATASJA WEITSZ, GETTY IMAGES

Alexander Litvinenko
The former FSB spy turned dissident, lying on his deathbed in a London hospital. He accused Putin of ordering his November 2006 murder by polonium. The case severely damaged relations between London and Moscow.

Anna Politkovskaya
Russia's most famous crusading journalist, shot dead outside her Moscow apartment in October 2006. Five years on, the Kremlin has been unable to identify the person who gave the order to kill her.

Natalia Estemirova
A leading human rights activist, Estemirova stood up to intimidation and threats from Chechnya's thuggish pro-Moscow president Ramzan Kadyrov. In July 2009 gunmen abducted her from her home in Grozny and executed her.

COLIN MCPHERSON, CORBIS

EPA

Russian tanks on the move
In August 2008 Georgia launched an ill-fated attempt to grab back the rebel Kremlin-backed province of South Ossetia. Russia responded with a full-scale invasion. Here, Russian tanks travel the road to Tbilisi, Georgia's capital.

Mikheil Saakashvili
Georgia's pro-western president. Putin promises to "hang him by the balls" but in the end refrains from capturing Tbilisi. Saakashvili – an ally of former US president George W Bush – was punished for daring to escape from Russia's grip.

SEAN SMITH, THE GUARDIAN

MONTSERRAT T. DIEZ, EPA

Georgian villagers fleeing
During the 2008 war Russian paramilitaries carried out a brutal campaign of ethnic cleansing on Georgian villages near and in South Ossetia. Georgian residents escaped on foot.

Gennady Petrov
Russia's top mafia boss, arrested in Spain in 2009. Spanish phone intercepts allege that Petrov had extensive connections with senior Russian government figures, including three ministers. So close are these illicit contacts that investigators describe Russia as a "virtual mafia state".

Moscow's Luzhniki stadium
My *Guardian* colleague Tom Parfitt and I kick a ball around Luzhniki stadium, the venue for the opening match, final and a semi-final in the 2018 World Cup, hosted by Russia. The decision to award the tournament to Moscow is mired in controversy.

Alexander and Evgeny Lebedev
Britain's most curiously dressed press barons, on their way to Downing Street and ownership of London's *Evening Standard* newspaper. Alexander Lebedev, a former KGB spy, became one of my best Moscow contacts. He first read the *Standard* in the late 1980s as an agent in the Soviet embassy.

Anna Chapman (*left*)
The glamorous Russian spy was one of 10 "sleeper agents" sent to infiltrate the US establishment. The FBI rumbled them early on, and they were swapped with Moscow in the summer of 2010. The FSB broke into my office after I wrote an article gently mocking its recruits.

Our Moscow home (*below*)
The garden of our cottage in Moscow. The *dacha* in Sokol was a refuge from the madness of Moscow. The FSB, however, broke in here, too, opening windows, disabling the central heating, and leaving a sex manual by the side of my bed.

ANDREY RUDAKOV/BLOOMBERG, GETTY IMAGES

Ruskin in Siberia (*below*)
The summer before my expulsion, we travelled by train to Siberia. We spent two nights camping in a yurt near the Mongolian border. Ruskin is standing under Aktru, a snow-covered 4,000-metre peak.

PHOEBE TAPLIN

PHOEBE TAPLIN

МИНИСТЕРСТВО ИНОСТРАННЫХ ДЕЛ
РОССИЙСКОЙ ФЕДЕРАЦИИ

УДОСТОВЕРЕНИЕ

корреспондента иностранного
средства массовой информации

г-н ХАРДИНГ ЛЮК

аккредитован при МИД России от
газеты "Гардиан"

(средство массовой информации)

Великобритания

(страна)

Действительно до
27.11.2010

По поручению Министра
иностранных дел Российской
Федерации
27.11. 20 09г.

ПРЕССА № К 021984

My annulled press accreditation
Russia's foreign ministry announced
in November 2010 it was not
renewing my press accreditation –
in effect, expelling me from the
country. Under Putin, the FSB has
gone back to using KGB tactics
with foreign journalists.

My office phone
The classic sign of an FSB
"intrusion". On this occasion the
agent has removed my phone and
laid it demonstratively across the
office table. The KGB developed
these psychological techniques,
also used by the Stasi, East
Germany's infamous secret police,
from the mid-1970s.

100 МИЛЛИОНОВ ЧИТАТЕЛЕЙ

ОШО

ЛЮБОВЬ

СВОБОДА

ОДИНОЧЕСТВО

НОВЫЙ ВЗГЛЯД
НА ОТНОШЕНИЯ

The sex manual (*top left*)
One of the more bizarre aspects of the FSB's harassment campaign. The agency left a book by the side of my bed by the Indian sex guru Osho. Someone had helpfully inserted a bookmark on page 110 – with advice on orgasms.

The video (*above*)
A video of a BBC *Panorama* programme on Litvinenko, recorded by a friend. The FSB erased the tape during a break-in. The voiceover was just audible but sounded like Mickey Mouse; the picture had disappeared.

The broken lock (*left*)
The FSB broke into our home for the last time in February 2011, just before we flew out of Russia. This time the agent didn't do a very good job, busting our front-door lock.

with my wallet intact. My Ingush driver takes me to an Ossetian colleague just across the border; she drives me back to Vladikavkaz.

Sitting in my hotel room, with a view of the Terek river and the bare Caucasus mountains, I reflect on the dismal events of the past few days. The Kremlin response to the metro bombings is vengeful. Putin calls for those responsible to be "scraped from the sewers". Medvedev visits Kizlyar, a town in Dagestan, where twin suicide bombers kill 12 people and injure 28 others. Security forces should "get more cruel", he recommends.

I flip open my laptop. I stare again at the photos of the dead garlic-pickers, posted by Memorial together with a one-page account of their killings. The images are gruesome.

I read that back in Achkoi-Martan it took relatives two days to discover what had happened to their loved ones. After hiding for 48 hours in a hole, fed by a spring, Adlan Mutaev crawled out of the forest. Local people discovered him alive on the edge of the wood. Russian commandos released his brother Arbi after two days. Human rights workers from Memorial arrived at the spot on 14 February. They interviewed dozens of witnesses and took photographs of corpses heaped up in the snow, next to sacks of garlic.

The photo of the Mutaev boys' friend Shamil Kataev reveals he was shot in the temple from close range. There's a neat hole. Someone stole his mobile phone and passport, as well as a letter from the head of Achkoi-Martan, granting the garlic pickers permission to be in the area. Shamil had gone to the forest in the hope of earning some money for his large, impoverished family, his relatives tell Memorial.

The body of Movsar Tataev is covered in gunshot wounds; he's a bloody mess. There are knife wounds to his spine and chest. His brother finds his body lying in the forest. One arm is curled up. The photograph is horrific. His last moments must have been sickening.

Unusually, Yevkurov – whom I fail to meet – acknowledges that several innocent civilians were killed in the special operation. He adds, however, that security forces succeeded in killing 18 genuine rebels, and says that the operation had served to increase "the stability of the region". Ramzan Kadyrov, Chechnya's president, pays compensation to the boys' families.

Movsar Dakaev's family have one of the saddest stories. They say they had no idea he was going into an area at the centre of a counter-terrorist operation. Dakaev asks one of his friends to take a photo of him in the woods. We know the time – *13.40 10.02.10* is stamped in red ink on the left-hand side of the picture.

Dakaev is wearing black gloves and a bright green fleece; he's standing against an escarpment of snow and bare trees. He looks rather serious, with his eyebrows slightly raised. He's very much alive, boyishly handsome, on the cusp of manhood. Two hours later he's dead. The second photo shows him lying in the snow. His face is yellow. There are flecks of blood. Dakaev's eyes are still open, I notice; he's staring at the sky as if life itself is an unfathomable dream.

A few days after the metro attacks, the FSB identifies the two women bombers. They are Mariam Sharipova, aged 27, and Dzhennet Abdurakhmanova, just 17. Both are from Dagestan, the largest autonomy in the north Caucasus. Sharipova comes from Balakhani, a mountain village known as a stronghold of conservative Islam. Abdurakhmanova is from the Khasavyurt area, in western Dagestan. Sharipova triggers the first explosion at Lubyanka metro station; Abdurakhmanova the second at Park Kultury.

Suicide bombing by so-called Chechen "black widows" was one of the grisly hallmarks of Putin's second Chechen war. But this is something new: the first time women from Dagestan have travelled to the capital, more than 1,000 miles away, and blown themselves up.

Abdurakhmanova's family details are somewhat hazy. After the bombing her mother disappears. But Sharipova's parents speak to *Novaya Gazeta*. They admit that their daughter was almost certainly the Lubyanka bomber. Her father, Rasul Magomedov, says he identified Mariam from a photo of one of the dead bombers released by police. He says that she had been missing for several days before the attacks, and adds that he recognised her immediately.

I call *Novaya Gazeta*'s reporter Irina Gordienko. We discuss the possibility of my travelling to Dagestan. She gives me several contacts. Over the subsequent weeks I find myself returning to the same question: why did Mariam Sharipova – an educated, sensible young woman from a solid and apparently happy family – blow herself and others up?

The trip is slow in coming together, but six weeks after the metro bombings I travel to Dagestan to meet Sharipova's father. I fly in an ancient Soviet plane to Dagestan's capital, Makhachkala. There I meet up with Yuri Kozyrev, a gifted Russian photographer who has just emerged from many years working in Iraq for the US magazine *Newsweek*. Magomed Shamilov, a former Dagestani policeman, travels with us. He knows the Sharipova family. And he has a Volga saloon, a tank-like car useful for negotiating the republic's hopelessly rutted roads.

The situation in Dagestan is gloomily similar to that in Ingushetia, Shamilov says. The republic, the biggest and most diverse in the north Caucasus, is also gripped by insurgency. Dagestan was once immune to the violence that erupted in neighbouring Chechnya in 1994. Now it seems to be in the midst of a small-scale civil war. This battle, characterised by daily shoot-outs and bomb attacks, is being fought between the Dagestanian police force and militant Islamist rebels. Caught in the middle are Dagestan's civilians. Shamilov says that several of his former colleagues have perished in these deadly skirmishes and that many serving police are decent officers trying to do a good job.

As we talk, we leave Makhachkala behind and drive across a green plain dotted with bungalows; gradually the shimmering Caspian Sea disappears. We head west into the mountains, passing through a landscape of sheer peaks and river valleys. Eagles float in a hazy sky above spruce trees; there are butterflies and birdsong. We stop at a roadside Sufi shrine decorated with coloured flags.

The journey takes four hours. Finally, we reach Balakhani. The village looks unchanged since the nineteenth century. There are houses of solid stone built alongside a river. There is something impregnable about Balakhani: the village sits beneath two sheer mountain flanks; donkeys plod between dark cobbled alleys and gardens of apricots and mulberries. Two men plough a maize field using a pair of bullocks.

Rasul Magomedov greets us in the courtyard of the family home. Washing hangs on the line, shoes are neatly stacked. There is a satellite dish; tree sparrows flit past a trailing vine. He shows us the ground-floor front bedroom where Mariam, his only daughter, lived. She decorated the walls herself – magenta. Her possessions are still there: L'Oréal moisturisers, a bedside table and a mirror. There are books in Arabic. More surprising is the heap of women's fashion magazines – *Health and Beauty*, *Good Advice* and *Glamour*. In photos, she is an attractive young woman – her hair parted in the middle and tucked behind her ears, with full lips, oval eyes and dark eyebrows.

We go inside. Sitting cross-legged on the carpet, Rasul tells me he thinks it impossible his daughter was a suicide bomber. "I don't know what happened," he says. "We, too, are seeking answers. She knows. Allah knows. That's it." He offers his condolences to the families of Muscovites blown up on their way to work. Typically, bombers leave a last testament before going on their final mission. But Mariam left no note of any kind. "We've looked everywhere. We've found nothing," he says.

Her background offers no clues as to why she would kill herself and murder others. Sharipova's parents are both members of what was once the Soviet intelligentsia: Rasul teaches Russian literature at Balkhani's junior school; his wife is a biologist. Sharipova was an outstanding student. His daughter's schoolbooks are covered in neat handwriting. She had been taking classes in Arabic. She was noting down verbs in her exercise book on 7 February – just weeks before her suicide. "She wasn't the kind of person who could do this. She was self-confident, someone who defined clear goals, and who wanted to achieve them," he says.

A bright girl, Sharipova studied mathematics at Dagestan's State Pedagogical University. She became the first person from her district to do a master's and took a second degree in psychology. In 2006 she started working at the village school. Her CV, then, has nothing in common with the tortured biographies of radicalised Chechen "black widows", who generally act from motives of personal revenge following the murder by security forces of husbands or brothers.

Was she, though, representative of a new kind of terror? Balakhani is known as a religious centre for Dagestan's Salafi community. This conservative form of Islam has been spreading rapidly across the republic. It is more radical than the traditional form of Sufism, or Islamic mysticism, that has existed in the region since the mid-8th century – far longer than in any other corner of Russia. There are growing sectarian tensions in Dagestan, with many Salafis critical of the local religious leadership, which they believe has grown too close to state power and too worldly.

The authorities, meanwhile, dub the Salafis extremists and "Wahhabists" and blame them for every anti-federal attack.

Sharipova's father tells me he condemns violence. At the same time, he talks eloquently of the unending 300-year struggle waged in the mountains of Dagestan against the encroaching Russians. He mentions Sheikh Mansur. In 1785 Mansur organised the first large-scale rebellion against Russian expansion into the Caucasus highlands. It was Mansur who issued a call for *gazavat*, or holy war, against the Russians, a slogan still used by today's webbed-up guerrillas.

The most celebrated anti-Russian military commander, Imam Shamil, surrendered just down the road after tsarist forces trapped him in the Dagestani village of Gunib. Shamil was also a spiritual leader: he saved his greatest criticism not for the infidel Russians but for his spiritually weak co-religionists. One hundred and fifty years later the same internecine conflict is being played out – with jihadist insurgents blowing up fellow-Muslim police officers they regard as apostates.

As Rasul sees it, Russia and its southern Muslims, subjects since the time of Tolstoy, are locked in an irreconcilable embrace – a deadly "historical spiral". "We've had war for 16 years in the Caucasus," he says. "We didn't join the Russian Federation willingly. It was annexation. But we don't want to leave either," he adds, paradoxically. He says he sees no difference between the "terrorists in the woods" – the rebels – and the "terrorists in epaulettes" – the security forces.

At the same time he is a fan of 19th-century Russian writers – he mentions Pushkin, Lermontov, and Tolstoy – all of whom served in the Caucasus. There is *Hadji Murad*, Tolstoy's extraordinary late novella. It tells of a famed Avar leader, Hadji Murad, who defects to the Russians and back again – the theme of disunity and betrayal a motif of Chechen history. I say I think it is Tolstoy's greatest work. "I admire Tolstoy's philosophy and his stand against violence," Rasul replies. "You can only end this war through political methods. Violent methods won't solve it."

In the afternoon we take a stroll around Balakhani. It's not unlike other villages I've visited in the mountains of Afghanistan and Pakistan: at the mosque we pass young men with white prayer caps and full beards. We walk alongside the river, filled with rubbish. We inspect the middle school where Sharipova taught – a whitewashed single-storey building.

Rasul rejects the official account of his daughter's death, and the Russian media's portrayal of her as a terrorist zombie. "It's rubbish. From my point of view this is all part of [Russia's] vile campaign against Muslims." It begins to rain. We shelter in the school's porch, as a group of boys kick a ball around the muddy yard.

Rasul believes Russian intelligence agents could have seized his daughter in Makhachkala. This is one version. But could someone else have persuaded her to kill herself? Russian investigators claim Sharipova was secretly leading a double life. They allege she was the bride of a top rebel leader, Magomedali Vagabov, whom the police shoot dead a few months after the metro bombings.

Secret marriages between rebel commanders and pious young women are real enough, with couples meeting every four months or so in a safe house for a brief moment of intimacy. The tragedy of Mariam Sharipova, I conclude, may ultimately be a generational one. Today's young Russian Muslims are less Sovietised than their communist-educated parents. As their disaffection grows, they are more ready to seek radical solutions.

I say goodbye to Rasul. Just before I leave he shows me his PhD thesis, written in 1975. Its subject is Avar poetry of the 16th and 17th centuries.

The FSB fails to get to grips with domestic terrorism. On 24 January 2011, a suicide bomber walks into Moscow's Domodedovo airport. Nobody challenges him. He blows himself up, killing 37 people and injuring 180.

The threat of a terrorist attack in Moscow is real enough – a constant beneath the surface. But another, more palpable form of intimidation stalks the city's streets. It targets those from the Caucasus – no longer perpetrators but victims – as well as anyone of non-Slavic descent. This spectre is Russian nationalism, furiously asserting itself.

CHAPTER 11

Rise of the Far Right

No 21, Block 2, Kedrov Street, southwest Moscow
16 April 2007

Let's clear out the garbage!
ELECTION SLOGAN, RODINA (MOTHERLAND) PARTY

At 9.10pm, Karen Abramian is returning home to his flat in southwest Moscow. He has been visiting his parents in a nearby tower block. The journey back takes five minutes – past a string of grey high-rise buildings, soaring into Moscow's packed skyline, a children's playground and up a modest flight of steps.

As he punches in the entrance code, two young men wearing baseball caps and bandanas approach him from behind. They stab him. They stab him again. And again: methodically slashing his head, neck, back and stomach. Abramian pleads with his attackers. "Don't do this. Please, take my money!" His assailants – two slight, boyish, almost nerdish figures – ignore him. They stab him a total of 56 times.

At this moment Abramian's wife Marta peers out of their ninth-floor apartment window. She looks down. She spots two boys beating a dark shape lying on the ground. This is her husband.

The couple's 14-year-old son Georgy, who has been playing nearby, finds his father in the entranceway. At this point Abramian is bleeding profusely. Georgy takes off his T-shirt – it is still winter in Russia and bitterly cold. He wraps it around his father and runs upstairs. Abramian is conscious when Georgy returns with a blanket and pillow. Together they wait in the gloom for an ambulance.

Abramian tells his son simply: "They were skinheads."

Four hours later, Abramian is dead. Doctors have tried to save him, but are unable to stem such colossal blood loss.

The names of Abramian's killers are Artur Ryno and Pavel Skachevsky. Both are 17. Their motive for murdering Abramian – the 46-year-old boss of a Moscow insurance company – is not criminal. It is ideological.

As they see it, Abramian's violent death is part of a national liberation movement – a quasi-mystical crusade to get rid of Russia's foreigners, in which they play the role of hero-warriors.

The boys had picked Abramian because he was an ethnic Armenian. His murder is an act of racist violence: Ryno and Skachevsky had spotted him on the street and impulsively decided to kill him. That they are apprehended is a coincidence: a neighbour witnesses the attack and runs after them. They escape on the number 26 tram. But the neighbour, a former investigator, flags down a passing police Lada and gives chase. Police officers halt the tram and arrest both boys. (Ryno and Skachevsky have turned their blood-soaked overcoats inside out; their victim, however, had managed to grab one of them by the arm, leaving behind a bloody print.)

Ryno and Skachevsky make no attempt to deny their crime. On the contrary, they are proud of it. In their rucksack detectives discover 25-cm-long knives. In custody investigators ask Ryno and Skachevsky whether they had committed other murders. To their surprise, the teenagers said yes, they have. They admit to having killed 20 people in a period of eight months, stretching between August 2006 and April 2007. They have carried out attacks on at least 12 others, who survived.

The police are initially sceptical, assuming that the boys are delusional. Gradually, however, investigators are able to confirm Ryno and Skachevsky's extraordinary claims. Prosecutors establish that the diminutive pair has indeed killed 20 people.

The case is shocking, exceptional. But it also suggests that the Kremlin's flirtation with nationalism – manifested in its periodic denunciation of foreign "enemies" – is having dark and unintended consequences.

Ryno and Skachevsky are among the worst mass murderers in Russia's modern history. Three hours before Abramian's random execution the pair had stabbed to death someone else – Kyril Sadikov, a Tajik. They ate some food, then set off in search of their next victim. The 45-page court indictment against them shows a disturbing, almost darkly symphonic, pattern – with the skinheads lying in wait next to different suburban metro stations and stabbing their victims as many as 60 times.

The victims all have one thing in common: they are not Slavs. Most are guest workers toiling in Moscow's building industry or cleaners in the capital's communal courtyards and urban parks. Nobody knows how many low-wage *Gastarbeiter* are currently resident in Moscow – a teeming metropolis of 12 million. Estimates range from 200,000 to two million. Many are unlicensed cab drivers working Moscow's clogged streets.

Typically the skinheads' targets have fled poverty and the impoverished former Soviet republics of Central Asia – Tajikistan, Uzbekistan and Kyrgyzstan. Others are from China. A few are "of Caucasian appearance", as the charge-sheet puts it – from Russia's troubled southern provinces of Chechnya or Dagestan.

Like all warriors involved in a holy war, as they perceived it, the boys sometimes made mistakes: several of their dark-skinned victims are actually ethnic Russians. One murder sticks out. Precisely a week before the murder of Karen Abramian, it's the turn of S Azimov, an Uzbek student (He is described simply as "S Azimov" in the indictment.) The skinheads ambush Azimov outside his flat in Moscow's bland northwest suburb of Voikovskaya. Azimov lived on Zoya and Alexander Kosmodemyansky Street – named after two Soviet partisans. Moscow's British International School is a short walk away – down a busy boulevard, past a TV repair shop and kiosks selling beer and kebabs. Middle class-parents in Range Rovers whiz past.

The skinheads stab Azimov 56 times. As he lies on the ground, his life ebbing away, they cut off his left ear.

Alexander Verkhovsky describes Ryno and Skachevsky's killing spree as "very unusual". Verkhovsky is an eloquent Russian with shoulder-length black hair and a 70s-style suede jacket. He is an expert on xenophobic violence. A fluent English speaker, he is also the director of Sova, a Moscow information centre that logs hate crime.

We meet in a Moscow cafe a few days before Ryno and Skachevsky's five-month trial for murder is due to end. Just around the corner around 300 neo-Nazi activists are holding a rally beneath the verdigrised statue of the 19th-century Russian playwright Alexander Griboyedov. (The venue is no accident: Griboyedov is a sort of early skinhead martyr. The author of the verse comedy *Woe from Wit*, he was stabbed to death in 1829 by a Persian mob.)

The skinheads wave black, yellow and white flags; a few clamber on the statue and launch Hitler salutes, shouting, "Russia for Russians!" I later discover that most Russian skinheads revere the *Führer* – believing that his only mistake was to attack the Soviet Union. The average age here is about 15 or 16; the style is baseball caps, Burberry scarves and Lonsdale – the uniform of the British far-right. One skinhead even has a Union Jack jacket. Among them are several young women.

The skinheads adhere to two ultra-nationalist groups – the Movement Against Illegal Immigration and the Slavic Union. The authorities will declare both illegal. A stall shows a photo of 15-year-old Anna Beshnova – a picture-book pretty blonde Russian schoolgirl raped and then murdered in October 2008 by an Uzbek city maintenance worker. Her death has ignited racial tensions across the city's already inflammable lower-middle-class suburbs and inspired several revenge attacks.

According to Verkhovsky, the phenomenon of racist violence in Russia isn't new. What makes Ryno and Skachevsky's case remarkable, he says, is the prolific scale of their murder spree – 20 deaths within eight months.

The fact that detectives solved these crimes has nothing to do with their investigative skills, he says, but is down to the teenagers confessing. "This isn't an example of good investigation," he notes. Verkhovsky says the crimes are an extreme manifestation of a pervasive racism. "There is a very widespread xenophobic prejudice in Russia."

"More than 50% support the idea that ethnic Russians should have privileges over other ethnic groups. More than 50% believe that ethnic minorities should be limited or even expelled from their region," Verkhovsky tells me. Under communism there was also prejudice towards non-Slavs as well as Jews, despite the polyethnic nature of Soviet life. In the 1990s, when many ethnic Russians returned from newly independent republics like Uzbekistan, prejudice continued.

But it is over the last Putin-driven decade that racism has grown to astonishing levels, Verkhovsky says. Russia's second war in Chechnya and the 1999 apartment block bombings, which killed almost 300 people in four Russian cities created this new xenophobia, he believes.

The Kremlin blamed the bombings on terrorist Chechens; others, including the late Alexander Litvinenko, believed the bombings were the work of the FSB. Soon afterwards, Putin used the bombings to justify his all-out attack on Chechnya, in what was to become the second Chechen war.

According to Litvinenko, who co-authored a book on the attacks, *Blowing Up Russia: Terror from Within*, active FSB agents planted the bombs. The first, on 9 September 1999, destroyed a nine-storey apartment building on Guryanova Street in southwest Moscow, killing 94 people and injuring 249. The second, four days later, exploded in the basement of an apartment block on Kashirskoye Highway in southern Moscow, killing 118 and injuring about 200. Two FSB agents were later caught planting another bomb under a building in the city of Ryazan. Nikolai Patrushev, the FSB director, said the agents had merely been carrying out a training exercise. He insisted the Ryazan "bomb" was made of sugar, not explosives.

Many Russians continue to believe that the attacks were indeed the work of the FSB, although the journalists Andrei Soldatov and Irina Borogan recently concluded the agency wasn't complicit in the plot. The site of the second bomb – next to the Moskva river and surrounded by garish modern tower blocks that survived the blast – is now home to a small timber-built orthodox church. When I walk past in 2010, a couple of kids are mucking about in its tower, ringing its bell.

Whatever the truth of the 1999 bombings, racism in Russia is now ubiquitous. According to Sova, at least 37 people were murdered in 2010 in racist or neo-Nazi attacks, with 368 injured; 60 were murdered in 2009. and 306 injured; and at least 110 people were murdered in 2008, with another 486 beaten or wounded. (The number of deaths was 50 in 2004, 47 in 2005, 64 in 2006 and 86 in 2007.)

Sova's research suggests that xenophobic prejudice has become mainstream, acceptable. And while most Russians don't support radical nationalist ideas in practice there are around 2,000-3,000 young skinheads prepared to attack and kill migrants, he estimates. Russia's law enforcement agencies, tasked with the job of catching these killers, share the prejudices of Russia's general population.

Typically police officers ignore race attacks – or classify them with the lesser charge of hooliganism. Verkhovsky says: "Enforcement is very weak. These young skinheads don't feel fear of the police since the risk of getting caught is small."

The bloody evidence appears to confirm his grim thesis. A few days before our meeting an unknown group, the Militant Organisation of Russian Nationalists, sends out a chilling email. The group says it has murdered a 20-year-old Tajik, stabbing him six times as he walks home from his job at a food warehouse. They have cut off his head, dumping it in a bin outside a council office in western Moscow.

The victim's body is discovered near the village of Zhabkino, a few miles outside the capital. The email includes an attachment. It is a photograph of the young man's head lying on a giant wooden chopping block. The picture is sickening, repulsive: taken in darkness, it shows the victim's face, covered in blood; his eyes clenched shut in agony.

The group says the murder is a protest against the authorities for their failure to deal with immigration or – as the beheaders put it – to rid Russia of its Caucasian and Central Asian "occupiers". Unless government officials deport "the blacks", their heads would "fly off" next, it warns. The beheading is reminiscent of another gruesome neo-Nazi attack that surfaced in 2007 via far-right websites. The online video – entitled "The execution of a Tajik and a Dagestani" – shows two men kneeling in an autumnal Russian forest, bound and gagged under a Nazi flag. Masked men saw off one man's head and shoot the other. Russian investigators initially dismiss the video as a hoax.

Later, however, it emerges that it is genuine. A man recognises the Dagestani victim as his missing brother, who vanished in Moscow several months earlier. During the same week in December 2008, meanwhile, unknown attackers in the southern city of Volgograd casually knife a black American teenager. Stanley Robinson, 18, from Providence, Rhode Island, had been in Russia on a school exchange. The attack leaves him critically injured; he is flown out of Russia to Finland for emergency surgery.

Back in south Moscow, it's another normal day. Suspected skinheads stab an 18-year-old Kazakh student, Yerlan Aitymov, as he waits for a bus near Kaluzhskaya metro station. Yerlan dies on the way to hospital.

Artur Ryno and Pavel Skachevsky do not fit the profile of classic serial killers. There isn't much in their upbringing to suggest they will turn into flamboyant teenage murderers. Ryno grew up in the southern Urals city of Yekaterinburg. His parents divorced when he was small; his father was from Russia's far eastern province of Chukotka. (Ironically, Ryno's own features were somewhat non-Slavic.)

At school Ryno showed an aptitude for drawing. Classmates describe him as a quiet, introverted pupil who struggled to make friends. He wore his hair long and sported a studded leather jacket. His lawyers claim that Ryno fell under the sway of racist ideas after a Chechen schoolmate beat him up. In 2006 Ryno moved to Moscow. Here he enrolled in Moscow's Arts Institute and studied icon painting. (Several of Ryno's icons hang in the church in Yekaterinburg built on the spot where the Bolsheviks shot and bayoneted Russia's last tsar and his family. The Romanovs feature in its kitschily overblown gold-painted iconostasis.)

In Moscow Ryno shaved off his hair. He met Skachevsky via an ultra-nationalist website, Format18.ru – the numbers 1 and 8 a reference to Adolf Hitler's alphabetic initials. The forum was popular with teenage skinheads who use it to swap videos of their racist attacks.

Skachevsky grew up in Moscow. The son of a deputy headmistress, he was a gifted student and even received a school prize for his academic prowess. Like Ryno, Skachevsky grew to hate "blacks". He would claim that several of his friends perished in the 1999 Moscow apartment block bombings. "I live in a house opposite Guryanov Street and the block which the Chechens blew up," he told friends.

At the time of the murders Skachevksy is a student at Moscow's College for Physical Education. Together, the pair have formed a gang of around a dozen like-minded skinhead-killers. They are a geeky-looking bunch – the tallest is a young woman, Svetlana Avvakumova, 22, who videos one of the gang's brutal attacks on a Chinese youth. Several wear glasses. Police get round to arresting Avvakumova in February 2008.

The trial of the Ryno/Skachevsky gang begins in July 2008. It takes place in room 408 of Moscow's modern-built City Court. It is a fine summer's day. Outside court, I meet Svetlana's mother, Yelena, who has turned up hoping to catch a glimpse of her imprisoned daughter.

Yelena expresses bafflement at her daughter's involvement, denying that Svetlana has anything to do with skinheads. After Svetlana's arrest, however, detectives show her the video, which faithfully records how the gang mercilessly kick and knife a Chinese boy as he lies helplessly on the ground. The boy is crying. Her daughter downloads the film on her home computer. The computer also contains snaps taken on the monastery-lake island of Valaam, during a holiday in Russia's picturesque north.

"Svetlana was always an innocent. As a girl she was a bit of a tomboy. She liked football and used to watch Spartak FC," Yelena says. Moscow Spartak will feature in Russia's worst ever race riots in 2010. Intriguingly, Yelena has a strong sense of where her daughter has gone wrong.

Skinheads are something of a paradox in Russia, a country that sacrificed at least 25 million people in the fight against Nazi Germany. "My father was a tank commander during the war. He was severely injured during the battle for Königsberg; it left him disabled. He personally fought fascism. Svetlana understands perfectly what fascism is. We still have her grandfather's medals."

According to Yelena, attitudes changed after the collapse of the Soviet Union. "My generation was a Soviet one. We were internationalist. We have Armenian relatives. My brother even married a Japanese woman. The problem is with this new generation. They don't understand the difference between nationalism and patriotism. They confuse the two."

Dmitry Dyomushkin is wearing a Ben Sherman T-shirt; he has ordered a plate of kebab and a bowl of *borsch* – beetroot soup. He speaks Russian with a slight speech impediment, and smokes a cigarette as he eats.

Dyomushkin is the leader of the Slavic Union, Russia's most radical ultra-nationalist organisation. Aged 30 when I interview him in 2008, he is a veteran of Russia's far-right scene. We meet in a pub in Marino – a sprawling dormitory suburb in southern Moscow, full of tower blocks, and at the end of Moscow's light-green metro line.

Both Ryno and Skachevsky had been members of the Slavic Union. (In Russian the organisation is called the *Slavyansky Soyuz*, the "SS".) "I didn't know them personally. They were young guys sitting in the corner at the meetings. They were quiet, mouse-like," Dyomushkin says. His group has 1,500 members across Russia – though experts suggest the number of far-right activists is around 50,000. The SS fights against illegal immigration and for the rights of Russians in Russia, he adds.

Dyomushkin says he has been disappointed by the radical actions of many of his members – more than 100 have been arrested and several are now serving life sentences for murder. (One of the group's leaders, Nikola Korolev, was jailed for blowing up the Moscow Cherkizovsky market in August 2006, killing 14 people and wounding 49 with a bomb left outside a Vietnamese cafe.)

"These tactics were wrong," Dyomushkin asserts. He also believes that Russia should be reunited with Ukraine and Belarus, reinstating the old western borders of Kievan Rus. Chechnya and other Muslim republics don't belong in Russia, he adds.

Dyomushkin is at his most plausible when he talks about the threat the Slavic Union now poses to Vladimir Putin. Over the past decade Putin has squeezed out virtually all independent political activity in Russia, he believes. There are now only two opposition movements left, argues Dyomushkin – the ultra-nationalists, and the democratic liberals.

Dyomushkin is scornful of the liberals – "many of whom are Jews" – even though he shares some of their anti-Kremlin stance. But while the democrats are weak, divided and marginalised, the far right enjoys much broader support. It is backed by elements deep inside Russia's powerful bureaucracy and law enforcement agencies, including the FSB. (Both Ryno and Skachevsky had links with a former far-right deputy in the Russian Duma. Officially they were working as his parliamentary researchers.)

Dyomushkin describes Putin's Russia as a "police state", which has retained the worst aspects of the Soviet Union while getting rid of the good bits. "It may seem a paradox. But our movement is now fighting for freedom. It is the nationalists who are fighting for freedom of speech and assembly. Nothing else has the strength to do this. Everyone else is frightened," he says.

Dyomushkin is co-founder of the "Russian March", a mass far-right gathering held on 4 November. In 2008 police and federal security agents break up the march in Moscow – arresting 1,000 people, including Dyomushkin. He is released after several hours in custody, however, and eventually fined 1,000 roubles (£23) – a paltry sum compared to the punishments dished out to some pro-democracy protesters.

Russia's authorities are clearly rattled by the rise of the far right – whose political appeal is growing as the country slithers into economic crisis and stagnation. As living standards tumble it is immigrants who get the blame. During my four years in Russia I saw no prospect of a pro-western orange revolution.

But the possibility of ultra-nationalist revolt against Putin's grip on power is real and growing. The skinheads – a pimply adolescent army of lower-middle class racists – pose a serious threat to the Kremlin's otherwise tight grip on power. As do the political parties that promulgate and enable xenophobia.

In 2005, the nationalist opposition Rodina party had been barred from taking part in Moscow elections after its campaign, which included the slogan "Let's clear out the garbage!", was deemed to incite racial hatred. While Putin supporters will have been relieved to see the Rodina challenge thwarted, its leaders hardly became outcasts. In 2007, Dmitry Rogozin, leader of Rodina in 2005 and author of the "clear out the garbage" slogan, is appointed Russia's ambassador to Nato.

In December 2010 Russia experiences its most serious racial unrest ever. The catalyst is the killing of a Spartak Moscow fan, 28-year-old Yegor Sviridov. He dies on 6 December following a brawl on Kronstadtsky Boulevard between Caucasian youths and a gang of Russian football supporters.

On 11 December, as many as 2,500 ultra-right activists gather on Moscow's Manezh Square, directly under the walls and spires of the Kremlin itself. They have come to show their support for Sviridov. Moscow's riot police are usually well-prepared to clamp down on any civil unrest: opposition demonstrators are often carted off to waiting police vans in a matter of minutes. But on this occasion the riot police are outnumbered.

Activists in the crowd begin attacking dark-skinned passers-by. When the police intervene the skinheads turned on the riot squad, using flares, knives and metal-rods. After a 30-minute battle in which the skinheads hold the advantage, reinforcements arrive. The police eventually prevail. At least 32 people are injured, including five police officers. Racial tensions explode across the capital and other Russian cities. They continue for several months.

In Moscow a young Kyrgyz man is stabbed to death. There are attacks on people of non-Slavic appearance on the Moscow metro. Russia's orthodox church warns grimly of "ethnic war". The police detain 60 skinheads – only to let them go again.

Putin pays a visit in darkness to Sviridov's grave, laying a bouquet of bright red carnations on the white snow. To liberals, the decision to pay his respects merely underscores the Kremlin's dubious relationship with nationalism

In reality, the ruling Russian regime has itself to blame for the simmering ethnic tensions. In public, of course, Putin and Medvedev have denounced ethnic violence. But Putin has also found it useful to play the nationalist card – attacking the west and other outside "forces" that supposedly want to make Russia weak.

According to Verkhovsky, there is clear evidence that in the past the authorities have encouraged and even directly supported ultra-nationalist groups.

In December 2010, the *Financial Times'* Moscow bureau chief, Charles Clover, reports that members of another neo-Nazi cell, the (since dismantled) National Socialist Organisation, are receiving 25,000 roubles a month

– just over £500 – "via a sophisticated system of untraceable bank cards". Who was paying them? Nobody knows. But one suspect is the FSB. The ascendancy of the far-right, some may reason, justifies the need for firm Kremlin rule.

But Verkhovsky suggests this strategy has dangerously misfired. "I think that often an official thinks he is manipulating a certain neo-nationalist group, but the group may be manipulating him," he tells the Americans in November 2009, according to a leaked US State Department cable. The cable, signed by the US ambassador in Moscow, John Beyrle, points out that the Russian government is now trying to "edge away from the nation-alist date" it brought to the dance. This may "prove difficult", he remarks.

In December 2008 Ryno and Skachevsky are given 10 years in jail – the maximum sentence permissible for juveniles. Five other members of their gang get between six and 20 years. The jury acquits Svetlana Avvakumova and one other male gang member. During the trial the skinheads show no remorse: they frequently giggle at the families of their victims.

Ryno makes a final speech to the jury. In a rambling address, he explains that he committed the murders for the "tsar, country, and monarchy". Later he explains that after prison he intends to embark on a new career. He wants to be a politician.

Marta Abramian shows me the family photographs. In one, Karen is dancing with their daughters at a party; other snaps reveal the family of five relaxing on holiday in Egypt, next to a camel; there are black-and-white photos of her husband's boyhood in Baku, Azerbaijan. The couple met and courted in Baku – but in the late 80s moved to Moscow after war erupted between Azerbaijan and Armenia. Karen studied at Moscow University and then joined an insurance firm, Garmed – rising to become its general director. He wrote poems and composed songs.

"He was a wonderful father, a wonderful son and a wonderful husband," Marta says. She adds: "I never thought this could happen to my husband. We considered ourselves real citizens of Russia. We work here. We pay taxes. This is our country."

We meet in the apartment of Karen's parents, Asya, 75, and Georgy, 76; the elderly couple sit together on the sofa holding their son's framed photo; their son's murder outrages them still. The family live in Moscow's south-west suburb of Yugo-Zapadnaya, a district popular with affluent Armenians. After an hour punctuated by phone calls from the court – the skinhead trial is just ending – Marta takes us to the spot where Karen was murdered.

Next to the entrance she has planted a small green fir tree. She and the kids still live upstairs on the ninth floor; they walk past the spot where he lay dying every day. "It's so we can remember Daddy," she says. "It's very difficult without him. There is just an empty shape. Nothing can fill the emptiness."

CHAPTER 12

The Neighbours

Cheremushki district, Osh, southern Kyrgyzstan
16 June 2010

*Russia, just like other countries in the world,
has regions where it has privileged interests.*

PRESIDENT DMITRY MEDVEDEV, SEPTEMBER 2008

When I arrive in Moscow my Russian is rudimentary. I begin learning the language while on sabbatical from the *Guardian* in 2006 and back in Oxford, having completed three and a half years as the *Guardian*'s Berlin correspondent. I start with a beginners' course. Its title is *Through Russia … with love*. Sitting in the kitchen of a rented house in Observatory Street, I listen to Russian CDs. The book has several interesting characters. They include an English journalist called Michael Cronin, who is visiting Moscow, and a gregarious Russian professor, Oleg Petrovich Belov. There is a family mystery, a cruise down the Volga river, and a brief history of the Moscow metro.

The first lesson includes a dialogue on how to get through Russian passport control:

Official: Are you Cronin?
Michael: Yes, I'm Cronin.
Official: Where is your passport?

Michael: Here, please, is my passport. This is my visa.

Official: Good, thank you. Here is your passport and visa.

Oleg waits to meet Michael at the airport. With him is his young ward Katya, a student.

Katya asks Oleg: "Is Michael not a spy?"

Oleg replies: "No, Michael is not a spy." Michael is not engaged in espionage but, Oleg explains, is a "journalist, musician and optimist".

It is the first time I encounter the domestic Russian assumption – widespread since the Soviet era – that all English journalists are spies.

Twice a week Phoebe and I have Russian lessons with Irina Duddell, a grey-haired Russian émigré recommended by the university's languages faculty. We sit in Irina's bright living room in her bungalow in Summertown. Irina introduces us to vocabulary that will prove useful in Moscow – we learn, for example, the word *tusovka*, party. We master the Cyrillic alphabet. This is surprisingly quick. I gain the mistaken impression that learning Russian will be easy. It isn't. Learning Cyrillic is like strolling in the foothills before an epic ascent of Mount Everest.

I only make real progress with the language after we get to Moscow. I begin lessons with Victoria Chumirina, a slight, elfin woman in her early 30s with dark, gamine hair, and intelligent soft-brown eyes. Vika is a member of the philology faculty at Moscow's prestigious State University. Her day job is teaching undergraduates; she gives lessons to journalists to supplement her meagre academic salary. Vika is an exacting teacher. I soon realise that she chooses her students, and not the other way round. We are neighbours; she lives with her mother, plus cat, in a book-filled apartment in Sokol, set back from Moscow's Leningradsky highway.

Gradually, we move through Russian verbs of motion, determinate and indeterminate as well as perfective and imperfective – y*ekhat/yezdit*, *lezt/lazit*, *plyt/plavat*. I learn about stress. (Emphasise the wrong part of a word and nobody understands you.) We start Russian classics. We read stories by Ivan Bunin, short pieces evoking a lost world of pre-revolutionary courtships and unhappy love affairs; prose works by émigré Soviet writers of the 70s and 80s such as Sergei Dovlatov, a master of terse irony; a novel by Lydia Chukovskaya, set in the 1930s at the height of Stalin's purges, which unfolds in slow, haunting passages. My grammars grow dog-eared. I drop a story by Viktor Pelevin in the snow.

One of my favourite texts is *At the Dacha*. It is a simple prose piece by Anton Chekhov. A middle-aged husband receives a note from a mysterious woman summoning him to an assignation in an old summerhouse. The note reads: "I love you … Excuse me for this declaration of love but I cannot be silent any more. I am young, good-looking, what more could you want?" He arrives to discover his brother-in-law Mitya is already waiting in the same spot, having received an identical note … The story is a delightful mini-satire on male vanity and female guile, in which the women get the upper hand.

I enjoy our Russian conversations. In winter, lessons take place in my dingy office. But in summer we sometimes work at home, sitting outside in the garden under the birch tree. Vika and I chat for 20 minutes before turning open a grammar book. We talk about the destruction of old Moscow and the loss of the lindens that once graced its boulevards; the rapacity of Moscow's mayor, Yuri Luzhkov; the general climate of political hopelessness. I already know the Russian for lily of the valley – *landyshi*. But when a pair of nightingales nest over our front door, singing liquidly in the early summer hours, I learn another alluring Russian noun – our winged guests are *solovi*.

Vika is the perfect interlocutor. She is sympathetic (so long as I express myself in correct phrases), and forbearing of my unhappy attempts to roll a Russian "r". We don't always agree on politics – she is appalled at Nato and its bombing of Belgrade, for example. But we find an agreeable mutual space. As my Russian becomes more fluent, the grammatical challenges grow harder. We spend months on prefixes. Prefixes become a fugue; they repeat in my head on the metro to work – variations of *za*, *pro*, *na*, *ot*, *pere* – as I clatter through the city's dark tunnels.

An academic points out that our Moscow flat exists within a cultural tradition of Soviet haunted houses. In 1921 Anna Akhmatova – the celebrated poet whose husband was shot and son imprisoned, and who herself wasn't allowed to write for decades – penned a poem. It eerily describes a similar setting: an intruded room, open windows, the strange position of things, a sense of fear. Later, Boris Pasternak – another Russian author persecuted by the state – recalled how he developed a habit of saying "Hello" whenever he entered an empty room. He knew that "walls had ears".

I don't pretend to be Dr Zhivago. The 19th-century satirist Mikhail Saltykov-Shchedrin wrote that "arbitrariness, hypocrisy, lying, rapacity, treachery and vacuity" rule Russian society. All this I understand without tuition. But it is from Vika I begin to understand, and then to love, Russia's tragic lyricism.

I knew before my Moscow assignment I would need Russian to read the Russian press and to carry out interviews. What I hadn't figured is that two decades after the end of the Soviet Union Russian remains the lingua franca of all post-Soviet states, with the exception of the three Baltic countries (although Russian is still spoken there as well).

You can hear the Russian language in Astana, Kazakhstan's steppe-capital, and in the Baltic city of Riga, thousands of miles away in Europe. Then there is the lingering influence of Russian culture.

Russian also comes in handy when reporting from the further reaches of the former Soviet empire. In June 2010 the small, impoverished Central Asian republic of Kyrgyzstan erupts in a bloody ethnic war. Two decades on, the country still lives in the shadow of its communist past.

Rioting breaks out in the southern city of Osh, with reports of gun battles raging between Kyrgyz and Uzbek youths. Witnesses describe how mobs of Kyrgyz men are burning Uzbek villages, slaughtering residents and storming police stations. Thousands of terrified ethnic Uzbeks flee to the border with Uzbekistan after their homes are torched. For the first three days I report the story from Moscow. But as the violence spreads, and threatens to ignite a regional crisis involving Kyrgyzstan's neighbours, I fly to the Kyrgyz capital, Bishkek.

The packed Aeroflot plane arrives in Bishkek at 5am local time. After a few hours sleep in a Bishkek hotel, I take a domestic flight to Osh, a dramatic flight across the snowy Tian Shan mountains. At Osh airport there are scenes of chaos: hundreds of Chinese workers are waiting in the court-yard, desperate to escape. The road from the airport to the centre of town has become a sniper's alley. It passes through an Uzbek village. There is no transport; it looks like I'll have to sleep in the car park. Eventually, Kyrgyz soldiers offer me a lift in the back of their army truck. I put on my flak-jacket. I lie flat. Tony Halpin, from the London *Times*, does the same thing. We drive through. We continue into the wrecked centre of Osh, and check in, post-curfew, at the Sunrise guesthouse.

The scale of the ethnic killing in Osh is grimly obvious the next morning, when I drive to the predimoninantly Uzbek neighbourhood of Cheremushki. Most houses are blackened shells; survivors take me to the burned-out street where one victim is still lying in his bed. Not much is left: only a jigsaw-like spine and hip. Round the corner, Uzbek survivors are busy retrieving the bodies of seven small children. They had been inciner-ated – together with their mother – while cowering in a dark cellar.

As I stand outside their home, eyewitnesses describe how the local Kyrgyz population attacked its Uzbek minority – an attempted genocide, they tell me. The violence erupted four days earlier, possibly ignited by a row in a casino. But much of it seems carefully co-ordinated, they say. The attacks took the prosperous outlying Uzbek areas of town, lined with garden bungalows and under a dramatically sprawling mountain, completely unawares.

An Uzbek lawyer, Rustam, tells me what happened. "It started on Friday lunchtime," he says. "It came in three distinct waves. The Kyrgyz entered Cheremushki district driving an armoured personnel carrier. This paved the way. Several of them were wearing army uniforms. At first we felt relieved. Someone had come to rescue us, we thought. Then the BTR [armoured transporter] opened fire and started shooting people randomly."

Rustam continues: "Behind them was the second wave. This was a mob of about 300 Kyrgyz youths armed with automatic weapons. Most were very young – between 15 and 20 years old. The third wave was made up of looters and included women and young boys. They stole everything of value, piling into cars. Then they set our houses on fire."

Evidence of this pogrom is everywhere. Neighbours recount how the mob surged down an alley of neat rose bushes and halted outside the house of a young Uzbek woman, Zarifa. They broke into her courtyard. After confirming she was an ethnic Uzbek they stripped off her clothes and cut off her fingers. After that they killed her and her small son – chucking their bodies into the street. Then they moved on to the next house.

I stand in Zarifa's courtyard, next to a burned cherry tree. "They were like beasts," Zarifa's neighbour Bakhtir Irgayshon recalls, pointing to the gutted bed-frame where Zarifa had been raped. A few pots and pans remain; the rest of the family home is a charred ruin. Zarifa's husband Ilham is missing, Irgayshon says, probably dead.

According to Rustam, the official death toll from the riots – 178 dead and 1,800 injured – is a woeful underestimate. He believes around 2,000 Uzbeks died, as the pogroms quickly spread from Osh to the neighbouring town of Jalal-Abad, 30 miles away, and to other Uzbek villages in the south. (An international inquiry later puts the death toll at 470 – higher than the official tally, lower than Rustam's estimate.) "I carried 27 bodies myself. They were just bones," Rustam says. "We are talking about genocide."

With the violence largely spent, and only the occasional gunshot disturbing Osh's evening curfew, I ask the survivors of Cheremushki whom they blame. Some finger Kyrgyzstan's ousted president, Kurmanbek Bakiyev: they describe the violence as a premeditated attempt by Bakiyev to revenge himself on the country's struggling new leadership. Bakiyev fled the country in April 2010 after bloody protests in the Kyrgyz capital. His supporters remain in control in much of the south. They dominate Osh's mono-ethnic Kyrgyz police and power structures, and also control the local mayor's office.

Many say the riots took place with the local administration's connivance. This looks very likely. But I suspect that other, more long-standing historical grievances are also at play. Ethnic Uzbeks make up 15% of Kyrgyzstan's 5.6 million population. They dominate the towns of Osh and Jalal-Abad. These ancient settlements near the Fergana valley ended up in modern Kyrgyzstan by accident – when Stalin dumped them there in the autumn of 1924.

Stalin's idea was that by adding these Uzbek urban areas the nomadic Kyrgyz would be encouraged to abandon their traditions, and to find their place in the new proletarian ascendancy. But he had another motive. This was to divide Central Asia's mosaic-like nationalities – leaving them weak, rivalrous, and therefore dependent on the centre. The Ferghana Valley was once under the control of a single feudal ruler – Stalin split it between Uzbekistan, Tajikistan and Kyrgyzstan. His internal boundaries worked under communism. But this Soviet legacy, transformed into anomalous state borders, is now a ticking time bomb.

"We're hard-working people. We were never nomadic like the Kyrgyz. We never lived in yurts. For the past two thousand years we've built stone houses," Rustam tells me, as we walk past the charred remains of a BMW by the house of a successful Uzbek businessman. He acknowledges that the town's Uzbeks were usually better off than their Kyrgyz neighbours. "Since the Silk Road, we've been involved in commerce and trade. We are successful. The Kyrgyz are jealous and resent this."

I watch as residents who survived the onslaught pick through the rubble. Swallows flit past spacious but now gutted family villas; someone's pet cockatoo takes refuge in the hedgerows; the sun is fierce and bright. The events of the previous week make no sense, Rustam says – heralding a return to barbarism in an age seemingly governed by international rules and institutions. "We were bombarded for three whole days," he says. "It was the state against us. It was the whole system. Everything."

I drive to the centre of Osh, which boasts a giant statue of Lenin. Here I find most Uzbek enterprises lie in ruins. Someone has firebombed the Jupiter restaurant. They have also ransacked the next-door supermarket, where a dog is busy rootling among a few charred oranges. On the walls Kyrgyz graffiti reads: "Uzbeks fuck off" and "Death to Uzbeks". Shops marked with "KG" for Kyrgyz escape the inferno.

When the trouble started thousands of panicked Uzbeks fled to the border with Uzbekistan, just 5kms from Osh, along a road that passes tall poplar trees, agricultural settlements and fields of maize. Not everyone made it: one eyewitness recalls how two Uzbek youths drove unwittingly into a Kyrgyz mob in the centre of town. "They pulled the two Uzbek boys out of the car, and killed them in less than five minutes using sticks and knives," says Maya Tashbolotova. "Then they dumped them in the Ak-Bura river." She saw this happen by peering over her fence, about 25 metres from my guesthouse.

I drive to the crossing with Uzbekistan. Tens of thousands of refugees have already fled, in what looks like a major humanitarian crisis. At the beginning of the Uzbek district I get out: our Kyrgyz driver is too scared to continue. Local Uzbeks manning a checkpoint give us a lift in their BMW. We drive up a mountain track to the border. On the Uzbek side uniformed soldiers patrol a 5ft-high barbed-wire fence. Nearby, on the

Kyrgyz side, Uzbek refugee kids are washing in a stream; an old lady beaten in the face is being treated in an improvised medical centre. The mood is one of anger, traumatised disbelief and betrayal. Many of the girls arriving at the border have been raped, witnesses tell me.

In the medical centre, a 35-year-old Uzbek doctor is crying quietly in the corner. "Why did I train to be a surgeon? Was it for this?" he says. The doctor says that many of the Uzbek victims have been shot in the face and head. A nurse shows me footage from her mobile phone of an Uzbek man who had been doused in kerosene and set alight. His head and arms are blackened stumps. He has no eyes. He is waving his arms feebly, a parody of life. He died in agony two days before I arrive.

"We've been discriminated against for 20 years," the doctor says, alluding to ethnic riots that erupted near Osh in 1990, just before the break-up of the Soviet Union. Recently, he says, Kyrgyz chauvinism has been growing. The weakness of the new transitional government in Bishkek has fuelled it, together with a fear among Kyrgyz politicians that the Uzbek minority has come under the influence of secessionist-minded leaders, the doctor believes.

I see few signs of humanitarian relief. Kyrgyz drivers are too scared to enter into Uzbek neighbourhoods. Uzbeks have demarcated their territory by felling maple trees and building makeshift barricades with burned out cars. Back in town Kyrgyz soldiers set up checkpoints in a post-facto show of strength. Some Kyrgyz locals I talk to blame the riots on Uzbek youths, whom they say ransacked a local casino in a dispute over money.

Back at my guesthouse that evening I write a dispatch for the *Guardian*. Few people outside the immediate region can locate Kyrgyzstan on a map – or even spell it. But the story of mass murder played out among women and children unable to flee is moving and important. There have been two revolutions in the country within five years, in 2005 and 2010, and now this, the worst ethnic unrest for two decades.

I also find myself mulling over Kyrgyzstan's astonishing ethnic diversity, long after the Soviet Union has vanished. Many Russians living in Central Asia moved to the new Russian Federation after 1991. But millions of ethnic

Russians remain outside it, left behind by the receding tide of Soviet history. The fate of ethnic Russians living in Estonia, Lithuania and Latvia is a source of constant tension between the Baltic States and Moscow.

The following day I drive to Jalal-Abad. Up near another part of the Uzbek border, the village of Bekobat, I find 6,000 ethnic Uzbek refugees camping out. There is still no international aid. The refugees say they fled after the pogroms spread from Osh to Jalal-Abad, Kyrgyzstan's third biggest city. They add that they are baffled by the international community's failure to respond to, or even notice, their plight.

One woman, Adina Haidarova, tells me how she escaped when the flames reached her home in Lenin Street, Jalal-Abad's main thoroughfare – the name another echo of the Soviet past. Outside a Kyrgyz mob was busy torching Uzbek property. Adina fled her home with her two grandchildren and ailing husband Zatulam. They left via the back door, stumbling across fields, and joined a weeping column of women and children heading for the Uzbek border. She walked for 14 hours – a wretched, footsore, terrifying exodus. At one point a Kyrgyz military helicopter buzzed overhead. In the distance, fires from the Uzbek quarter lit up the night sky. "We thought they were going to shoot us," says 56-year-old Adina. "We tried to hide. But they didn't shoot. Instead we heard them laughing at us."

The family eventually found sanctuary in Bekobat, an agricultural settlement a couple of miles from the border. For the first four nights they slept in a grassy open field next to a walnut tree. After that they moved into a tiny one-room cottage with a television, teapot and a geranium plant. Zatulam, who has heart problems, got the only bed. When I arrive there, it is home to 15 adults and children. "There's not enough space so we sleep in shifts, with the kids on our laps," Adina explains. "We have absolutely nothing. The children are hungry. We have scarcely any food. The only thing we have to eat is what the locals give us." Adina shows me a meagre plastic bag containing half a kilo of scruffy potatoes and an unimpressive cabbage. She adds: "How am I supposed to feed 15 people with that?" Others say they have no medicines, running water or nappies; Zatulam grumbles that the kids have peed on his mattress.

The ethnic attacks displace more than 400,000 Uzbeks, according to non-governmental agencies. When I get there 100,000 Uzbeks are living in temporary camps in neighbouring Uzbekistan. The world community's lack of interest in the region is a common complaint. "We're on our way to becoming a second Afghanistan," says Farkat Matsakov, a spokesman for the village's impromptu relief committee. The country's Uzbek minority feels utterly betrayed, he adds: "We don't trust anybody any more. The local administration, the police, the west, they all failed us."

Talking to Farkat, it's hard not to conclude that Kyrgyzstan's future is bleak. Most Uzbeks put their faith in the country's new interim administration, led by one Rosa Otunbayeva, a career diplomat and former Kyrgyz ambassador in London. She took over from the deposed Bakiyev, who had himself ousted the previous incumbent in the 2005 "tulip revolution". Months after the latest government assumed responsibility, shadowy nationalist forces, working with the military and police, staged their own furious pogroms against the country's Uzbeks.

I return from the border to Jalal-Abad. I learn the riots were similar to those in Osh – with armoured personnel carriers used to kill defenceless civilians and clear the way for a knife and stick-wielding mob. "What happened in both cities was a genocide, a holocaust," Alisher Karimov, a local Uzbek journalist says; we meet outside an administration building. "It was very well organised."

I invite Karimov for lunch. We find a cafe near the bazaar serving plates of fried eggs and sausage. For the Kyrgyz population, life is almost back to normal, with flatbreads for sale on colourful tables. On the edge of town I spot Kyrgyz herders wearing striking national hats, nudging their cattle up a mountain road towards green summer pastures. But for Uzbeks the nightmare goes on. Over lunch Karimov's hands tremble; he scarcely touches his food; he lights a cigarette, and talks and talks. At the end of our meal he starts to cry. Among other survivors I find a similar mood: angry, disbelieving, defiant. Refugees show me mobile phone footage of a dead Uzbek teenage boy shot in Osh. A round from the gun of an armoured personnel carrier had blown off one side of his head.

Adina tells me she has no intention of leaving Jalal-Abad, even though her home no longer exists. The town is named after Jalal, a 13th-century Uzbek warrior-hero, she points out. "We want to stay here. This is our country. This is our town. We are not leaving it. They [the Kyrgyz] are the arrivistes." How can she live side by side with the people who have torched her home? "We can't. They are our enemies."

In 2007, William Burns, the US ambassador in Moscow, identifies five "principles" of Russia's foreign policy. The Kremlin's number one principle, Burns notes in a leaked diplomatic cable, is "gaining international recognition as a great power and maximizing Russia's global influence". Second is "defending the territorial integrity of sovereign states", and, third, "promoting the inclusion of all stakeholders, even the 'undesirables' in peace settlements". Fourth and fifth are "minimising the prospects for further expansion eastward of Nato" and "expanding Russian exports, including arms, to any country with the cash".

The US embassy in Moscow also provides helpful briefing notes for visiting US officials, explaining the mentality of their Russian hosts. These briefings lay out the grudge-driven backstory behind Putin's assertive, and often confrontational, foreign policy, and his barbed dealings with the west. Putin's most memorable exposition of this comes during a speech in Munich in 2007, in which he launches a blistering attack on US power. He denounces the "unipolar" world in which the US is top dog, and calls instead for a "multipolar" world.

Russians across the political spectrum still nurture a grievance over their perceived "humiliation" by the Americans and Europeans, during Russia's period of acute weakness in the 1990s, the US says. They also feel that important gestures by Putin – such as its help in staging the US-led war in Afghanistan post 9/11 – go unreciprocated. Moscow remains vehemently opposed to the US basing missile defence sites in former Soviet states. It believes these sites undermine Russia's national security and threaten its "great-power" status. In 2008 the Obama administration scales back US missile defence plans in Europe in an attempt to assuage Russian concerns. Three years, later, however, the Kremlin is still unhappy. Medvedev even hints Moscow is prepared to tear up the new Start treaty with the US on nuclear arms reductions.

In a dryly amusing cable examining Russia's global arms export industry, Burns puts much of Moscow's prickliness down to its "inferiority complex with respect to the United States". In recent years the Kremlin has sold billions of dollars of military equipment to countries like Venezuela, Iran, Syria and Sudan. Burns writes: "It is deeply satisfying to some Russian policy-makers to defy America, in the name of a multipolar world order, and to engage in zero-sum calculations ... While profit is still seen by experts as Russia's primary goal, all note the secondary thrill of causing the US discomfort by selling weapons to anti-American governments in Caracas and Damascus." Lurking under the surface of these weapons sales is Russia's quest "to be taken seriously as a global partner".

Over four years in Moscow I write numerous articles on Russian foreign policy. During this period Putin resurrects the Soviet practice of showing off missiles, tanks and heavy weaponry during the Kremlin's annual Victory Day parades in Red Square. After my first year in Moscow, I receive few official invites of any kind; the foreign ministry blacklists me from its annual party.

But inexplicably I receive a white card with gold lettering to watch the Red Square parade every year; I'm even allocated a spot close to Lenin's tomb next to the VIP tribune. I write stories when Putin tears up a treaty limiting conventional armed forces in Europe, lays claim to a large chunk of the Arctic, and holds war games with China and four Central Asian nations. He also resumes long-distance patrols over the Atlantic, Pacific and Arctic Oceans by Russia's elderly fleet of TU-95 nuclear bombers. Western experts are unimpressed by the gesture. "It's willy-waving. That's what it is," one tells me.

The most vexed area of US-Russian competition is not bomber patrol missions, however, but Russia's "near-abroad." The phrase encompasses the former Soviet republics that are now Russia's sovereign neighbours – the three Baltic States, Ukraine, Georgia, Belarus, and Moldova, Armenia and Azerbaijan, and the five Central Asian "Stans". The foreign policy expert Dmitry Trenin points out that after the collapse of the Soviet Union, Russia shed communism and lost its historical empire. Ever since, it has been strug-gling to find a role. In the meantime, Trenin writes, Russia has behaved as if it has gone through two doors simultaneously: one into the globalised markets of the 21st century; the other back into the 19th-century world of the imperial Great Game.

A month after the war in Georgia, Medvedev articulates Russia's new foreign policy doctrine – that it enjoys a "zone of privileged" interests in neighbouring countries. In other words, Moscow has the right to influence their internal affairs. The Obama administration rejects this. Indeed, Barack Obama tells Putin the idea belongs in the 19th century, rather than the 21st. Nonetheless, the Kremlin remains deeply hostile to US encroachment in its "near abroad". And – as the 2008 war in Georgia demonstrates – it is prepared to defend its interests using military force. It is also viscerally opposed to Nato expansion.

Russia has numerous strategies to pile pressure on its neighbours. But its most potent weapon is energy. On two occasions while I'm correspondent in Moscow, Russia turns off the gas to neighbouring Ukraine – in 2006 and 2009. There are numerous other politically motivated cut-offs (or threatened cut-offs) to the Baltic states, Belarus and Turkmenistan. "Under the USSR, we had the barrel of a gun pointed toward us. Now, we have the barrel of a pipeline pointed toward us," Lithuania's foreign minister, Petras Vaitekunas, grumbles, according to a leaked diplomatic memo, after Moscow halts gas supplies to Lithuania in the summer of 2006.

But Moscow doesn't always get its own way. Its attempts to create a regional political system with Moscow at its core are frequently unsuccessful. None of Russia's immediate neighbours follows Moscow's lead in recognising the independence of South Ossetia and Abkhazia. Even Belarus, Russia's staunch ally, refuses, as relations between the Kremlin and the Belarus dictator Alexander Lukashenko descend into mud-slinging.

Russia remains an important strategic partner for all the former Soviet states. But behind closed doors Central Asian leaders rail at what they regard as Russian racism. In 2009 Uzbekistan's president Islam Karimov tells a visiting top-level US delegation that Russia was seeking to re-establish a zone of "privileged interest." Why, he asked them, according to leaked cables, does Russia treat Finland as an independent country but not Uzbekistan? Russia's biggest problem remained its "imperial ambitions," he charged, along with racist "chauvinism" exhibited toward ethnic minorities.

Central Asia is of great strategic importance to the US, too, principally because of the war in neighbouring Afghanistan, and the US-led struggle against the Taliban. In the spring of 2009, I travel to Tajikistan, the most impoverished country in the area. Like Kyrgyzstan, Tajikistan is a staging post for logistical support to US troops fighting next door.

I fly to Dushanbe in late March – from the freezing and snow-bound streets of Moscow to spring in Tajikistan's warm capital. The pavement cafes are full, the sky a deep blue, the temperature – it's 24 C – perfect. I find a driver and set off towards the border with Afghanistan. We drive for two hours. The road passes a shimmering mountain pasture. It then dips down steeply to a new US-built bridge. Over on the other side, across the languid Panj river, is Afghanistan and the dusty northern town of Kunduz. On this side is Nizhny Panj, a previously sleepy crossing point.

It's here, at what used to be the remote boundary of the Soviet empire, that the US and Nato are planning a new operation. In the weeks after my visit, Nato trucks loaded with non-military supplies start rolling into Afghanistan from this northern route – avoiding Pakistan's perilous tribal areas and the ambush-prone Khyber Pass. This northern corridor is essential if President Obama's Afghan-Pakistan strategy is to work. With convoys supplying US and Nato forces in Afghanistan regularly attacked by the Taliban on the Pakistan route, the US is again courting the ex-Soviet republics of Central Asia – Tajikistan, Uzbekistan, Kyrgyzstan, Kazakhstan and Turkmenistan.

Just before I arrive Nato signs a transit deal with Tajikistan. It also negotiates bilateral agreements with Uzbekistan and Kazakhstan. Pakistan remains the primary route. But the quiet Tajik-Afghan border crossing at the village of Nizhny Panj – harried in winter by hungry wolves from the local forest – becomes a focal point in Obama's Afghan push. I try to talk to the Tajik commander. He is unavailable. We drive on to the nearest hamlet. "We used to cross the river by boat. Then the Americans built a bridge," Rasul Nematov, 35, says, gesturing at the river crossing. Next to his front garden, past a line of washing and a trailing vine, is a Tajik sentry tower.

The Pentagon has given Dushanbe $10 million to beef up security on its mountain border – a key conduit for Afghanistan's biggest export, opium. (Russian border guards – stationed here until the summer of 2005 – used to take a lucrative cut of the heroin trade, WikiLeaks cables suggest.) Nematov tells me he has no objections to Nato increasing its activities. But, he adds, "What we really need here is a minibus to take our kids to school." He points out: "It's five kilometres away. At the moment they walk."

Up until 2009 only a few dozen Afghan drivers crossed the bridge every day. At Dushanbe they filled up their Kamaz trucks with sugar and other goods. They then headed home. Now Tajikistan has allowed up to 250 Nato lorries a day to cross here. Driving along the same route I pass fields of cotton, small boys selling fish, donkeys and willow and poplar trees. Fluffy seeds – in Russian the evocative word *pukh* – float across a fragrant green spring landscape. "This road to Tajikistan is good. It's safe, quiet," says Said Muhammed, a truck driver from the northern Afghan city of Mazar-I-Sharif. "The problem is with the road south from Kabul to Kandahar. I don't drive it. It's dangerous. The Taliban dragged my friend out of his truck and set it on fire."

Casting a long shadow over the latest US attempts to get a foothold in Central Asia is the region's former colonial power – Moscow. Formally, Russia offers to help Obama in his attempts to deal with the deteriorating situation in Pakistan and Afghanistan. It agrees, for example, to the shipment of non-lethal supplies destined for Kabul across Russian territory. Informally, however, Russia has moved decisively to reassert its influence in Central Asia, a region it still regards as its backyard.

In 2001 Putin and the then-US president George W Bush cut an informal deal to co-operate over the war in Afghanistan, with Moscow allowing the US military to set up several Central Asian bases. Soon, however, the Kremlin came to see itself as having been betrayed, by what it regarded as US-engineered pro-western revolutions in Georgia and Ukraine. It hit back by sealing backroom deals with Central Asia's autocratic rulers. In 2005 Uzbekistan's president, Islam Karimov, fed up with western criticism of his dire human rights record, kicked Washington out of its military base near the border town of Termez.

Back in Dushanbe I have a cup of tea with Parviz Mullajanov, Tajikistan's foremost expert on international affairs. Mullajanov says that Russia still has the advantage in Central Asia's new Great Game. "It's up and down. Since 2001 the Americans have had the upper hand in Central Asia. Now the Russians are getting back what the Americans have lost," he tells me. "In reality the US never won the game. Since the collapse of the Soviet Union Russia has managed to preserve its leading position in Central Asia."

According to Mullajanov, Moscow has significantly boosted its military, economic and intelligence activity across the region. It has other advantages too, he says. "All post-Soviet countries live in Russian-speaking informational space. The majority of people watch Russian TV and read Russian newspapers. They see the outside world through Russian eyes. This is a very powerful tool." The American position, by contrast, is "very weak", Mullajanov suggests. Washington's attempts to reach out to civil society and opposition groups have made little progress in Central Asia – a region run by a series of variously repressive super-presidents, all apparently in the job for life. The US faces another headache in the shape of China, an ambitious pre-imperial contender in the region.

Just before my trip the Brussels-based International Crisis Group issues a gloomy report on the region. It questions how wise Obama is to rely on his new partners, and suggests that Central Asia is little better than crisis-gripped Pakistan – and a "seriously risky bet". The report's author, Paul Quinn-Judge notes: "Its leader are all former Soviet apparatchiks ... most of the citizens live in deep poverty, and the countries' economies are for the most part feeble and fragile."

He adds: "Worst-case scenarios include state collapse, the disintegration of national infrastructure, chaotic succession struggles and Islamic insurgency."

From his giant monument overlooking Sevastopol, Lenin gazes out towards the Black Sea. Down in the harbour, elderly ladies in floral swimming costumes bob in the warm lilac water. Shimmering in the distance is the Russian battleship *Moskva*, just back from the war in Georgia. The port of Sevastopol is on the rocky southern coast of Crimea, an autonomous republic within Ukraine, and home of Russia's Black Sea fleet. After the break-up of the Soviet Union, Ukraine said it would allow Russia to retain Sevastopol as a base until 2017. When I visit, however, Viktor Yushchenko, Ukraine's pro-western president, wants the Russians out.

My trip to Ukraine in the autumn of 2008 coincides with wild speculation that Crimea – after South Ossetia and Abkhazia – could become the next target of Russian ambitions. More than half of its population is ethnically

Russian. Yushchenko's officials accuse Russia of distributing passports to ethnic Russians in Crimea, as it did in South Ossetia. They fear a row over the use of the base could be used to stir up separatist sentiments, with Crimea seceding from Ukraine after a referendum.

In Sevastopol, I discover, the popular mood isn't simply pro-Russian. A more fitting description would be pro-Soviet, with nostalgia for the USSR almost universal. The locals are also vehemently opposed to Yushchenko's ambition to join Nato – plans that will be comprehensively sunk when the voters oust Yushchenko in early 2010.

I call on Anatoly Kalenko, chairman of Sevastopol's veterans' associations. "The majority of the population here supports the presence of the Black Sea fleet," he tells me. According to Kalenko, locals would resist any attempt to get rid of the Russian fleet, especially if Nato ships would then control the base instead. "We categorically don't want other vessels here. Not the Americans, not the French and not the Turks," Kalenko explains. He goes on: "Britain has a tradition of seafaring. We respect that. We remember Nelson. But frankly we don't want you here either."

The Russian fleet employs 25,000 people, Kalenko says. His association is categorically opposed to any attempt to rip down the Soviet memorials that adorn the town's hilly streets. I notice a USSR map is pinned to his wall; above his desk is a portrait of Lenin. Popular feeling against Nato is hardly surprising, he says, since it is an "aggressive military bloc".

Many of the peninsula's politicians admit they would like Crimea to join the Russian Federation. "It's a myth that Ukraine is not part of Russia. We don't believe it," Oleg Rodilov, a pro-Russian deputy in Crimea's autonomous parliament, informs me. We meet in a pavement cafe near the parliament building in the regional capital of Simferopol, talking – as ever – in Russian. It would be wrong to call his views "separatist", he says. "For you, Ukraine and Russia are *a priori* different states. For us they are *a priori* the same," he explains. The links of culture, language, and orthodox religion make Ukraine and Russia an indivisible entity, he suggests. "We don't believe there is any difference. We have been together for 350 years."

That is a view echoed by Vladimir Putin, according to leaked cables. He considers Ukraine a "cobbled together country", with six million Russians, according to Poland's foreign minister Radoslaw Sikorski.

Catherine the Great established a naval citadel in Crimea after defeating the Turks in 1783. Since then the port has been synonymous with Russian and Soviet military glory. But, as in the case of Kyrgyzstan, it is the Soviet past that explains today's simmering divisions. In 1944 Stalin deported Crimea's Tartars and several other much smaller groups to Central Asia. He replaced them with Slavic inhabitants from Russia or Russian-influenced parts of eastern Ukraine. Most of the newcomers were from poor urban backgrounds; they moved into homes vacated by deportees. They had weak ties with Ukraine. Even before 1991, many of the Crimean Tartars – the peninsula's original Turkic-speaking Muslim inhabitants – had come back. Well-educated and politically organised, they now number 300,000, 15% of Crimea's population.

The Soviet leader Nikita Khrushchev transferred Crimea to the Ukrainian Soviet Socialist Republic in 1954. Russia has reaffirmed Ukraine's modern borders several times since. When I visit I find nationalist Crimean MPs in an excitable mood – predicting that Crimea will declare itself independent should Yushchenko press ahead with his plans to join Nato.

"If Yushchenko declares that Russia is the enemy Crimea won't accept it. In Crimea there will be a war, maybe even a world war," Leonid Grach, a pro-Russian MP, tells me, when I drop into his surgery in Simferopol. Grach is a larger-than-life figure. He has slicked-back white hair and an ebullient manner. Ukraine should renounce Nato, agree a friendship and co-operation treaty with Russia, and prolong the lease for Russia's Black Sea fleet, Grach says. This is exactly what happens in April 2010, when Viktor Yanukovych, Ukraine's new pro-Russian president, extends the lease with Russia for 25 years. In exchange, Moscow gives him a discount on Ukraine's gas bill.

But Russia's attempts to exert pressure on its near abroad don't just include blunt gas cut-offs. In the wake of Ukraine's 2004 orange revolution, Moscow begins a systematic, organised campaign to finance pro-Russian groups in Crimea. Its aim is to foster inter-ethnic discord and ensure tensions on the peninsula keep boiling. According to leaked US diplomatic memos, Russia's military intelligence wing – the GRU – takes the lead in passing money to local NGOs carrying out Russia's wishes. (The FSB, one memo notes, restricts its activities to counter-intelligence operations, and keeping tabs on "western visitors".) Much of this money comes not from Kremlin coffers but from Mayor Luzhkov and his Moscow city government. City hall officials insist they are not supporting Russian nationalism – merely encouraging Russian language and culture.

Just up the road from Sevastopol's museum I spot the offices of the "Russian community", one of several non-governmental organisations that promote the Russian language. Its chair, Raisa Taliatnikova, rejects the suggestion that she runs a front organisation for the Kremlin. "This is our land. My father and uncle fought for this territory during the great patriotic war," she says, invoking the Russian name for the second world war. "Why should we leave? Nobody asked us whether we wanted to live in Ukraine. None of us are intending to go anywhere." She admits she wouldn't be unhappy at Ukraine's demise. "Personally I wouldn't be too sad if it breaks apart. Everything would be in its right place again."

CHAPTER 13

Batman and Robin

Trial of Mikhail Khodorkovsky, Khamovnichesky Court, Moscow
31 March 2009

*Moscow is a city rich in rumour and impoverished
in hard data, and those who report on the political scene
there struggle perpetually to distinguish between fact, educated
speculation, planted rumour and just plain rumour.*

SERGE SCHMEMANN OF THE *NEW YORK TIMES*,
QUOTED IN *THE MOSCOW CORRESPONDENTS*

As soon as I get to my office, it's clear something odd has happened. My friends from the FSB have paid another nocturnal visit. The agent (or agents) has left a trail of deliberate minor clues. The window in my study is open. (When I closed up the previous evening at 9.45pm it was locked. It has two inner catches; there are bars on the outside.) When I try to log on, the internet doesn't work. This, in itself, is hardly evidence of a conspiracy. But when I check the modem I see someone has unplugged it from the wall. And then there is my office phone. It's off the hook. My uninvited guest has removed the receiver from its cradle and laid it demonstratively on my table.

By now I'm a veteran at puzzling out what the FSB is trying to tell me. The break-in – with its troika of low-key clues – is a reminder that I am once again pursuing stories the agency regards as unacceptable. It is 30 June 2010. The day before, I had written a long article for the *Guardian* on the astonishing arrest of 10 undercover Russian spies in the United States. The Russians were part of a network of long-term "sleepers". They included Anna Chapman, a glamorous young Russian woman who had lived in London and was briefly married to an Englishman. The arrests are deeply embarrassing for the Kremlin. They come three days after a visit by President Medvedev to California and amid an upswing in US-Russian relations.

My story reads:

The 55-page FBI dossier reveals in humiliating detail the frequently amateurish and bungling behaviour of Moscow's agents in America – who lived in a series of leafy suburban homes in Boston, New York and Washington DC. The FBI said the spies were urged to adopt Americanised names as part of their efforts to blend in, and ferret out information from think tanks and government officials.

Far from staying hidden, however, the FBI appears to have known about the espionage ring since at least 2000 ... FBI agents secretly observed numerous encounters conducted in Manhattan coffee bars, in which the spies would send data to their Russian handlers via wireless transmissions from their laptops. Often, however, the technology broke down. This prompted desperate pleas to Moscow to sort the problem out.

I also mention the "stiltedly textbook spy-craft" used by the Russians to identify their own side. In one comic encounter Chapman is told her contact will ask: "Excuse me, but haven't we met in California last summer?"

To which she is to reply: "No, I think it was the Hamptons."

The Russian spies are soon on a plane back home. It is the biggest spy swap between Washington and Moscow for decades. On her return, and seemingly without pausing for breath, Chapman removes most of her clothes for Russia's *Maxim* magazine. She also embarks on a political career as a cheerleader for the Putin-led United Russia party. Putin greets his returning agents with a patriotic singsong.

I wasn't the only journalist to treat the story with some lightness, in the spirit of a cold war melodrama. My Moscow-based colleagues wrote articles similar in tone. The huge increase in Russian spying activity overseas since

Putin came to power, with the FSB's budget tripled, looked like a job-creation exercise for the well-connected offspring of Russia's elite. (Chapman's father is a high-ranking "foreign service" official.) The British *Daily Telegraph* got hold of Chapman's ex-husband. They even printed her wedding photos. But for some unknowable reason, I was again singled out for special punishment. I record this latest FSB "intrusion" on the back of my blue medical folder. There isn't much space left. I have to squeeze the details in the margins.

By the summer of 2010, I have a strong presentiment that my career as a Moscow correspondent might not go on for much longer. It seems likely that, should I complete my tour of duty in the normal fashion, the FSB may well debar me from returning. With this in mind, we decide to go on one last family holiday inside Russia. We head to Siberia.

I queue for an hour at Belorussky railway station. Eventually I manage to buy tickets: from the Urals city of Yekaterinburg to the old Siberian capital of Tobolsk; from Tobolsk to Omsk; and from Omsk to Tomsk – a name made magical for a generation of middle-aged Britons by the 1970s BBC children's series *The Wombles*. The journey involves three night trains on the trans-Siberian railway. We are not going all the way to Vladivostok. I never make it there. With its foggy climate and reputation as a criminal fiefdom this seems a loss I can bear. But we are completing a chunk of the world's longest train journey, part of the 5,752-mile route between the capital and the Pacific coast.

Train travel is one of the most uplifting aspects of our Russia experience. In a country plagued with corruption and bureaucracy, the trains are clean, well organised and efficient. In Yekaterinburg we turn up at the station two hours before the trains do, not knowing that Russia Railways, operating in multiple time zones, operates its schedule to Moscow time. On the express to Tobolsk we have a coupe; the kids grab the upper bunks. A *provodnitsa* provides towelling slippers, a newspaper, and snacks; for 25 roubles she brings black tea with lemon in a glass cup with a silver filigree holder.

The landscape outside is classically Russian: birch trees, villages of decaying *dachas* and dirt tracks leading off indefinitely into the taiga. At one stop I buy smoked fish, beer and crisps; local women sell buckets of earthy potatoes and the bitter seeds from pinecones. It is high summer. The sun scarcely sets. It's light by 4am. By day the Siberian sky is limpid and vast.

Tobolsk turns out to be small and charming, with a well-preserved old town and baroque cathedral. It has a large population of Tartars – Siberia's original Muslim inhabitants. We are its only tourists. In Omsk it's raining; the children find an urban playground next to the river. Otherwise it's a dump. Tomsk, by contrast, is a gem: a university town with a European flavour and several pizzerias; we tour its old wooden cottages on a municipal tram. To my disappointment, and the children's relief, I find Tomsk's gulag museum shut.

In Novosibirsk, Siberia's modern capital, we pick up a jeep and a driver, Sergei Kudrin. Kudrin runs a business taking tourists to the Altai mountains, a remote region of southern Siberia 2,000 miles from Moscow. An accomplished Soviet alpinist, now in his late 50s, Kudrin has climbed most of Altai's peaks. Russia's Altai republic sits on the fringes of Central Asia, at the vertiginous intersection of Mongolia, Kazakhstan and China. The area is popular with middle-class Siberians, who go rafting, glacier-climbing and horse-riding; it gets few European visitors.

It takes us 14 hours to drive to Altai's northern tip. By Russian standards Altai is beautifully unspoiled. Its lush alpine valleys give way – the closer you get to the Mongolian border – to eerie semi-desert and desolate frontier towns. In one, we spot a gold statue of Lenin. A family of goats sit surreally next to him. Everywhere we pass unmistakeable signs of early human habitation. Nomadic Scythian tribes lived here for dozens of centuries, well before the Bolsheviks turned up. They left behind distinctive stone burial mounds known as *kamennye baby*, or stone grandparents – tall, haunting tombstones incised with strange Turkic faces.

Stopping on the M52, Altai's main highway, we inspect one of the *kamennuyu babu* abandoned in a wide valley. Giant scarlet-winged crickets leap in the air, sounding like deranged football rattles. The pasture all around us is a buzzing insect carpet; several tumuli are nearby. The tombstone has stylised slanting eyes and a large nose. (It lacks the distinctive Terry-Thomas moustache we'd seen in other examples in the museums in Omsk and Tomsk.)

Further along the highway, Kudrin invites us to scramble up a steep, scree-covered hill. Pulling back weeds, the kids reveal a deer petroglyph engraved in the rock. Further up there are more prehistoric carvings: some done using a blunt object, others worked more elaborately in florid graffito. There are deer, ibex and wild boar, all instantly recognisable and brought to life out of the ancient stone.

In the evening, we arrive at our camp in the shadow of Mount Aktru, a 4000-metre-high snow-covered peak. This turns out to be the highlight of our trip. The camp is located in a larch forest beneath the mountains. The children go off and build a den. Above us a black-winged kite hovers in an emerald sky; from the ramshackle observation post on a nearby hill you can see across the mountain valley towards Mongolia. The camp is basic but cosy, with a wood-burning bathhouse, or *banya*. We sleep in a yurt. The only drawback is the billions of Siberian mosquitoes.

The night is cold. The following morning we set off for the mountains. The drive is spectacular: across a rickety wooden bridge into conifer forests filled with dazzling alpine flowers. Phoebe spots gentians, clustered bell-flowers, bedstraw and meadowsweet. Leaving our jeep near a river, we hike in the foothills. On one side Aktru rises from a snowy ridge of glaciers; on the other there is a languid cycle of summer lagoons and small lakes. On the way back Ruskin and I stop for a dip in a fast-flowing turquoise stream.

Moscow – and all its surveillance and sinister shadow-play – feels a long way away.

One of the books I read in Siberia is *The Moscow Correspondents*. Its author is Whitman Bassow, a fine American journalist who lived in Soviet Moscow in the late 1950s and again in the early 60s. Bassow chronicles the ups and downs – it is mostly downs – of the 300 US reporters who covered the Soviet Union since 1921. All experienced some degree of harassment from the KGB and its predecessors. There are numerous other privations, during what one reporter dubs "the cruellest assignment". The list is long: interminable hours, a meagre diet, a lack of toilet paper and the gruelling physical environment of post-war Moscow – a drab, grey and depressing city then and today.

But one of the biggest obstacles to reporting from Russia was the sheer lack of information. During the Brezhnev and post-Brezhnev period, Kremlinology – the famous science of puzzling out what is going on inside the Politburo – reached its high point. Starved of official news, reporters resorted to ever more inventive methods. When Yuri Andropov, Brezhnev's successor, fell ill, reporters lined the route of his drive to work along Kutuzovsky Prospekt, hoping to catch a glimpse of the ailing leader in his limo.

On the evening of 9 February 1984, one enterprising journalist, acting on a hunch that Andropov had died, drove the streets of Moscow seeking confirmation. He found the lights blazing in the offices of the KGB, the defence ministry and the General Staff headquarters. He filed an exclusive overnight story saying that Andropov was dead – an event confirmed the next day.

During this period, meeting Soviet bureaucrats was almost impossible. It became slightly less trying with Gorbachev and glasnost in the mid-1980s, but the real change came with the – often chaotic – presidency of Boris Yeltsin. My predecessors at the *Guardian*, Jonathan Steele and David Hearst, were able to talk freely with senior Kremlin officials and meet government sources. Chrystia Freeland, an enterprising reporter for the *Financial Times*, became pally with oligarchs and cabinet ministers; she parlayed her energy and charm into a highly readable book on the inside dealings of Yeltsin's court.

But with Putin Russia goes backwards. There is a squeeze on the independent media. Old KGB habits of secrecy return. There is less information under Putin, one veteran journalist tells me, than he encountered when he first reported from Brezhnev's Soviet Union in the late 1970s: "Back then we had *Pravda*. At least you could read between the lines." By the time Dmitry Medvedev is anointed as Russia's third president in May 2008, Kremlinology is back.

True, there are newspapers, magazines, and radio stations to report political events and to illuminate Medvedev's apparently reformist and modernising agenda. Russia also boasts an impressive cadre of political commentators and academic pundits. Some – such as the political technologist Gleb Pavlovsky and the thoughtful United Russia Duma deputy Sergei Markov – are close to the Kremlin and reflect official opinion.

Others, however, are robustly independent. Both camps are good for educated speculation.

Nonetheless, in a city prone to rumours and conspiracy theories, it is fair to say that during the Medvedev period very few people in Moscow really know what is going on at the top of the Kremlin. Even Russia's Cabinet seems largely in the dark.

In part, this is due to Russia's unusual ruling arrangement: the tandem. The tandem means that instead of having one ruler Russia now has two – Medvedev and Putin, with Putin, the prime minister, nominally subordinate to Medvedev, the president. This model is not merely atypical in terms of Russian history. It is unprecedented – a break with the centuries-long authoritarian tradition in Russia and the Soviet Union of one man – and occasionally one woman – rule.

The eras of Stalin, of Khrushchev and of Brezhnev all conformed to this pattern, with each new leader denouncing his predecessor. So did the era before that: of Peter I, Catherine II, and Alexander III. Between 2000 and 2008, President Putin restores Russia's classic authoritarian leadership model, following Yeltsin's experiment in quasi-democracy. Putin's regime is strongly "personalist" in character. Everyone knows who the ultimate arbiter is. Now, though, there are two arbiters.

This strange duopoly leaves commentators, journalists and diplomats scrambling to work out which of the two rulers is really running things. To begin with, the near-universal assumption is that Putin is still the boss. But within weeks of Medvedev's inauguration the speculation starts: could Medvedev – shoehorned into the job by Putin – escape from his master's Darth Vader-like shadow? And are Medvedev's speeches on ending "legal nihilism" and battling corruption in Russia for real, or merely the liberal yang to Putin's hawkish yin?

Looking for signs of dissonance inside the tandem becomes a favourite Moscow parlour game. There are plenty of false clues but few real ones. Even those inside the Kremlin appear not to know. At one point I ask Natalia Timakova, Medvedev's press spokesperson, what kind of relationship the president and the prime minister have with each other. She is unable to answer. "Good?" I inquire, helpfully. "Yes," she says.

As I soon discover, US diplomats stationed in Moscow are engaged in the same guesswork, the same groping, as everyone else, albeit of a refined and intelligent kind. Surprisingly, the US appear not to have any genuine sources inside the corridors of Russian power: they are talking to the same small group of experts that I was. Where are the American moles?

Understanding the nature of the tandem is, admittedly, a challenge. But it has generated some of the most fecund and imaginative descriptions to be found in the cache of more than a quarter of a million US diplomatic communiques sluiced out by WikiLeaks. In November 2008, after a speech by Medvedev to the federal assembly, US deputy chief of mission Eric Rubin sends a cable to Washington setting down the various views on the fledgling Medvedev-Putin power relationship, then just six months old. There are, he tells Washington, "three, very divergent camps":

> The first group views Medvedev as ascendant, slowly accruing power as he plays to his strengths managing the economic crisis. The second, more sceptical, group argues that Medvedev continues to play Robin to Putin's Batman, surrounded by a team loyal to the premier and checked by Putin's dominance over the legislature and regional elites. Adherents to the third group see no essential difference between Putin and Medvedev, taking at face value the tandem's unanimity in purpose and vision.

Rubin rightly notes that it is impossible to work out which view is the right one: "All are hindered by the impenetrable nature of Kremlin politics and the fertile field of speculation and rumour that the information vacuum creates." In his field reporting Rubin reflects the widely held view in Moscow that Medvedev is the "junior partner" – not just Robin to Putin's Batman but, in the words of one scathing opposition politician, "the Lilliputian to Putin's commander-in-chief". It is Putin who is "pulling the strings". Another delightful comparison likens Putin to Cardinal Richelieu with Medvedev as King Louis XIII.

The emblem of the Russian Federation is the double-headed eagle – an ancient Byzantine symbol whose confused heads – like Russia – face both east and west. But some are sceptical that Medvedev is actually the second head on the eagle. One analyst tells the Americans the president is actually "the number three guy". Medvedev, he says, is less important than both Putin and the deputy premier, Igor Sechin, head of the *siloviki* clan and the Kremlin's powerful bogeyman.

It was Sechin, US diplomats believe, who engineered the demise of Khodorkovsky's oil company Yukos – "a signal turning point in Putin's approach to governance". Sechin is thought to have orchestrated "the hard-core statist and *silovik* opposition to foreign investment in strategic sectors, especially oil and gas", and is "widely believed to have directed oil exports towards Kremlin-favoured traders like Gunvor".

With little hard information to go on, journalists and struggling commentators poke through Medvedev's CV in search of clues. When Putin took over as president in 2000 he was relatively unknown, prompting the question: "Who is Mr Putin?" In late 2007, after Putin gave his endorsement, the question became, "Who is Mr Medvedev?" I offer my own stab at an answer in a profile of Russia's future president for the *Guardian*. In it I note that Kremlin spin doctors have cast Medvedev as a representative of Russia's new and aspiring middle-class – a modest, internet-savvy, cosmopolitan leader, who holidays on the Black Sea and likes to groove to 70s rock music. (Medvedev is famously a fan of the superannuated British rockers Deep Purple).

I write:

Like his mentor and friend Putin, Medvedev grew up in Leningrad, now St Petersburg. He spoke lyrically of his ordinary Soviet childhood in the proletarian suburb of Kupchino in an interview with the magazine *Itogi*. His parents were university teachers, who didn't have money but weren't starving, either. His teenage dream, he said, was to own Pink Floyd's *The Wall* and a pair of Wrangler jeans.

Medvedev and his wife Svetlana met at school; they have a son Ilya, born in 1995. Medvedev recalled working as a labourer and a snow sweeper while studying for a law PhD at Leningrad State University. "I never strived for, or dreamed, that the world would know about me," he said. He met Putin in 1991 when both worked for St Petersburg's liberal mayor Anatoly Sobchak.

But Medvedev's real personality is an enigma. Observers agree that, having survived the shark-pool of Kremlin politics, first as Putin's campaign manager during the 2000 presidential elections and then as his chief of staff, he is no patsy. Most experts believe his platform is substantially the same as Putin's with any differences merely stylistic.

One of my favourite commentators, Grigorii Golosov, of St Petersburg's European University, tells me he doesn't think Medvedev will be a "puppet". "It does seem he has a will and an intellectual capacity." But, he adds thoughtfully: "Whether this will be consequential in any way we have to wait and see."

A profile penned by William Burns in December 2007 later fills in some of my gaps. Burns begins: "Despite his prominence as first deputy premier, Gazprom board chair, and earlier as head of the presidential administration, Medvedev remains only somewhat less of an enigma than his mentor Putin was when the latter was picked as Yeltsin's successor eight years ago."

The next passage has the heading: "The Un-Putin?" Burns writes:

Medvedev appears not to have Putin's ambition or "hard" edge, possibly because he has less to prove. Whereas Putin grew up in a working class family living in a communal apartment, Medvedev's roots are in St Petersburg's academic community ... Putin learned judo to fight neighbourhood toughs; Medvedev lifted weights and focused his energies on western "heavy metal" music, then considered "subversive". Medvedev also succeeded in winning the hand of Svetlana, the girl his contemporaries considered "the prettiest" in school.

(US diplomats later devote an entire cable to Svetlana. They describe her as exerting influence on her husband "behind the scenes". Mrs Medvedeva is "more active" than Putin's almost invisible wife Lyudmila but "less flashy" than Gorbachev's wife, the late Raisa.)

Burns concludes that Medvedev will occupy the role of Putin's "capable assistant". Capable assistant or not, the Obama White House uses every opportunity it can to boost Medvedev and the "liberal faction" he is supposed to represent. Washington's idea is to nudge Russian foreign policy away from its hawkish Putin vector towards a more constructive multilateral approach. In June 2008 I cover President Obama's first visit to Moscow. It follows a period of mutual US-Russian acrimony during the last years of the Bush White House.

Medvedev and Obama hold a joint press conference. The venue is the impressive gilded palace rooms inside the Kremlin. The sheer difference in stature between the two leaders is hard to miss: next to the lanky Obama, Medvedev looks like a small schoolboy collecting a prize from the headmaster.

The substantive part of the two leaders' talks concerns a new nuclear arms reduction treaty to replace the Start agreement. But, inevitably, one reporter asks Obama which part of the tandem he thinks really runs Russia. Obama deadpans: "Medvedev is the president and Putin the prime minister." Obama seems to me tired, after a long transatlantic flight from Washington. He praises Medvedev but has problems pronouncing his host's name, addressing him on one occasion as "Mededev".

While the talks are going on, I wander round the Kremlin. The two delegations appear to have dropped from different worlds: oversized Chevrolet minivans belonging to the White House park themselves directly in the Kremlin's courtyard, opposite a 15th-century cathedral with gold domes. Inside the Kremlin, I watch several members of Obama's team pause to snap photos of a painting. It depicts Russian archers slaughtering their enemies in a medieval battle scene. Despite much talk of a "reset", Russia's state media are still stuck in cold war battle mode. They downplay Obama's trip and relegate it to the nether regions of the news schedule.

In private exchanges US officials harbour few illusions about Medvedev's limitations. But they stress that Obama should treat Medvedev as his "primary interlocutor". The officials express cautious hope that by making Medvedev the focus of US interaction they can give a boost to "more progressive" forces aligned with Medvedev and strengthen Medvedev himself.

A dispatch by John Beyrle, Burns's successor, puts it like this: "We are not advocating circumventing Putin; to the contrary, we cannot imagine improved US-Russian relations without his concurrence. Instead we will need to thread the needles of managing Putin and his ego so that US engagement with Medvedev is seen as constructive, rather than interference in Russian domestic politics." Beyrle warns that *siloviki* elements are out to wreck the improving US-Russia relationship. He complains of "thuggish intimidation" by the FSB against USAid, Washington's aid-giving body, and "harassment" of its National Democratic Institute.

Fast forward two years, and American diplomats are still busy explaining the dynamics of the tandem relationship. But by this point hopes that Medvedev would preside over a partial liberalisation of Russian society are either dead or barely twitching. Most correspondents – myself included – have stopped reporting Medvedev's speeches, which have become repetitive and boring. The president's themes are still upbeat; he talks of innovation, tackling corruption and the "rule of law". But his initiatives hardly ever translate into concrete political deeds. One of his few "achievements" comes early in his term when he extends Russia's presidential term from four years to six. But this is a democratic step backwards. It is widely seen as teeing up the conditions for a potential presidential comeback in the spring of 2012: Putin's.

Looming over Medvedev's presidency, meanwhile, is the spectre of Mikhail Khodorkovsky, the jailed oligarch who in 2009 goes on trial in Moscow for a second time. Khodorkovsky, and his business partner, Platon Lebedev, have been in prison since 2003, following their arrest and conviction for tax evasion. With the prospect of parole looming, prosecutors slap a second set of charges on the defendants, accusing them this time of embezzlement. The purpose is to keep Khodorkovsky in jail; the author of the charges Putin himself. Everyone realises the trial is political. It stems from Putin's deep personal hatred of the oligarch.

But the trial poses an obvious problem for Medvedev. He has repeatedly called for an independent judiciary. An acquittal means that Medvedev must be taken seriously. It's also a positive signal to the international community, good for Russian civil society, and a fillip to the president's dwindling credibility. But the opposite also applies. If Khodorkovsky is convicted, then Medvedev is left looking like a fake. The case is a bellwether for Russia's direction: forward to a more liberal vision of society, or backwards along the same lugubrious KGB track as before.

In March 2009 I go along to the opening day of Khodorkovsky and Lebedev's trial. There is a large scrum of reporters at Moscow's Khamovnichesky Court; the defendants, prosecutors and lawyers gather in a small, stuffy room on the third floor. I sit in an overflow room below. There are closed-circuit television screens showing the proceedings. As the court rises, however, an irascible female official comes in and turns the live-feed off. One of Khodorkovsky's lawyers, Robert Amsterdam, tells me: "This case is of immense importance because of what it will say to all of us about where Russia is going." Unable to watch, I interview a handful of demonstrators outside. "I think Putin is afraid of Khodorkovsky. He's envious of him," says 73-year-old Irina Nabatova. The Khodorkovsky supporters break into an ironic chorus. "End legal nihilism," they chant.

I have better luck when I return to the trial a few months later. I find a seat inside the crowded courtroom. Khodorkovsky is sitting with Lebedev in a glass cage; he looks pale but cheerful. His hair is severely cropped in convict fashion; his rimless glasses lend a professorial touch. He is chatting with his lawyers. Seven guards armed with Kalashnikovs stand guard. But the oligarch hardly looks like he is about to attempt to escape. Khodorkovsky's parents sit in the front row. Just before the session begins a guard comes up to Khodorkovsky's elderly father and takes away his chair.

It is painfully obvious. This trial is nothing more than a tableau of political vindictiveness – designed to keep Khodorkovsky in prison when his eight-year sentence expires. The case against Khodorkovsky is so feeble and contradictory as to be surrealistic. (The prosecution alleges the two men embezzled 350 million metric tons of oil worth over $25.4 billion and laundered over $21.4 billion. The defence team maintains that the charges are absurd to the point of incomprehensibility. Khodorkovsky allegedly stole all the oil that his company, Yukos, produced.) The oligarch's real crime is to have challenged Putin and to have broken the unwritten covenant– a kind of omertà – that Russian businessmen, especially rich ones, should stay out of politics.

US diplomats who attend the Khodorkovsky trial on 28 April 2009, give their own droll account. They clearly find the trial as monotonous and impenetrable as I do. They write:

A stupor settled over the courtroom as the prosecution's designated reader droned on ... The prosecutors frequently hesitated and stumbled over their words, and had trouble reading from their own documents, as well as finding the items they needed ... As the prosecutor's reader delved into mind-numbing detail regarding a particular set of Yuganskneft shares that had followed a convoluted path through a series of Yukos's subsidiary companies, we asked a fellow spectator sitting next to us:

"Are you following this?"

He replied, "No, I am not; and neither is the person reading it."

US officials remark that it's "facile" to compare the Khodorkovsky trial to the show trials of the Stalinist era. (In 1938, for example, Bukharin and Yagoda were taken out after theirs to be shot.) Khodorkovsky's PowerPoint defence is available on the internet; his supporters are allowed to attend hearings. At one point the oligarch produces a jam jar full of crude oil, prompting the judge to exclaim: "How the hell did that get in here?"

The case leaves the Kremlin with little wriggle-room: any move that pleases liberals will enrage conservatives, and vice versa. But – as the diplomats conclude after their stultifying day in court – "nobody believes that the judge will make his decision free of GOR [government of Russia] influence."

They add: "As a result, the world is watching the case in order to learn about the GOR's political intentions rather than the judge's legal intentions."

This prediction turns out to be depressingly correct. The trial of Khodorkovsky and Lebedev grinds on for 16 months. On the day of the verdict, intelligence officers escort the judge, Viktor Danilkin, into court. He duly pronounces both defendants guilty. Khodorkovsky is jailed until 2016. (He gets 14 years, to be served concurrently with his original sentence, later reduced by one year.) A few weeks later the court's clerk, Natalya Vasilyeva, reveals that someone else wrote Judge Danilkin's verdict for him. He had originally planned to sentence Khodorkovsky to 10, rather than 14 years. Khodorkovsky was previously incarcerated in Chita, in distant Siberia. This time he is sent to a penal facility in Karelia, an area of forests and lakes in northwest Russia near the Finnish border.

Vasilyeva's decision to speak out is brave. She tells the independent TV station Rain: "As for Khodorkovsky and Lebedev, I don't think they should be in prison. I don't pity them, but I do sympathise. I realise that they were just unlucky enough to fall into the mincer, as it were."

By 2010 the analogies used to describe Medvedev have become even more disrespectful. At one seminar in London I hear an expert describe Russia's ruling model not as a tandem but as "a bicycle with a child's seat in the front". Other commentators compare Medvedev to Putin's shadow – or even his shoelaces. Critics point out that during his four years as president oppression has actually got worse. New laws have been passed classifying opposition members as "extremists", and the number of political prisoners has grown. The impression that Medvedev is a wimp is widespread.

Some believe there is a Medvedev camp within Russia's bureaucracy, comprised of liberal-leaning civil servants at odds with the ex-KGB guys. One witticism doing the rounds, however, says that there are serious doubts whether Medvedev is actually in the Medvedev camp. According to the Americans, the well-intentioned Medvedev is at risk of being dismissed as "a seat-warmer for the prime minister" or "permanently subservient to Putin".

The US embassy reports another cruel joke circulating in Moscow:

Medvedev sits in the driver's seat of a new car, examines the inside, the instrument panel, and the pedals. He looks around, but the steering wheel is missing.

He turns to Putin and asks: "Vladimir Vladimirovich, where is the steering wheel?"

Putin pulls a remote control out of his pocket and says, "I'll be the one doing the driving."

In the autumn of 2010 the only political question is whether Medvedev will be allowed to stand for another presidential term. Or, as seems more likely, will Putin get his old Kremlin job back? By this point analysts have stopped reading the tea leaves for signs of an intra-leadership struggle between Russia's weak president and powerful prime minister. Instead, there is a more cynical consensus: that Medvedev is simply the exportable version of

Putinism. His talk of reform and modernisation goes down well with what Garry Kasparov dubs the "western appeasement crowd" – western European nations like Germany, France and Italy that place friendly relations with the Kremlin above human rights concerns.

In dispatches to Washington, it is clear that the US embassy believes it is Putin alone who will decide the candidate for Russia's 2012 presidential election. This doesn't necessarily mean that Putin will become the president again – although all the signs point in this direction – but that it is in his power to decide. Diplomat Susan Elliott predicts that Russia's "bicephalous ruling format" is unlikely to be long lasting, given Russia's history and "current tandem dynamics". Her analysis is that "Medvedev and Putin work well together, but Putin holds most, and the best, of the cards in the tandem relationship. His return to the Kremlin is not inevitable, but should things remain stable Putin remains in a position to choose himself, Medvedev or another person to become Russia's next president."

Several factors make a Putin return likely. The Kremlin is more prestigious than the White House and gives Putin an international platform. But, more importantly, as president, Putin can exercise full control. One contact tells the Americans that Putin needs to ensure that he is in a position to "crush anyone who might initiate de-Putinisation, or suggest that Putin had a hand in unsavoury deeds, such as the murder of journalists or the 1999 apartment bombings". Another mentions Putin's secret assets. Putin will decide who gets to be president depending "on his perception of being able to control Russia's political-economic system and protect his financial interests". The tandem, then, appears to be fizzling out.

Confirmation of the tandem's painful death comes in September 2011 at the annual congress of the United Russia party. Medvedev announces that the party's next candidate for president will be...Vladimir Putin! Russia's two leaders are swapping places. Medvedev is standing aside. As a consolation, Medvedev will get Putin's old job of prime minister.

The news is, somehow, a bombshell and no surprise whatsoever. On stage, before cheering supporters, the two men hug. (Medvedev's grin, admittedly, looks strained.) Putin reveals that back in 2007, Medvedev secretly agreed to serve just one presidential term. The job swap announcement is a moment of humiliation for Medvedev, the ultimate patsy. Twitter users deride him using the hashtag "pathetic".

And then in November 2011 something extraordinary happens. No-one had quite foreseen it. For the first time in 12 years, Putin is himself humiliated. The occasion is a martial arts fight at Moscow's Olimpisky stadium. When Putin steps into the ring to congratulate the winner there are jeers and catcalls from the audience. Lots of them. Kremlin spin-doctors try to explain away the heckling by claiming the fans needed to go to the bathroom. But the reality is this: Putin's popularity is beginning to slip. Cracks are appearing in the Kremlin edifice.

It gets worse. On December 4th the United Russia party suffers a humiliating reversal in Duma elections – with its share of the vote tumbling from 64 per cent in 2007 to below 50 per cent. This "result" is only achieved by industrial-scale fraud: carousel voting, ballot box stuffing, even the use of invisible ink to rub out votes for the "wrong" parties.

Violations in Russian elections are nothing new. But it appears that Russia's populace – especially its middle-class representatives – have had enough of the cheating, lying and feudal disdain that have characterised the Putin era. Tens of thousands take to the streets of Moscow in the largest anti-government protests since the fall of the Soviet Union. Their demands are simple: a re-run of the Duma poll and fair elections. And most want Putin to resign.

Despite these unprecedented demonstrations, Putin's "reelection" in March of 2012 is virtually guaranteed. The most likely scenario is that his rule will continue. Following Medvedev's changes to Russia's constitution it is entirely "legal" for Putin to remain in the Kremlin until 2024 – in theory, serving two more six-year presidential terms.

The comparisons are with Leonid Brezhnev: he presided over another epoch of political stagnation and high oil prices; there was also a war (Afghanistan) and an Olympic Games (Moscow 1980). After news of Putin's "return", liberals post a photo of him mocked up to look like Brezhnev – complete with military uniform, patriotic Soviet medals and a hammer and sickle. Putin even gets Brezhnevian eyebrows.

At the start of 2012 Putin shows few signs of departing from power voluntarily. His strategy, instead, appears to be to tough the crisis out – denigrating the protesters and appointing trusted former KGB allies to key government posts. This may work. Or not. The Brezhnev era ended only when the General Secretary's body was carried out horizontally from office.

One other cloud darkens the Kremlin's horizon. In November 2009 a 37-year-old lawyer working for the asset management company Hermitage Capital dies in prison after being refused medical treatment for acute pancreatitis and gallstones. His name is Sergei Magnitsky. Hermitage and Magnitsky had accused Russia's interior ministry of stealing $230 million in taxes that Hermitage paid the Russian government the previous year. The scam involved 60 senior Russian officials. After Magnitsky testified against them, the same officials arrested Magnitsky and kept him in prison for almost a year without charge.

Despite Medvedev's promises to punish those responsible, no action is taken against the corrupt officials involved. In Europe and the United States, however, the case sparks outrage. In the US, a bipartisan group of senators proposes a new law named after Sergei Magnitsky. The law would revoke US visa privileges and prohibit financial transactions for Russian officials involved in human rights abuses. The proposed legislation rattles Moscow and even provokes one of those on the list – Vladislav Surkov, the Kremlin's chief ideologist – to fly to Washington for urgent private talks. In July 2011 the US state department goes ahead and imposes visa bans on Russian officials. The move is actually an attempt by the Obama administration to avoid the far more sweeping sanctions the bill envisages. Moscow is furious. Medvedev orders his foreign ministry to retaliate and draw up a list of US citizens banned from Russia. The draft bill correctly identifies the Russian regime's Achilles heel – its assets in the west.

Giving evidence to the US House committee on foreign affairs, Gary Kasparov argues that the "common refrain", that the civilised world had no leverage with the Kremlin, is wrong. He says: "The principle refutation of this line exists because Russia today is not the Soviet Union. Putin's closest allies, those who keep him in power, are not faceless grey Politburo members who aspire to nothing more than a nice house or car. Putin's oligarchs own global companies, buy real estate in London, Biarritz, New York. The money they have pilfered from Russia's treasury goes to buy art, yachts, and American and British sports teams. In short, they wish to enjoy the spoils and that makes them vulnerable. Putin needs the west's support because that is where they all keep their money."

One investigator comes up with a new and arresting description for Putin's Russia. He calls it a "virtual mafia state."

CHAPTER 14

WikiLeaks

Secret bunker, the *Guardian*, Kings Place, London
28 October 2010

*Grinda stated that he considers Belarus, Chechnya and Russia
to be virtual "mafia states" ... One cannot differentiate between the
activities of the government and OC [organised crime] groups.*
SPANISH PROSECUTOR JOSÉ GRINDA GONZALEZ, 13 JANUARY 2010

My mornings in Moscow acquire a comfortable routine. After the school-run, I take the metro four stops to Belorussky station. I have breakfast in one of its cafes. My favourite place is a simple pancake bar in the station's subterranean passage. I order a *blin* (pancake) with condensed milk and, for 55 roubles, a small cup of black coffee. I chat with the staff: a young Russian woman and her Kyrgyz assistants. The cafe is non-smoking. This is unusual for Russia. Often it's empty. For 20 minutes I sit and read quietly and pleasurably: a novel or a short story by Bunin or Nabokov.

I return my tray, walk five minutes down Gruzinsky Val, a car-choked street, and cut through a small park, past a kiosk selling groceries and a knitting shop. The *Guardian* office is located in a 1970s former diplomatic compound owned by the state property agency UPDK. The building is now home to a jumble of low-ceilinged offices and private flats. A security guard stands next to the entrance and the *Shlagbaum* – the word for a raised barrier comes from the German. In winter he clamps his hands together to keep warm.

Our office is No 75-76 – two pokey residences knocked into one to make a small workspace. I collect the morning's newspapers from the post-box outside. (Someone broke the lock long ago; we didn't bother to get it fixed. Much of the time my post never arrives. Inefficiency or interception? It could be either.) I share the office with my colleague Tom Parfitt and a succession of bright young assistants who suggest story ideas and handle the accounts – Yulia, Sergei and Olga.

Every morning we plough through the morning papers. We start with the independent ones – the English-language *Moscow Times*, *Kommersant*, *Vedomosti*, and *Novaya Gazeta*. Mid-morning I make coffee in our dingy kitchen; its window looks on to a small spot of green popular with dog-walkers. Then we go through the pro-government newspapers: *Komsomolskaya Pravda* and others, whose pages are a daily bulletin of Putin and Medvedev. Lastly, I read *Izvestiya*. Once a vigorous independent title, *Izvestiya* has turned into a dull Kremlin propaganda sheet since being bought by the energy giant Gazprom.

On the morning of 25 October 2010, however, *Izvestiya* surprises me. It carries an interesting article. Its subject is Julian Assange, the editor-in-chief of the whistleblowers' website WikiLeaks. I'm aware of Assange's reputation for spilling secrets: the *Guardian* and other international media partners have – in July and October respectively – published confidential military logs from the wars in Afghanistan and Iraq.

This time, however, Assange promises revelations concerning Russia. Assange tells *Izvestiya*: "We have [compromising materials] about Russia, about your government and businessmen." Another WikiLeaks spokesman, Kristinn Hrafnsson, goes further. He tells *Kommersant*: "Russians are going to find out a lot of interesting facts about their country." Hrafnsson, an Icelandic journalist and one of Assange's key lieutenants, adds that WikiLeaks will soon be targeting "despotic regimes in China, Russia and Central Asia". There will be fresh document dumps, he says.

I am intrigued. Could we get hold of these documents? The suspicion of corruption at the very top of the Kremlin is widespread, but up until now there has been scant proof. Even with inside information, an army of gifted lawyers, a detailed knowledge of offshore banking structures, and five years to research and investigate, following the money trail would be almost impossible, I suspect. But Assange's "materials" would be a good place to start. I email the *Guardian*'s deputy editor, Ian Katz:

> Dear Ian
>
> Julian Assange has given an interview to *Izvestiya* newspaper here saying he's sitting on incriminating material involving Russia. He doesn't elaborate but says that the information is from a US source.
>
> It's not clear if it's linked to the Iraq war or something else. Either way it would be worth getting hold of. Could you let me know how we might proceed: should I drop him a note directly (and if so how?) or is this something you might mention to him?
>
> Luke

Katz sends a cryptic reply:

> Hi Luke
>
> I think we know what this is referring to. Suggest you don't approach Assange but I'll ask David Leigh to fill you in.
>
> Ian

David Leigh is the *Guardian*'s investigations editor. He is a colleague and friend. In the late 1990s we co-authored a book on the Conservative politician Jonathan Aitken. (Aitken was jailed after lying on oath in the High Court in a Kamikaze libel action he brought against the *Guardian*.)

It appears the *Guardian* already has sight of Assange's mysterious "materials". Leigh emails me extracts from a diplomatic cable sent by the US embassy in Rome, with conspiratorial instructions to delete the email as soon as I've read it. It concerns Silvio Berlusconi and his relationship with Vladimir Putin. I read that Berlusconi and Putin have "close personal ties", based on "mutual commercial interests". It seems that, according to the Americans, Berlusconi is benefiting "personally and handsomely" from Russia's prime minister. In other words – gulp! – Berlusconi is on Putin's payroll. This might explain the Italian premier's readiness to act as Putin's mouthpiece in European negotiations, and Italy's curious role as Russia's warmest EU ally.

The Americans don't like this much, I discover. The US Rome mission, for example, writes in 2006:

> We are concerned that this relationship could weaken international criticism of Russia at a time when the Russian Federation is reversing democratic reforms ... We should highlight to Berlusconi that Russia's pattern of resisting democratic change, undermining international organisations, manipulating internal politics in neighbouring countries, and using its fuel exports for political purposes, is a threat to global stability and requires direct and sometimes public criticism.

The material is sensational indeed. But what else has the *Guardian* got? I email Leigh. Given the security issues raised by the Assange cables, and the FSB's intrusive surveillance of my home and office, I offer to fly back to London. Leigh agrees. "Come over," he writes. Within 24 hours I'm back at the *Guardian*'s offices in Kings Place near King's Cross station. It's 28 October 2010. Leigh explains that the *Guardian* and other international publications – the *New York Times* and Germany's *Der Spiegel* magazine – are co-operating again with WikiLeaks on another clandestine project. This project has been under way for some months. Secret files from Afghanistan and Iraq were "packages" one and two. But there is also "package three".

Package three is the biggest and most sensational yet – more than a quarter of a million secret diplomatic communiques sent by US embassies and consulates from around the world. A disillusioned 22-year-old army intelligence analyst, Bradley Manning, has allegedly downloaded the dispatches from a US military and defence server in Baghdad. He then passed them to WikiLeaks, it is claimed.

They come in five categories. There is secret/noforn (that is, not to be read by non-Americans); secret; confidential/noforn; confidential; and unclassified. There is no top-secret bracket: this layer of super-sensitive material had been omitted from the original SIPRNet database, used by the US State Department and department of defence to swap information securely. Most of the cables concern the last five years. The most recent is dated 28 February 2010.

This is the biggest leak in history. The plan to publish a series of articles based on this extraordinary data-spill is already well advanced. As I arrive in London, two other European newspapers, Spain's *El País* and France's *Le Monde*, have just joined the three-headed international media consortium publishing the cables. Secretly, the five media partners and WikiLeaks have agreed to publish simultaneously on 28 November 2010. Several *Guardian* foreign correspondents are already busy sifting through these telegrams region by region – the Middle East, Afghanistan, Iran, Yemen.

My job is to look at Russia and the former Soviet Union. I install myself in the *Guardian*'s fourth-floor secret bunker. It is an overheated room with a bank of computers. There is a free coffee machine nearby. There is also a relaxation room. I log on to the *Guardian*'s internal "leakserver". I tap in a search term. I try "Litvinenko". The system spews out dozens of results. Bingo! I click on the first one. I feel a bit like the English archaeologist Howard Carter setting foot for the first time in Tutankhamun's tomb, realising he has stumbled on treasures. I begin reading. Several hours later I'm still reading, engrossed and amazed. The material doesn't disappoint. It is a trove of information on one of the world's most secretive states.

The US embassy cables paint a desperate picture of Russia under Putin. It is well known that corruption is widespread, and that on democracy and human rights the country has slithered alarmingly backwards since 2000. But the cables go further. They suggest that Russia has metastasised into a brutal, autocratic kleptocracy, centred on Putin's pre-eminent leadership, and in which officials, oligarchs and organised crime bosses are bound together to create a "virtual mafia state".

Arms trafficking, money laundering, personal enrichment, protection for gangsters, extortion and kickbacks, suitcases full of money and secret offshore bank accounts in Cyprus and Switzerland: the cables unpick a dysfunctional political system in which bribery alone totals an estimated $300bn a year, and in which it is often hard to distinguish between the activities of government and organised crime.

The Americans, I read with interest, also believe that Putin has secretly amassed a large fortune. There are several references to his "alleged illicit proceeds", hidden abroad. Privately, it seems, US diplomats in Moscow take the same bleak view of the Kremlin that I do: that it isn't so much a state as a private-sector moneymaking business, in which stealing is a pathological habit. AD Miller – the author of Snowdrops – describes the logic of the ruling class like this: in theory Russia must be great, but in the meantime this particular Russia is a contemptible mess – and if we don't plunder it, someone else will.

Most of the cables I sift through come from the US embassy in Moscow. But one from Spain also pricks my curiosity. Sent by a Madrid-based American diplomat, William Duncan, it reports on a briefing by one of Spain's top experts on the Russian mafia. His name is José "Pepe" Grinda Gonzalez. Grinda is a national court prosecutor. For the past 12 years he has had the unenviable task of fighting organised crime in Spain and bringing mafia dons to justice.

On 13 January 2010, Grinda gives a frank presentation to a new US-Spain counter-terrorism and organised crime group. The session is held behind closed doors. Just two months earlier Grinda had wrapped up his prosecution of Zakhar Kalashov, a Georgian-born Russian citizen and a notorious *vor v zakone*. (The term means "thief in law" and signifies the highest rank in Russia's organised crime network. Russian observers familiar with the criminal underworld say that these days Russian *vory* are more sophisticated than Dima – a burly, tattooed, tennis-playing money-launderer, from a criminal family in Perm who features in John le Carré.)

Grinda is also the prosecutor in several other high-profile Russian mafia cases. This fact makes him understandably nervous about his physical security and, I read, "suspicious of penetration attempts by intelligence services".

Grinda begins by conceding that the term "Russian mafia" is something of a misnomer, since these criminal gangs often involve Ukrainians, Georgians, Belarusians or Chechens. But he says that the phrase is the most appropriate one, even though the Russians dislike it and prefer the more neutral term "Eurasian mafia".

The prosecutor then makes the following statement, according to the cable:

Grinda stated that he considers Belarus, Chechnya and Russia to be virtual "mafia states" and said that Ukraine is going to be one. For each of those countries, he alleged, one cannot differentiate between the activities of the government and OC [organised crime] groups.

According to Grinda, there are two reasons to worry about the Russian mafia. First, he says, it exercises "tremendous control" over certain strategic sectors of the global economy, such as aluminium. The second, he says, "is the unanswered question regarding the extent to which Russian PM Putin is implicated in the Russian mafia and whether he controls the mafia's actions".

Grinda doesn't give a definitive answer to this. But he implies that Putin may indeed be involved in the Russian mafia's activities. He cites a thesis by Litvinenko, an expert on organised crime, who met secretly with Spanish intelligence agents a few months before his mysterious poisoning in London in 2006. Grinda puts forward Litvinenko's view that the Russian intelligence and security services – the FSB, SVR and GRU – "control organised crime in Russia". The cable says: "Grinda stated that he believed this thesis [by Litvinenko] is accurate."

The prosecutor goes on to say that the FSB is "absorbing" the Russian mafia but can also "eliminate" them in two ways. The first is to kill "OC leaders who do not do what the security services want them to do". The second is to put them behind bars "to eliminate them as a competitor for influence". The crime lords can also be put in jail for their own protection.

The cable offers persuasive evidence of what critics of the Russian regime have long been saying: that under Putin, the government, FSB and criminal elements have melded together to run Russia. Citing wire taps, witnesses and information received from intelligence services, Grinda further claims that "certain Russian political parties operate 'hand in hand' with OC". He names the far-right Liberal Democrats – the party of Litvinenko's alleged killer, Andrei Lugovoi. The KGB and its successor agencies created the party, Grinda says, adding that it is now "home to many serious criminals". He goes on to allege that "there are proven ties between Russian political parties, organised crime and arms trafficking".

Grinda cites the mysterious mid-2009 case of the Arctic Sea ship, which the Russian government claims was hijacked by a group of Estonian pirates in the Baltic. Grinda asserts instead it was "a clear example" of arms trafficking. The Russian government denies this, and says the pirates diverted the boat to Africa and the Cape Verde islands. Grinda doesn't give details. But his remarks indicate he believes organised criminals acting under orders from Russia's intelligence agencies used the boat to smuggle arms. (There has been speculation the ship was carrying S-300 missiles destined for Iran. Others have suggested rockets, smart bombs or even nuclear missiles.)

After more than a decade investigating organised crime, Grinda has strong views about the relationship between the state and the mafia. He says that "whereas terrorists aim to substitute the essence of the state itself, OC seeks to be a complement to state structures". Top Russian mafia bosses, for example, enjoy access to senior government officials and "high-level ministers", he claims. The cable continues: "He summarised his views by asserting that the GOR's [government of Russia's] strategy is to use OC groups to do whatever the GOR cannot acceptably do as a government."

Two other cables from Spain give intriguing details of Russian mafia activity. Mafia dons began entering Spain in the mid-1990s. By 2004 they had become so pervasive that Spanish prosecutors were forced to devise a formal strategy to "behead" them. These individuals, the cables say, had no known jobs or known sources of income, and yet they lived in large mansions. Spanish prosecutors concluded their money came from money-laundering. The challenge was how to prove this.

Spain conducted two major operations against Russian organised crime – codenamed Avispa (2005-2007) and Troika (2008-2009). They resulted in the arrest of more than 60 suspects. Among them were four top mafiosi: Gennady Petrov, Alexander Malyshev (Petrov's deputy),Vitaly Izgilov (a key lieutenant, out on bail following a previous arrest) and Kalashov. They allegedly formed the leadership of one of the four largest mafia networks in the world and the largest Russian organised crime network. The cable, dated 31 August 2009, asserts: "Spain served as the group's safe haven from authorities and rival OC networks in Russia." The gang's illicit activities were breathtaking – contract killings, arms and drug trafficking, extortion, coercion, threats and kidnapping.

The cable claims that those recently arrested in Spain were involved "in a complex web of shady business dealings and enjoyed a murky relationship with senior [Russian] government officials". Much of the information on this appears to come from Litvinenko – a further possible motive for his polonium assassination in Britain. According to *El País*, Spain's centre-left daily, Litvinenko tipped off Spanish security officials on the locations, roles, and activities of several "Russian" mafia figures with ties to Spain during a May 2006 meeting. Six months later Litvinenko was dead.

During its two-year investigation, the Spanish government's security services tapped "thousands" of mafia conversations. The contents of the wiretaps, according to unnamed sources cited in the Spanish press, "will make your hair stand on end". They are said to give details of Petrov's "immense power and political connections", and disclose that mafia leaders "invoked the names of senior GOR officials to assure partners that their illicit deals would proceed as planned". So sensitive is this intercept evidence that only 10 Spanish officials are reportedly aware of their contents – fearing, reasonably enough, that their wider release could be a disaster for Spain's bilateral relations with the Russian government.

Nonetheless, a few details do emerge. They are fascinating. One of Petrov's intercepted phone conversations suggests that the Russian trade attache was sailing on Petrov's yacht on 6 September 2007. (The Russian ambassador to Spain publicly denies this.) In October 2008, Spanish authorities raid the Mallorca vacation mansion of Vladislav Reznik, chair of the Duma's financial markets committee and a deputy in the Putin-led United Russia party. The cable states: "There is some debate about whether Reznik bought the house from Petrov or whether it was a gift. In any event, the two were regularly seen together on the island, according to press reports."

Spanish prosecutors issue an EU-wide warrant for Reznik's arrest. He remains in Russia. Here he enjoys immunity. The prosecutors link him to the Tambov crime family and an audacious plot to kidnap the eldest son of a Spanish construction magnate. Citing *El País*, the Americans say the Spanish government has compiled a "secret list" of Russian prosecutors, senior military officers and politicians – including current and former ministers – who may have been involved with the network investigated in the Troika operation. The chain allegedly involves "three ministers". It stretches to the very top of Russia's defence ministry.

I also learn that the Spanish deliberately left Moscow "out of the loop" on the Troika investigation because they were afraid of leaks to mafia targets. This secrecy is understandable. In 2005 Kalashov and Tariel Oniani – also a Georgian-born Russian citizen – were tipped off hours before a Spanish police raid as part of Operation Avispa. (The presumed culprits behind the leak were the Russian security services or corrupt Spanish officials.) They fled the country. Kalashov was detained in 2006 in Dubai and extradited back to Spain. The Americans estimate Kalashov has a personal fortune of €200 million. They say he also owns a significant share of the Russian energy giant Lukoil and was instrumental with Oniani in bringing it to Spain in 2003-2004.

The picture is an extraordinary one. Crime dons, trade attaches, ministers, money laundering, smuggling, kidnapping, and a security service that employs the mafia for its own opaque missions. Here, in diplomatic telegrams never meant for publication, is the corrupt nexus at the heart of the Russian state.

I begin writing a battery of stories about Russia based on the WikiLeaks documents. Of all the material to emerge from this remarkable archive, the Russian cables are the most compelling. Upstairs, still stuck in a room with broken air-conditioning, I explain my discoveries to Leigh and Katz. I am excited. So are they. The broad theme of our soon-to-be-published Russia WikiLeaks coverage is obvious: corruption, Litvinenko, and the mafia character of the Russian state.

But among the cables I find colourful vignettes that illustrate Russia's post-Soviet progress – or lack of it. When searching for the word "Lenin" I find a cable sent by the US mission in Burma. It details a meeting in September 2005 between the US's charge in Rangoon and the Russian ambassador to Burma, Oleg Kabanov. The venue is the Russian embassy compound – "a Stalinist-style bunker next to the foreign ministry in downtown Rangoon".

The ambassador and the charge don't agree on Burmese politics. ("The Russian mission's views ... seem stuck in the same Stalinist frame," the charge notes. Kabanov says that western countries are "too impatient" to see change in Burma and adds that democracy would only "lead to chaos and collapse".)

At the end of this unhappy courtesy call, the US charge learns that the Russian diplomat is a fan of Lenin: "Kabanov seemed nostalgic for the era when his country was also an autocracy; he told the charge that he keeps a 55-volume set of Lenin's collected works in his office, noting that it took years in exile for the Bolsheviks to plan and organise 'reform' of the Russian political system." Lenin, then, doesn't just live on in Russia's dusty provincial squares. He clearly inspires nostalgia among Putin officials sceptical of western values and more at home with authoritarian ones.

A cable sent by the US embassy to the Vatican offers further evidence of lingering Soviet thinking. Written by the US ambassador to the Holy See, Jim Nicholson, it recounts a meeting with the Vatican's Russia director, Archbishop Alberto Tricarico, in 2002. Tricarico is "unhappy and agitated". The Russians have refused to grant visas to two senior Catholic clergy – a slap in the face for those within the Vatican who want reconciliation with the Russian orthodox church.

Tricarico complains that attempts at rapprochement with the Russians have so far been "one-sided". Indeed, other cables confirm that Putin's desire to assert Russian influence also extends to the spiritual and Episcopal realm. The archbishop complains that "Catholics had been persecuted in Russia for 80 years, thrown into the gulag and many martyred, and 'this is our reward?'" He concludes by alluding to allegations that Russia's then-patriarch, Alexy II, used to work for the KGB. The cable says: "Tricarico averred that Russian orthodox clergy suffered from "socialist ways of thinking; they were all collaborators in the past and can't shake old ways".

The cables also record unsatisfying encounters between European Union officials and their Russian counterparts. The two sides meet twice a year for EU-Russia summits. But these summits, held alternately in Brussels and in showcase Russian towns like Khabarovsk or Khanty-Mansiysk, make little progress and are increasingly a waste of time.

Part of the reason is European disunity. There are two different camps on how to deal with a resurgent Russia: realists who think the EU should accept Russia as it is and not annoy it, and moralists who believe Russia should observe European standards. At a meeting of Nato's advisory body on terrorism and espionage in 2009, for example, the British raise the threat from the Russian security services. (Nato earlier that year had expelled two Russian diplomats for activities inconsistent with their status.) The French, however, complain that this amounts to a "cold war" viewpoint.

Part of the difficulty is down to a lack of agreed vision when it comes to the EU and Russia's common neighbourhood. I read one cable that says the EU wants to advance its "shared interests" with the Kremlin in Ukraine, Moldova, Belarus and the southern Caucasus. The cable dryly notes the EU "encounters difficulty overcoming Russia's belief in exclusive spheres of influence". One Russian government official bluntly tells the EU that these countries of the "near abroad" are "relatives" who are "very near to our heart". To the EU "they are merely neighbours and new ones at that".

These EU-Russian frictions worsen in 2005 when Moscow dispatches a new, energetic ambassador to Brussels, Vladimir Chizhov. A dispatch to Washington says that Chizhov has shaken up the Russian mission and "delights in needling the EU". Russian diplomats had grown used to Chizhov's laid-back predecessor. Now, the cable notes pityingly, they are "minding their p's and q's, and lavishly greeting Chizhov as 'your excellency' and asking how his wife, children and dog are doing each day." Asked about Chizhov, one EU staffer groans: "He's a nightmare."

The EU's mandarins have moments of amusing indiscretion. It is recorded that in 2004 Chris Patten – at the time the EU's external relations commissioner – has a gossipy lunch of "rubbery fish" with a US diplomat at a German thinktank. Patten had been in Moscow a week earlier, and had just concluded EU-Russian ministerial consultations in Brussels.

The cable states: "Patten said Putin had done a good job for Russia mainly due to high world energy prices, but he had serious doubts about the man's character. Cautioning that "I'm not saying that genes are determinant", Patten then reviewed Putin's family history: grandfather part of Lenin's special protection team, father a communist party apparatchik, and Putin himself determined from a young age to pursue a career in the KGB. "He seems a completely reasonable man when discussing the Middle East or energy policy, but when the conversation shifts to Chechnya or Islamic extremism, Putin's eyes turn to those of a killer."

One other cable is a gem. In April 2008, William Burns, the US ambassador, pays a visit to Alexander Solzhenitsyn, the Nobel-winning writer and dissident. The meeting takes place at Solzhenitsyn's Moscow *dacha*; Solzhenitysn's wife, Natalya, is also present. Burns finds the legendary author, now aged 89, to be "alert" and "actively engaged with the events of the day" but in visibly declining health. "A stroke has left his left arm paralysed, and his hand gnarled," Burns reports.

The conversation turns to politics. Thrown out of the Soviet Union in 1974, it emerges that Solzhenitsyn is an unexpected fan of Putin's.

"Solzhenitsyn positively contrasted the eight-year reign of Putin with those of Gorbachev and Yeltsin, which he said had "added to the damage done to the Russian state by 70 years of communist rule". Under Putin, the nation was rediscovering what it was to be Russian, Solzhenitsyn thought, although he acknowledged that many problems remained; among them "poverty and the widening gap between rich and poor". Solzhenitsyn died four months later.

These cables are illuminating. But as well as sniffing out potential stories for the *Guardian*, I use the WikiLeaks database to learn more about the FSB – the shadowy organisation that for almost four years has decided to treat me as an enemy. The search term "FSB" produces a jackpot of results. I begin to collect the reports referencing Russia's security agencies on a memory stick. I call the file "ghosts".

I don't have a specific goal in mind. The WikiLeaks documents contain more than 200 million words. They offer an unparalleled insight into the thought processes of American diplomats and the world's only superpower, and lay out a rich mosaic of life and politics in the 21st century. But I'm optimistic that among the torrent of analysis and top-table gossip there will be clues to some of the questions I set out to answer after the first mysterious visitation in 2007 – namely, who are the FSB agents who broke into my flat? Who sent them? And whom else have they visited?

Within hours of beginning my search I make an enlightening discovery. On 9 November 2009, John Beyrle, the US ambassador, sends a secret telegram to the FBI's director, Robert Mueller. Mueller is about to visit

Moscow; Beyrle's job is to give him a frank assessment of the Russian security service and law enforcement chiefs he is due to meet. The ambassador starts by noting that US-Russian relations are "improving markedly after hitting bottom in the summer of 2008" – in other words, during the dog days of the Bush administration and the Russia-Georgia war. Since then, however, both Barack Obama and Hillary Clinton have visited Moscow, established a new bilateral presidential commission, and generated "more positive momentum in bilateral ties than I have seen in over a decade".

The bad news, though, is the obstructive attitude and "cold war mentality" of Mueller's Russian counterparts. They are FSB director Alexander Bortnikov, SVR director Mikhail Fradkov and interior minister Rashid Nurgaliyev. All three, Beyrle says, represent institutions that feel "ideologically and materially" threatened by the improvement in relations. Beyrle dubs them influential opponents of the White House's "engagement agenda". In a paragraph headed "State Security" he also reports that independent analysts believe "individuals within the security services are linked with organised crime".

Russian security services had dramatically stepped up their efforts against the US and other western powers in response to pro-democracy revolutions in Georgia and Ukraine, Beyrle writes. They believe the west incited the protests.

> Their officers maintain constant vigilance against the US government representatives through active surveillance and they have sought to stifle US humanitarian programs in the north Caucasus. MVD [interior ministry] forces harass and intimidate political opposition parties while "investigations" against western-supported NGOs for trumped-up charges (like using pirated software) have hindered the work that those organisations seek to accomplish.

The most interesting revelations are to be found in the section describing the daily difficulties faced by American diplomats stationed in Moscow. Under the heading, "A Challenging Relationship", Beyrle reviews some of the problems his staff and local hires have faced:

While portions of the FSB are working co-operatively with US law enforcement, some sections, particularly those dealing with counterintelligence, are not. Harassing activity against all embassy personnel has spiked in the past several months to a level not seen in many years. Embassy personnel have suffered personally slanderous and falsely prurient attacks in the media. Family members have been the victims of psychologically terrifying assertions that their USG employee spouses have met accidental deaths. Home intrusions have become far more commonplace and bold, and activity against our locally engaged Russian staff continues at a record pace. We have no doubt that this activity originates in the FSB. Counterintelligence challenges remain a hallmark of service at Embassy Moscow. This fact is unlikely to change in the medium term.

Finally, then, some kind of answer. The FSB's domestic break-ins have a name. They are home intrusions. At least this is what the Americans call them. And it's clear that I am far from being the only victim. It seems that half of Moscow has played host to the same uninvited guests. Across the Russian capital, Europe's largest city, FSB agents are actively picking locks, hiding bugs, skulking in stairwells, and using the flats of patriotic neighbours to spy on targets. If the intrusions are growing bolder and more commonplace, this means an increase in manpower. How big is the FSB's intrusion squad, I wonder?

Since most of their targets are invented enemies – rather than real ones – this activity must be a colossal waste of time. Putin's restoration of elements of the Soviet system is well known. But it also seems he has brought back another aspect of the inefficient communist past: the non-job. Reality is unimportant. What matters is Putin's worldview – in which diplomats, western journalists and internal critics are all dangerous spies.

Britain severs its co-operation with the FSB following Litvinenko's murder. But the Americans, by contrast, continue to do business with the agency, despite the fact that elements within it appear to be busy sabotaging the "reset" of US-Russian relations heralded by the Obama administration. The US co-operates with the FSB and Russia's interior ministry on counter-terrorism, organised crime, bio-terrorism and cyber-crime; Washington invites a Russian law enforcement officer to attend the FBI's national academy in Quantico. The FSB's elite Alpha Team, tasked with hostage rescue missions, also trains at Quantico with its US counterpart.

As part of the reset, meanwhile, Mueller brings with him an unusual gift: a small chunk of radioactive uranium. According to secret cables, in 2007 the Russian government requested that the US hand over a 10-gram sample of highly enriched uranium, seized in Georgia in 2006 during a nuclear smuggling sting operation. The FBI tells the Russians that director Mueller will bring it during his Moscow trip, and deliver it into the hands of the FSB. The US believes the uranium was stolen from a Russian facility. The Americans are hopeful that the lump of uranium will be interpreted as a goodwill gesture and encourage the Russians to greater nuclear co-operation. For its part, the FSB agrees to waive charges on Mueller's overflight and airport landing fees.

Despite this pragmatic working relationship, I discover that the White House is under no illusions about the nature of the FSB's activities. It is, in essence, a criminal organisation, offering protection to gangsters and extorting bribes from large businesses. This, at least, is what Beyrle alleges in another secret telegram sent to Washington on 12 February 2010. His subject is Yuri Luzhkov, Moscow's veteran 73-year-old mayor, whose grip on power is slipping. After 18 years in office, the Kremlin is increasingly fed up with Luzhkov – but at the same time acknowledges his ability to run the city smoothly, and to deliver votes for the Kremlin's United Russia party.

A discussion of Luzhkov is impossible without deconstructing the City Hall government he runs – a sleazy, crime-ridden, kleptocracy, in which senior, mid-level and even junior officials all demand backhanders. Beyrle describes the extent of Moscow corruption as "pervasive". Mayor Luzhkov sits "at the top of the pyramid", he says. The ambassador observes: "Luzhkov oversees a system in which it appears that almost everyone at every level is involved in some form of criminal behaviour." Luzhkov may also have dubious "connections" to organised crime, Beyrle adds, and alleges a "murky" connection between bureaucrats, gangsters and even procurators.

I read with fascination as the ambassador gives a forensic account of Russia's well-developed system of bribe-taking:

> The Moscow city government's direct links to criminality have led some to call it "dysfunctional", and to assert that the government operates more as a kleptocracy than a government. Criminal elements enjoy a *krysha* (a term from the criminal/mafia world literally meaning "roof" or protection) that runs through the police, the Federal Security Service (FSB), Ministry of Internal Affairs (MVD), and the prosecutor's office, as well as throughout the Moscow city government bureaucracy. Analysts identify a three-tiered structure in Moscow's criminal world. Luzhkov is at the top. The FSB, MVD, and militia are at the second level. Finally, ordinary criminals and corrupt inspectors are at the lowest level.

According to Beyrle, all businesses in Moscow are forced to pay protection money to law enforcement structures, in a virtual parallel tax system: "Police and MVD collect money from small businesses while the FSB collects from big businesses." An FSB *krysha* is the most sought after, Beyrle says, with the FSB even protecting the Solntsevo Brotherhood, Moscow's top organised crime gang.

The sleaze goes all the way to the top of Russian power, I read, with bribes distributed upwards under Putin's "vertical" system. Beyrle quotes one source who says that Luzhkov and many mayors and governors "pay off key insiders in the Kremlin". The source alleges that officials enter the Kremlin "with large suitcases and bodyguards". The suitcases, the source speculates, "are full of money". Another source disagrees. He points out that it is simpler to pay bribes "via a secret account in Cyprus" – a favourite offshore route with rich Russians. This system of bribery also functions in Russia's provinces.

Not surprisingly, the criminal world and the political world intersect, the cable says – with deputies generally having to buy their seats in parliament. This arrangement is straightforward: the deputies need money to get to the top, but once they are there, "their positions become quite lucrative money-making opportunities". Moscow police heads, meanwhile, also preside over "a secret war chest of money", used to solve problems for the Kremlin, such as "rigging elections" or paying off people when necessary.

This sounds similar to allegations I hear later from another source: that state corporations such as Gazprom and Rosneft secretly pay in money to a Kremlin slush-fund. The fund is kept at VTB bank. It is used to give second salaries of up to $70,000 a month to key government and law enforcement officials.

The scale of corruption is staggering. Beyrle cites Transparency International's figures for 2009. Bribery costs Russia $300 billion a year, the organisation estimates, or 18% of the country's gross domestic product.

A month before I return to London to examine the WikiLeaks cables Medvedev fires Luzhkov. It is one of the few daring acts of his presidency. In the run-up to his dismissal, Russia's state-run TV channels accuse Luzhkov and his wife – the billionaire property developer Yelena Baturina, now living in London – of massive corruption. Medvedev, however, fails to mention corruption as a reason for Luzhkov's sacking. Instead, he offers a more nebulous explanation – that the mayor has lost the president's trust.

His reticence is understandable. After all, if Luzhkov had been corrupt for the previous 18 years – 10 of them under Putin – why did the Kremlin keep silent all that time?

My stories on corruption from WikiLeaks are not going to go down well in Moscow. This much I know. Truth telling isn't popular in Russia. But I fail to anticipate the Kremlin's vengeful response.

CHAPTER 15

'Thanks to Dima and Vlad'

Russian foreign ministry press and information department,
Old Arbat, Moscow
16 November 2010

*Everyone is guilty of some misdeed, whether political
or economic back-sliding of some sort or petty corruption.*
HEDRICK SMITH, *THE RUSSIANS*

The phone call, on Tuesday 2 November 2010, is unexpected. I'm in London, immersed in reading the secret WikiLeaks cables on Russia. On the line is Nikolai, a junior apparatchik from the Russian foreign ministry's press department. "You must come to a meeting at the foreign ministry at 10am tomorrow," he says, in Russian. I explain I'm in Britain, on a temporary assignment at the *Guardian*'s offices in London and won't be back in Moscow for some time. I ask what it's about. He refuses to say. A week later Nikolai (I never learn his full name) rings again. The ministry still wants to see me.

The phone call is clearly a harbinger of something. But what? Its timing is curious: my annual accreditation with the Russian ministry of foreign affairs (MFA) is soon to expire, on 27 November 2010. I have applied – as in previous years – for a renewal. On 28 November, the *Guardian*, plus the international consortium of publications including the *New York Times*, is due to publish the first of a series of extraordinary revelations from the US

State Department cables. Does the Kremlin know what's coming? And is this an attempt to dissuade us from publishing? Intimidation, perhaps?

The *Guardian*'s intranet server on which the WikiLeaks cables are stored has several levels of security. But the Russian state has an army of accomplished hackers, for whom regular firewalls pose few difficulties. The same week I meet Julian Assange, WikiLeaks editor-in-chief. He is of the view that the Russians and the Chinese, and "possibly the Iranians", are already in possession of the State Department files.

Nevertheless, it strikes me as improbable that the ministry will take the dramatic step of expelling me from Russia. Surely this would be a public relations disaster, a throwback to the bad old days of the Soviet Union? Instead, I prepare myself for another official scolding. I fly to Moscow from London on Saturday 13 November. We agree that I will call in at the foreign ministry on Monday 15 November. The MFA mysteriously postpones by 24 hours. Its leadership is "unavailable".

The following morning, Tuesday 16 November, I report at 11am to the MFA's press and information department in the historic district of Old Arbat. The classically faced building is a short walk away from the modernist British embassy and the main Stalin-era foreign ministry building, a super-sized edifice towering like a Gothic monster over the Boulevard Ring. Pushkin lived in Arbat for three months after his marriage; the area was fashionable with Moscow's pre-revolutionary intelligentsia. These days Arbat is a tourist trap, with stalls selling Soviet memorabilia, hats made from rabbit fur, and *matrioshkas*, or Russian dolls, featuring Putin, Gorbachev and Sponge Bob.

I meet Nikolai downstairs. He escorts me in a creaking lift up to the second floor. Nikolai ushers me down a red-carpeted corridor into a small reception room. The walls are decorated with framed pencil drawings of old Moscow. There is a sofa and a couple of drab wooden chairs. The window looks down on to cobbled Denezhniy Lane. The atmosphere is institutional and distinctly Soviet. I get the impression this gloomy room isn't used much. Oleg V Churilov, the head of the press department, appears with his deputy Alexander S Kuznetsov. Churilov is a man in late middle age. These two bland government functionaries are to deliver a message.

Churilov begins in a superficially affable tone. We speak in Russian. He remarks on Moscow's unseasonably warm weather. (It's 11 C and mid-

November; by now Moscow's streets are typically covered in thick snow.) Two years earlier, Churilov's press department colleague Boris Shardakov bawled at me using "ty", the impolite Russian "you" – a deliberate snub. But Churilov is calm and mildly spoken. He uses "vy", the formal "you", and addresses me politely as "*Gospodin* Harding" – Mr Harding. My sense of foreboding grows.

What follows is a kind of surreal pantomime – a black comedy that might have flowed from the pen of Gogol, the supreme chronicler of bureaucratic absurdity. Churilov explains that "certain problems" have arisen in connection with my accreditation. Growing solemn, he produces a thin, fawn-coloured leather folder. It appears empty. Then I notice two A4 pieces of paper. Over the next 20 minutes Churilov explains that I "violated" migration rules when I travelled to Russia's Arctic on a Greenpeace press tour.

I remember the trip well. In October 2009 – two months before the Copenhagen summit – I had flown with 30 other journalists to the Yamal peninsula. Our purpose was to study climate change. We spent two nights camping with Nenets reindeer herders. The Nenets had roamed this remote area of the sub-Arctic for thousands of years. But their migratory lifestyle was coming under increasing stress from warming temperatures.

The expedition was memorable. I ate reindeer with pasta, swam naked in a Siberian lake, and interviewed an expert on woolly mammoths. I also flew by helicopter over a wilderness of ancient ice ridges laid out in a series of emerald polygons. Our final destination was the Kara Sea – one of the most extreme places on earth. I asked a Russian meteorologist here whether he'd noticed any differences in the thickness of the sea ice. What about climate change? He replied: "Climate change is a fantasy made up by bored Europeans."

My *Guardian* colleague John Vidal had been due to go on the trip. At the last minute he pulled out. I travelled instead. The *Guardian* had a valid permit for the region – in John's name. At the arrivals section of Salekhard airport I stood meekly in line. Airport officials from the Federal Border Agency – an arm of the FSB – examined our permits. Amie Ferris-Rotman, a Moscow-based reporter for Reuters, also had a piece of paper issued in the name of her male bureau chief.

An official sifted us from the others. He explained we were to be driven to the agency's headquarters: a modern single-storey building on the edge of town, fronted with smart black-painted double gates. It was late afternoon in early October; the sky was overcast and grey. Ice – a harbinger of early winter – was already starring the muddy potholes.

Inside, in a warm side-office, a second FBA official explained that our "crime" wasn't serious: we merely needed to sign a *protokol*, or form, and could rejoin the rest of the group. First, however, there was an interrogation. What was my nationality? What was I doing in Yamal? I explained I had flown to Yamal with a large group of foreigners. Our mission was to seek out clues indicating climate change, a concept with which the official was unfamiliar.

I produced my passport, ministry of foreign affairs press accreditation card, and a dog-eared copy of my registration address in Moscow – another piece of Soviet bureaucracy that has survived in modern Russia. He carefully photocopied my documents. We left and headed to Salekhard's "North Pole" hotel.

More than a year later, here is my *protokol!* I point out to Churilov that other journalists on the trip also "broke" the rules. My offence – if it was an offence – was evidently a trivial one. I also point out that the Federal Border Agency didn't bother to fine me. "I can't exclude that the budget situation of the service was healthy at the time," Churilov counters.

Churilov then produces the second piece of paper. It concerns my trip to Ingushetia in March when FSB agents detained me near the republic's main city, Nazran. I point out that the agents arrested three other journalists from the news agency Agence France-Presse earlier the same day. All of us had taken reasonable precautions and were unaware that Nazran had – days before – been declared off-limits. I had informed the local authorities ahead of my trip. In Ingushetia, the republic's president, Yunus-Bek Yevkurov, had invited me to interview him. I had even phoned the local FSB. "How am I expected to interview the president of Ingushetia without travelling to Ingushetia?" I inquire.

Churilov is unable to offer advice. And he admits that no action has been taken against other correspondents who "broke" the same rules at the same time. As with other critics of the regime, it appears that justice in my case is going to be selectively applied. At this point my patience runs out.

"Am I going to get new accreditation or not?" I ask.

The answer, expressed in painful bureaucratese, is no.

"As a foreign citizen you have twice infringed administrative legislation. You have fallen onto the list of those foreigners whose visas are not to be prolonged. This decision has been taken."

It has taken Churilov 23 minutes to get to the point – that the foreign ministry is expelling me from Russia. Even then he can only muster the courage to break the news using the anonymous passive voice.

Churilov, it seems, is reluctant to identify the real body that has given the order to kick me out – the FSB. I ask him directly: which agency has decided I now have to quit Russia? And does the presidential administration – apparently keen to attract foreign investors and modernise Russia's economy – know of this decision?

He replies with another impressive piece of circumlocution: "This decision is taken by the bodies in charge of applying the relevant legislation. You can examine our statutes to see which organs are competent for implementing the laws on entering and leaving the country."

"So it's the FSB then?"

"Yes," he finally confirms.

The foreign ministry, I discover, would like the *Guardian* to make a "virtuous substitution" – in other words to replace me with another, presumably less critical, correspondent sent from London. I think of Muggeridge: "It is even not unusual for agents of the Soviet Union to bring pressure to bear in editorial offices when the correspondent in Moscow is not to its satisfaction."

"We are prepared on a friendly basis – *po chelovecheski*– to allow you to stay in Russia until the end of the year," Churilov says.

"The point is, as you know, that I have two children who are at the British school here in Moscow. It's the middle of the school year. My visa finishes on 27 November. Are you saying we don't have to leave on the 27th?"

"We are talking about a reasonable time," Churilov replies.

"What about until next summer?"

"I'm afraid not."

Somewhere in the background, in the grey streets outside, a car alarm goes off.

The conversation is an unhappy one. Two decades after the cold war was supposed to have ended I am being slung out of Russia for having the wrong paperwork. In fact, my expulsion follows the same Soviet-style legalism used against other regime critics. The Russian government routinely takes similar legalistic measures to harass and close down foreign NGOs, debar opposition candidates from registering for and competing in local and national elections, and to punish businesses. All have committed fictitious "offences".

This tactic has been around for a long time. In the 1970s Hedrick Smith pointed out that nobody could abide by the Soviet Union's myriad laws and regulations. The system is deliberately designed so that the authorities permanently have the upper hand, leaving Russian citizens confused, disempowered, and on the back foot. Smith wrote:

> It is impossible, as Russians often commented to me, for them to live faultless lives in a society with as many rules as the Soviet system imposes. Everyone is guilty of some misdeed, whether political or economic back-sliding of some sort or petty corruption. The authorities use this sense of guilt and vulnerability, my friends said, to keep ordinary people on the defensive.

I tell Churilov: "I'd like to say on record I was working perfectly legitimately. I don't believe these infringements are in any way serious. We both know this isn't the real reason [for my expulsion]. It is just a pretext to get rid of me. I don't understand why you are doing this. But I think it's a mistake."

Churilov repeats that "facts are facts" and that I am guilty of "violations".

"I regret the decision. I will now contact the British embassy and the British government and we will make representations at a political level.

What I find strange is that at a time when bilateral relations between Britain and Russia are improving you take this negative step."

Almost as an after-thought, I add: "You do realise there is going to be a big scandal?"

Churilov is unmoved by this. I get the impression that whoever has decided to kick me out of Russia is more senior than he is. How senior, I wonder. And for every moderniser inside the Kremlin who cares about Russia's international reputation, there is a hardliner who enjoys – even relishes – confrontation with the west, even on the petty level of a foreign correspondent. I understand that Churilov's job is to pass me the bad news. I don't find him in any way evil. Like other members of Putin's vast bureau-cratic system, in which unquestioning loyalty is the key to advancement and a good career, his deficiencies are human ones: weakness, complacency, self-deception, and – above all – cowardice.

As I get up to leave Churilov strikes a conciliatory note: "I understand for a journalist this isn't pleasant. We are sorry. After some delay there is no reason why you can't apply for a visa again."

"Do you have anything else to say?" I ask. Churilov doesn't respond.

"Thank you." I shake his hand. I walk out, leaving the two pieces of paper – evidence of my grave crimes against the Russian state – lying on the glass table.

I am not the first reporter to suffer this fate. In fact, in the days of the Soviet Union it happened all too frequently. The Soviets kicked out Whitman Bassow – author of *The Moscow Correspondents* – in 1962 for violating unspecified regulations. Half a century earlier his expulsion foreshadowed my own. In his case another unsmiling press department official, Alexei V Popov, accused him of "violating the standards of behaviour of foreign correspondents of the USSR" and writing "crudely slanderous dispatches about the Soviet Union, which have evoked the righteous indignation of Soviet opinion".

Popov informed Bassow he had to leave Russia within seven days. Bassow also protested. There was no protocol handshake. His career as *Newsweek*'s bureau chief was abruptly over. His expulsion took a few minutes; mine drags on for almost an hour. Bassow didn't make it back to Moscow until 1984. On his return he found his old office as "seedy and run down" as when he left.

The Kremlin's justifications for expulsion vary. But the classic Soviet excuses include currency speculation, espionage, and working against the interests of the state. In 1923 watchful agents of the Cheka – the granddaddy of today's FSB – slashed open a leather diplomatic bag and discovered dispatches written by four US correspondents. What horror! The correspondents were caught red-handed circumventing the Bolsheviks' strict rules on censorship. All four were expelled. They were the first of many, Bassow noted, to be thrown out by Red Moscow over the next six decades.

In 1956, the Associated Press correspondent Roy Essoyan was thrown out. His crime? "Violating the rules regulating the activities of foreign correspondents." In the 1960s and 1970s the pretexts changed to dissidents and the demands of Soviet Jews seeking to leave for Israel. But the same tactics were applied, with more reporters told to leave. In 1969 it was the turn of Raymond Anderson of the *New York Times* and Anatole Shub of the *Washington Post* ("slanderous articles"). Three more expulsions followed over the next year-and-a-half.

The expulsions took place when relations with the west were in fairly good shape. In 1977 George Krimsky, an energetic AP reporter who covered the dissident beat and was friendly with the dissident Andrei Sakharov, got the boot. (He was accused, among other things, of espionage; Jimmy Carter's White House evicted the TASS correspondent from Washington in protest.) Krimsky's expulsion was a warning to other correspondents to tone down their coverage of the Sakharov story. By now, expulsion had become a sort of Moscow ritual: at the airport expelled correspondents would make farewells to fellow reporters, as well as to friends, diplomats and a few brave Soviets, Bassow recorded. Their departures took place under the watchful eye of the KGB – men in fur hats, their faces hidden by scarves.

The Kremlin continued to use expulsion as a weapon well into the post-Brezhnev 1980s. In 1986, under Gorbachev, KGB agents swooped on Nicholas Daniloff, a correspondent for the *US News & World Report*. They dragged him off to Lefortovo prison. Daniloff spent 13 days in a cell before

President Ronald Reagan and General Secretary Gorbachev struck a deal: Daniloff was freed in exchange for a Soviet UN employee accused by the US of spying. He then left the country. British journalists got similar treatment. In 1989, Angus Roxburgh, then of the *Sunday Times*, was expelled when the Thatcher government kicked out Russian diplomats from London. He was accused of "unacceptable activities" – in other words, spying. Happily, Roxburgh returned to Moscow months later, after the Soviet Union imploded.

Throughout the Soviet era, there was an ideological assumption that all western journalists were spies. In part this appeared to be the product of mirror thinking – given that many Soviet journalists who worked in the west, or were attached to trade delegations, did have links with Soviet intelligence.

The communist system may have collapsed. But the spy-mania that characterised the Soviet era has endured. Putin has expressed his admiration for spy thrillers including *Seventeen Moments of Spring*, a book and popular 1970s mini-series featuring the exploits of Max Otto von Stirlitz. Stirlitz is a Soviet spy working in the heart of the Nazi foreign ministry.

Today's successors to the KGB seem equally convinced that western journalists are all undercover operatives working for British or American intelligence. As agents of influence whose real task is to denigrate Russia, correspondents deserve whatever the FSB chooses to throw at them. They are fair game. Or so the thinking goes.

To a western eye, the *siloviki*'s outdated cold war worldview seems positively barmy. But it is, at least, historically consistent – the Kremlin has mistrusted foreign journalists ever since Britain and other allies supported the White Armies during the Russian civil war. Writing about the 1970s, a period of US-Soviet détente, Bassow observed: "Foreign journalists were still regarded as hostile, nosy probers seeking only to portray the negative aspects of the USSR … The traditional suspicion that correspondents were spies and therefore fit subjects for surveillance, provocations and dirty tricks remained unchanged, especially within the KGB."

A decade later, during his 1984 Moscow trip, Bassow was surprised to discover that the KGB was still employing the same crude methods he experienced as a journalist in early post-Stalin Moscow. Not all of them were unpleasant. In 1958, on an overnight train to Leningrad, Bassow found himself sharing a coupe with an attractive, well-endowed blonde. Her name was Karolina. At about 11pm Karolina wriggled out of her clothes and wrapped herself in a diaphanous robe. Bassow – with a pleasing eye for detail – noted the robe is "of foreign origin".

"I like you," she told him, breathlessly. "You are an intelligent, handsome man. I have always wanted to make love to an American. I hope you will not deny me the opportunity." Bassow rebuffed Karolina's advances and pointed out he was married with a child. When she asked why he didn't want the opportunity to find out "what a Russian women is like" he offered: "I already know what they're like. I've read *Anna Karenina* and *War and Peace*."

But the KGB's honey-traps – followed by blackmail attempts for those who succumbed – were the glamorous end of the challenges faced by Moscow correspondents. Other forms of harassment included physical surveillance, bugging, and even beatings. "'Continuity and change', the hallmarks of Russian and Soviet history, were clearly evident in the way the Kremlin had dealt with foreign correspondents over the previous two decades," Bassow wrote of the late Soviet period. "Through crude intimidation and threats, the Soviets were still attempting to control reporters and reporting. KGB agents continued to slash tires when correspondents sought out the few dissidents in Moscow." He added: "Apartments of several reporters were burglarised to signal that no place was off-limits to the KGB."

These are methods with which I am familiar.

I am stunned. But my expulsion is not, I reflect, a surprise. It's something I had always accepted as a real if far-fetched possibility. Western correspondents in Moscow meet at least once a month in a series of informal gatherings known as the "hack pack". After more than a decade as a *Guardian* foreign correspondent I realise that the more ugly the regime, the greater the sense of solidarity between its beleaguered diplomats and journalists. (The wildest parties I ever encountered were in Kabul under the Taliban, where drinking is outlawed. The UN club served only spirits since the beer had all been drunk.)

These meetings are a useful opportunity to blow off steam. They attract an eclectic crowd of scruffy reporters and slim Russian blondes working for the state news agency RIA Novosti. Six months earlier a young woman doing an internship at the MFA turns up at hack pack drinks. The venue on this occasion is an upmarket cafe selling croissants and cakes. Normally, the drinks take place in smoke-filled subterranean Moscow bars, where pints of mediocre yellow lager cost 300 roubles, or £6. Asked which journalist the ministry hates most, the intern unwittingly replies: "There's a guy called Luke Harding. They really hate him."

I am not the only journalist in Moscow to write on sensitive issues such as corruption. There are many other correspondents – both western and Russian – who report with integrity and courage as Russia moves from the chaos but relative freedoms of the Yeltsin years to the "managed democracy" of the vertical Putin epoch. The taboos are well known: the wealth of Putin and his team, the activities of the security services, and human rights abuses by federal and local troops in the north Caucasus. Others also break these unwritten rules.

But I am sometimes taken aback by the timidity and accommodationist tendencies of some of my western colleagues. The BBC Moscow bureau in particular is extremely reluctant to report on stories that might offend the Kremlin. Despite the efforts of some of its braver reporters the corporation has so far entirely slumbered through what the economist Anders Aslund describes as the "greatest corruption story in human history".

Reuters and other news agencies – with correspondents in the Kremlin press pool – also strike me as too willing to take the pronouncements of Kremlin spin doctors at face value. They are worried, understandably perhaps, about the future of their bureaus. Many correspondents in Moscow have Russian wives or girlfriends, and Russian in-laws – a fact that makes them more susceptible to self-censorship. Are the BBC and some other Moscow-based news organisations guilty of self-censorship? Probably. Do they lack balls? Absolutely.

I had broken all these informal Kremlin "rules" on what journalists should and shouldn't report from Moscow. And then there was WikiLeaks and the US State Department's view of Russia as a deeply unappealing kleptocracy. These, then, were my crimes. I had become an irritant and someone – who? – had decided to get rid of me.

My four years in Russia end, then, in dramatic fashion: with a textbook Soviet-style expulsion. It appears I am the first western staff correspondent to suffer this fate since the end of the cold war. I walk out into the street. I sit down in the nearby McCafé. I phone Phoebe. I tell her we are being kicked out. Phoebe – who is en route to a Russian literary group (this week's book is *Anna Karenina*) – appears in the cafe a few minutes later. She is shocked, disbelieving.

I call James Barbour, the press attache at the British embassy in Moscow. James arrives soon afterwards. He also seems surprised by the news. The FSB's campaign of harassment against me is known inside the embassy, and to the British Foreign Office in London. But this is an unexpected development. What does it mean?

Two hours later, we take the green line metro to Voikovskaya and then travel by trolley-bus to the British school in Moscow. We tell Ruskin that we are leaving Russia for England. He reacts coolly. I explain this means that he will no longer be appearing as a junior crow in Miss Marina's Christmas production of *The Snow Queen*. We walk over to the school's senior building, where Tilly is attending an after-school writers' club. When she emerges she immediately senses something is up: both her parents are there to meet her, an untypical event. We sit in the Spanish classroom. I tell her we are leaving Moscow. I have to assure her this isn't a joke. After a decade of travelling the world – Tilly has lived in India, Germany and Russia – she is finally going to the UK. She is stunned. "Wow," she says.

Over the next few days we are caught uncomfortably between two different worlds: the personal and the public. The British ambassador in Moscow, Anne Pringle, makes diplomatic representations to her MFA counterparts. We, meanwhile, pack up to go. At our Moscow *dacha* we begin clearing up – throwing away old newspapers, clothes and children's toys – the debris of four years of life in Russia. In London, the *Guardian*'s editor-in-chief Alan Rusbridger writes to the British foreign secretary, William Hague.

The *Guardian* also drafts a press release. In it, Rusbridger says: "We are extremely disturbed that the Russian authorities have, in effect, expelled our Moscow correspondent, Luke Harding. He has, over the years, faced harassment over his reporting from Russia and the surrounding region but it is very worrying that the government should now kick out reporters of whom they disapprove. Russia's treatment of journalists – both domestic and foreign – is a cause of great concern."

I add: "My expulsion has nothing to do with these spurious explanations. It is punishment for reporting what the Kremlin considers off-limits." We agree to publish an article about my expulsion once we're on a plane back to Heathrow, beyond the reach of the FSB.

We book tickets to leave Moscow on Wednesday 24 November. The packers arrive. Within hours they have boxed up and bubble-wrapped most of our cottage's contents: books, paintings, a framed map of early Moscow, and a wall-clock featuring Putin and Medvedev hung, as a humorous greeting for my FSB visitors, next to our front door. We abandon the television, our double bed shipped from India, and a couple of mattresses. The children's rooms are stripped bare.

Twenty-four hours before our departure my phone rings. It is Nikolai – the junior press department diplomat.

"Mr Harding, do you have children?' he asks.

"You know I do," I reply sourly.

He continues: "I have good news for you. We are willing to give you a visa for six months so your children can finish school."

"What happens after that?"

There is a pause. "After that you have to leave Russia."

It appears I am to be temporarily un-expelled, before being re-expelled later.

In a state run by a secretive and paranoid oligarchy, it is usually impossible to find out the real reasons behind any administrative decision. Having decided on my expulsion, the Russian state appears to have reversed its decision – or at least postponed it. The reasons are unfathomable. This could be a pragmatic victory for the Kremlin's liberals. It's also possible that British diplomacy has done the trick. (At a time of improving relations between Moscow and London, the MFA can present its "concession" as a goodwill gesture to Britain's new coalition government.) More probable is that someone has woken up to the looming PR disaster of my expulsion.

It's only later, I reflect, that the climbdown may always have been the plan. The FSB's decision has turned our life as a family upside down. Previous measures against me have proved ineffective. I come to suspect this was always the agency's cynical intention. Phoebe is on her way to pick up the children from school when I tell her of Nikolai's phone call. Tilly has just said a final goodbye to her friends. Her English teacher, Mrs Semyanik, has given her a copy of *The Little Prince*; she is clutching her school-leaving certificate. Phoebe breaks the news that we are staying in Moscow after all.

Tilly goes beserk. She runs off across the playground. "You've fucking ruined my life," she shouts. "I'm not fucking going back to my old school!" Miss Smith – Ruskin's teacher, a wise and warm British woman in her early 60s – is not at all scandalised by Tilly's behaviour. "She's got a point," Miss Smith says.

At home, Tilly barricades herself in her bedroom. She is 13 years old. She writes:

On our wall, in the entrance room there is a boring plastic clock on which are the faces of Vladimir Putin and Dimitry Medvedev. My dad always says it's an ironic joke that we have this clock, along with the other bits and pieces of political satire scattered around our house.

When your father is the Russian foreign correspondent for the *Guardian*, there is certainly no shortage of political humour. I remember one time when my dad asked me to put a sign saying Duck House on our front gate, as a joke about the crooked expenses.

But when we joke about Russia's government, we don't expect anything to come of it. For some reason we consider ourselves untouchable. We laugh about "Dima and Vlad" but we don't expect them to do anything about us, short of glaring at my dad a couple of times and making some quiet threats.

So it came as a complete and utter shock, when one unassuming Tuesday, just after I'd finished writers' club, that my mum and dad both appeared at my school and announced rather sheepishly that we were going to be leaving Moscow and moving to England.

It was an alien concept to my mind. Leave Moscow? Leave? Leave Moscow with its churches and cathedrals and operas and towering metro stations? Leave Moscow with its traffic jams and pollution and icy winter and terrible food? Leave my friends, my house, my school, for something completely mysterious and unknown?

When were we leaving, I asked, when were we going? My parents replied that we would be leaving in two weeks. Two weeks? Wow, two weeks. That wasn't very long. Why, I asked carefully, why did we have to leave? My dad answered with a nervous smile, trying to assure me that it was not his fault, that the Russian Foreign Office was refusing to renew his visa on account of him violating some Russian laws. He claimed this was just an excuse to get him out of the country and stop him reporting on corruption and rigged elections and wars. I had no trouble believing that.

In complete shock, and not at all sure this wasn't some sort of elaborate practical joke, I left the school, zombie-like. We informed my brother of the news who simply said, "That's cool." And resumed blowing up aliens on his computer.

The next few days were a haze of tears, disbelief and Facebook messages as I hurried to tell my friends the news. As I watched my parents frantically scanning the web for any schools that might accept me and my brother at such short notice, trying to get affairs in order, desperately looking for places we could stay. My dad, while not outright saying it was secret, had impressed on both me and Ruskin the need to keep our sudden departure quiet.

"Just wait a little time to tell your friends, OK?" He said to me. I couldn't not tell my friends. How could I leave without saying goodbye? It was impossible, so I ignored him.

My dad was spending large amounts of his time in his room with my computer, typing up stories, and when he wasn't he was either angry with us for revealing too much to friends or sad when he realised that he had, once again, wrecked all our lives. It took a couple of days for my brother to finally crack and shed a few tears over leaving, and my mum moped around depressed. Leaving Moscow would mean losing her job with the *Moscow News*, in which she wrote [about] tours and walks around Moscow's few idyllic green areas. It was, she said, what everyone dreamed of. Being paid to do what you love doing.

Two days in and I finally got over the shock. The worst part was not really being able to tell anyone. Two days in, under two weeks to go and my mum had still not told her employers she would be leaving. She has a large mailing list who she mails every week and she couldn't tell any of them, aside from a few close friends. My dad told me not to tell my close friend Danya, quite yet, as her dad was a journalist and might write something. I ignored him and told her anyway, but asking if she could keep it a bit of a secret for now. I couldn't tell her why we were leaving either, and it felt to me ridiculous. But, despite the outrageousness of the situation, we were all coming round to the idea. "We think," they said "We'll live in London, but we're not quite sure. If we do, you'll like London. It's got loads of Thai restaurants and things. There's a lot to like." I didn't think much of London. I'd been on the Tube and compared to the forgotten splendour of the Moscow metro (however, somehow, the trains always seem to come on time) it seemed, well, rubbish. But London was the city I was born in and I felt that going there couldn't be a bad thing.

Those two weeks until we left seemed to stretch ahead. All that waiting. "We're going to have a pretty huge mortgage when we first buy a house, we're going to have to be a bit frugal. But don't worry, you'll be alright," they said "Come take a look at this school ... look, it's international. You should fit right in."

It was on that same Thursday, two days after I heard the fateful news, that my dad pronounced (with another one of those guilty grins) that we would in fact be leaving, not in two weeks, but next Wednesday. In five days. Seven days since we heard we would be leaving. As one of my best friends, Nicole, said, "We've done so much together. All that, and then, seven days? Oh my gawd, next Wednesday, that's so soon." But the news also came with a sort of pleasure. No more agonising, drawn out wait. Just a couple more days and we'll be off. But I think it wasn't until the packers arrived that I really believed we were going. I came home from school and realised that my room had gone. All my furniture had gone. Vanished. All the books that had surrounded and comforted me for so long. Vanished. My desk, my clothes, my old school books. Gone. It was a shock to say the least, and I spent a couple of minutes wrapped in my blanket rolling about, going, "My room is emptyyyyyyyyyyyyyyyyyyyyyyyyyyyy!" But then I was looking forward to leaving. Looking forward to a new start and a new home. "You're going to be home-schooled for about a month when we get there," they said "Until we have a chance to find a school. It'll be fun, Gran can teach you bird watching ..."

So the final day of school dragged by, with a leaver's certificate and cake and hugs from my friends, it was with a sad smile on my lips that I walked away from my school for four years for what I thought would be the last time. I reached the gates of my brother's school, only to be met by my mother wearing smart clothes with that all too well known guilty expression on her face. She stopped in front of me and said ... "We might not be leaving after all ..." The taxi home was 20 minutes of screams and confusion as I tried to figure out what was going on after all. It seemed that my dad had gone to see the Russian Foreign Office one last time, telling them that what they were doing was ridiculous and for some reason they obliged. They told us that they would extend my dad's visa until May, so we could finish the academic year (not realising that for us the academic year ended in July) and my dad's bosses at the *Guardian* advised us to take the opportunity. We would be taking a two-week trip to England to talk about it, visit schools and figure things out.

By the time we got home the movers were already unpacking all our stuff, without a word. When I got over the initial horror and shock I reluctantly accepted the plan, seeing that it would be a better solution in the long term, leaving us much more preparation time for leaving. But the idea of going back to my school after having a leaver's party, saying goodbye to everyone, well the idea was repellent, not to mention embarrassing. My parents decided we could have one day off school to deal with the shock before returning. This did not sound good. In the one day we stayed home, the packers unpacked the rest of our stuff, leaving it dumped everywhere in the wrong places. After finally shifting my shelves back to their positions, I stared in despair at the massive piles of books everywhere, stuff left all over the place, and all the sorting out I would have to do to get through it all. As I told my mum: "This would drastically exceed my limits for 'Doing Stuff'."

As I sat in my room, staring at the crumpled and messed up things all around, I realised exactly what was going on. All that time my dad had spent holed up in his room, he was writing a story about how we were being forced to leave so suddenly. He was going to publish the whole thing, tell the world about it, but the Russian government couldn't take that. They couldn't reveal that they had kicked out a family simply because they didn't like what my father wrote. So they extended his visa. They get kicked out in May, big deal. It doesn't matter. They're clever and they're crafty, but they just shattered my life twice in a row. "Stop playing mind games Mr Medvedev," I whisper. "Stop wrecking our lives Mr Putin," I say. We meet up to discuss what we're going to do and we laugh together, but we're laughing in desperation. Stop messing with our minds, I want to say.

And now that clock on the wall is no longer just a harmless piece of political satire. Now, whenever we enter the house that clock receives glares of frustration and anger. Now that clock is the source of all our problems.

So our lives have been wrecked twice in a row. And it's all thanks to Dima and Vlad.

I read Tilly's article and weep.

CHAPTER 16

Enemy of the State

Passport control, Domodedovo international airport, Moscow
5 February 2011

*Under Putin, the FSB returned to KGB
methods to deal with foreign journalists.*

ANDREI SOLDATOV AND IRINA BOROGAN, AGENTURA.RU

The flight back from London to Moscow is unremarkable. Phoebe, Tilly and Ruskin return to Russia after the first week in January, so the children can resume school; I stay behind in Britain to finish a book about WikiLeaks. Russia's foreign ministry grants me a six-month visa until 31 May 2011. After that I have to leave the country. The reasons for the ministry's climbdown are mysterious, as is practically everything in Putin's murky bureaucratic system. But there's an agreement of sorts, a truce almost: I'll remain in Moscow until early summer, before quietly packing up and leaving Russia with my family – presumably to the ministry's enormous relief.

In the meantime, the *Guardian* publishes hundreds of stories based on the US State Department's secret cables. For the Kremlin they are not happy reading. In early December 2010 Putin reacts badly on CNN to suggestions by a US diplomat that he plays Batman to Medvedev's Robin. The comparison is "unethical", evidence of US "arrogance", and an attempt to drive a wedge between him and the president, he tells CNN's Larry King. Medvedev, meanwhile, dismisses the leaks as "not worthy of comment".

After a week of torrid revelations that see Russia depicted as a "mafia state", the Russian government changes its mind. It concludes that the biggest loser from WikiLeaks is an embarrassed United States, which is suffering an enormous loss of face before its global allies and partners. In the zero-sum world of Russian diplomacy what's bad for Washington is good for Moscow. Moreover, the Obama administration's angry condemnation of WikiLeaks is further evidence – from Russia's perspective – of US hypocrisy and double standards on the issue of free speech.

When Medvedev travels to Brussels in December, one member of his entourage comes up with an idea to compound the US's loss of face. He mischievously suggests that Julian Assange – whom the Pentagon is trying to nail for treason – could be nominated for the Nobel Peace prize. This is another slap in the face for, as the Russians see it, the two-faced Americans. Russia Today later gives Assange his own TV show.

My byline is on the *Guardian*'s WikiLeaks stories about Russia. They begin on 2 December 2010 under the striking headline "Inside Putin's 'mafia state'". Vladimir Putin stares out from the front page, every inch the former KGB spy, and wearing a pair of sinister-looking mirrored silver sunglasses. Other international publications including the *New York Times* report the same material, albeit more diffidently. (The *Times* outsources its Russia reporting to a former Moscow bureau chief now based in New York. It chooses the headline "In cables, US takes dim view of Russia".)

We briefly consider taking my name off the Russia stories, but then conclude that the Russians would regardless assume I'd authored them. Additionally, it's clear to any reasonable reader that the stories are based on the frank private assessments of senior US diplomats serving in Moscow. They aren't my views as such, though I broadly agree with them and their generally pessimistic sweep. Surely Russian officials will take the same grown-up view?

And yet, as British Midland flight 891 makes its approach to Moscow's Domodedovo international airport, I feel an unmistakeable sinking inside my stomach. After four years in Moscow, I'm under no illusions about Russia's capacity for nasty surprises. I had joked with colleagues that there is a "50% chance" officials at the airport will send me back. This is probably an overestimate, I reflect.

But Russia's track record in this respect isn't good: since 2000 around 40 journalists and human rights activists have been denied entry visas as a result of their professional activities. Russia runs not one but two international blacklists. One is with Belarus (if you are banned from one country you are automatically debarred from the other). The other is the Joint System. Operational since 2004, it includes six countries: Russia, Belarus, Armenia, Kazakhstan, Kyrgyzstan and Tajikistan. Once on the list, it is almost impossible to get off it.

For even the coolest of western correspondents, then, arriving back in Russia from a trip abroad is a moment of minor anxiety. Waiting in the queue at passport control, you wonder what your fate will be. Passport stamp and green light? Or something else? I banish these thoughts. I think instead of my wife and children. By this point we haven't seen each other for almost four weeks. This is the maximum period beyond which, as I know from long reporting stints in Afghanistan and Iraq, the family unit begins slowly to fall apart.

Ahead of me, Russian passengers clutch Harrods shopping bags and large bottles of duty-free cognac. We get off the plane. We take a bus to the grey terminal building, its letters illuminated in art deco capitals. I follow the herd up to passport control, on the first floor: a row of booths, one of them for diplomats, in a sterile hall. I get in line. There isn't much of a queue. I hand over my battered British passport. (The lion on the front and the words *Dieu et Mon Droit* have disappeared; the gold unicorn is fading, though his horn remains.)

I read the name-badge of the Federal Border Agency official who checks my documents. She's called Liliya. Liliya is young – 25ish – and blonde; her attractive features offset her official olive uniform. Liliya taps in my details. She looks surprised. She calls over her boss. Both of them scrutinise my computer entry. Something strange happens: they exchange glances, and then break into an embarrassed giggle. It's as if they've been let in on a secret. (I've observed this on previous occasions, and wonder if something puerile, something mockingly unpleasant, is written on the agency's system next to my name. What? The bearer of this passport has a small cock?) Liliya tells me to stand to one side. The supervisor takes my passport. He vanishes into a side-room.

This doesn't appear too encouraging. While I'm waiting my mobile rings; it's Ruskin. "When are you coming home, Daddy?" he asks. I tell him – despite the fact my situation has taken an uncomfortable turn – that I'll see him soon. I send Phoebe a text. It warns: "They've taken my passport away. This doesn't look good." I SMS James Barbour, from the British embassy in Moscow. I ask whether he is around (it's Saturday afternoon) and tell him of my apparent problem at immigration. James pings a jocular text back. It reads: "Hehe – they're probably just messing with you! Keep in touch."

After a few minutes a second official – in his early 20s, scarcely out of school, with white pasty skin, and the same olive uniform as the sweet-faced Liliya – emerges from the side-room. I notice his name badge. He's called Nikolai. Nikolai is holding my passport.

Before I can ask what's going on, Nikolai launches into a speech, one he's clearly delivered before. The speech is brief: "In accordance with paragraph 27 of Russian federal law, you are refused entry to the Russian Federation," he says. Why, I ask. "For you, Russia is closed," he answers. It's clear he has no idea whatsoever why I've been placed on a list of undesirables. But I am now, officially, an enemy of the state. Nikolai explains I'm going to be put on a plane and sent back to London. He seems mystified by the decision to deport me and asks if I've done anything wrong. I can't think of an answer – unless writing articles sometimes critical of government is the reason – so I reply no.

As he leads me away, I try and console myself with the idea that things could be much worse. Compared to the fate suffered by some domestic critics of the Putin regime (assassinated, poisoned, beaten with baseball bats, left for dead) this is VIP treatment. It would even be perversely flattering, were it not for my family stranded in Moscow. I tell Phoebe: "I'm being deported." She texts back: "NO." I assure her that this isn't a stupid joke. I call my *Guardian* editor.

Nikolai – still holding my passport – leads the way against the flow of incoming passengers; we take the lift to the ground floor. I ask whether I can go to the loo – in order to make more telephone calls and perhaps get the decision stayed; he refuses. Instead, Nikolai leads me directly to a door with a sign in Russian and English marked "deportation zone". He accompanies me inside. He exits. He locks the door behind him.

The cell is a small, unremarkable L-shaped room; there are grey metal benches and a separate shower room and a toilet. It's more of a tucked away annexe to the airport building than a dungeon. Several other people are already inside: a small group of lost souls who, like me, are patiently waiting for their deportation. Through a picture window I can see slow-moving jets parked up against the terminal complex; mini-buses drive along service roads; there is the familiar machine rumble of ordinary life.

I introduce myself to my cellmates. One is Ruslan Minsafin, a Russian national who is being sent back to Italy after a problem with his passport. He's been here for 24 hours. There are four youths from Tajikistan and another from Kyrgyzstan. The Tajiks hail from Khujand, Tajikistan's second largest northern city; they are playing a game of *Durak*, or "fool", sitting cross-legged over heaps of cards. We chat about the new road Chinese labourers have constructed between Khujand and Dushanbe, Tajikistan's Soviet-built capital.

Next to the window is a Congolese woman. She's been here for a week already. The woman is reclining full-length on the bench, holding her mobile. She speaks neither English nor Russian; she is evidently bored, perhaps indifferent, and sunk into her own universe of misery. Outside it's dusk. I feel strangely calm. The sky is turning a soft, darkening purple; the clouds have a luminous tinge.

Ruslan and the Central Asians express amazement at my presence – I am, after all, a prosperous European, someone who has generally prospered in life's lottery. What am I doing here? I explain that I'm a journalist, that this probably has something to do with what's happened, but that the full reasons for my deportation are an enigma – at least to me. Ruslan is sympathetic. "Russia isn't Europe. You shouldn't be surprised that they don't observe human rights here," he says by way of consolation. "It's unjust that Moscow should suck up all the wealth," he adds, expressing disgruntlement at Russia's gross regional inequities.

According to Ruslan, conditions in custody aren't too bad: warders bring black tea with sugar (but without lemon), as well as food. There is no coffee. As we chat, in our narrow companionable space, it dawns on me this is probably my last ever interview in Russia. I've roamed across the Russian Federation, the world's largest country by geographical area – traversing all

11 time zones. I've gone from Kamchatka on the Pacific, with its smouldering volcanoes, lousy weather and salmon poachers, to the Altai Mountains of Siberia, and to Kaliningrad, with its university statue of Immanuel Kant wearing a faintly absurd tri-corn hat. But now my world is shrunk. The last destination in my Moscow reporting assignment is a five-by-10-metre cell.

After about 20 minutes Nikolai opens the door again. He brings in my luggage, a holdall and a small blue case. After a similar interval he reappears. He says it's time to go. In total, I've spent less than 45 minutes locked up – hardly an ordeal worthy of gulag literature. Outside, a middle-aged woman official with short-cut curly hair, greying at the edges, fetches me a luggage trolley; she parks it neatly and considerately outside the cell. It's a small gesture of kindness.

I shake hands with Ruslan. He congratulates me on my good fortune. I bid farewell to my new Tajik comrades, still stoically playing cards, feeling vaguely guilty that they are left behind. I think of the dungeon scene in *Life of Brian*, when Brian's hairy bearded cellmate, hanging in chains from the wall, taunts him with the words: "You lucky, lucky bastard."

Back in London, the wheels of diplomacy are beginning to turn. And in Moscow, my friend and colleague Clifford Levy, the *New York Times*'s bureau chief, is frantically phone-bashing his Kremlin contacts. But these efforts are not enough, it seems, to prevent the Federal Border Agency – an arm of the FSB – from fulfilling their patriotic order to bundle me out of Russia as quickly as possible.

Nikolai takes me through my own security control point, back to departures and gate No 1. I realise I'm being sent back on the same British Midland flight I've just arrived on. At the front of the plane I explain my situation to the stewardess. She is amazed: she can't think of a similar case. One of the crew signs a form undertaking to fly me back to Heathrow. Once the paperwork is complete, Nikolai hands my passport to the stewardess. He disappears.

I discover he has stamped my Russian visa with a large, if badly smudged, blue rectangle. On it is the word "annulled" and the date: 05/02/11.

There's one final gift from the Russian state. It's another piece of official-looking paper. I read: "Harding, Luke Daniel, a citizen of the United Kingdom, arriving on 05.02.11 at Domodedovo from London-Great Britain on flight 891 does not have the right to enter into Russia in accordance with paragraph 27 of regulations specifying proper entry and departure from the Russian Federation."

Just before the door shuts and we begin to taxi away my mobile phone rings. It's Alan Rusbridger, the *Guardian*'s editor-in-chief. Rusbridger had suggested at the time of our WikiLeaks publications that it might be wiser for me to remain in Britain. In hindsight, this was perhaps good advice. Rusbridger is, as ever, laconic and wry.

"They really don't like you, do they?" he says.

"No, Alan," I reply. "They really don't."

I'm in no doubt that the FSB, with what the US ambassador dubs its "usual light touch and unique sense of timing", has given the order to return me – the object of four years of state harassment – back to England. But they might have picked a better moment. Russia's foreign minister is due in a few days to visit London on the first official trip for nearly five years. It's part of an attempt by Britain's Conservative-led government to rebuild relations with Moscow.

Intentionally – or not – the decision to deport me is about to catapult the agency's clandestine war against its foreign "enemies" into a small international scandal.

On the flight back, I wonder who exactly signed my deportation papers. The FSB's director, Alexander Bortnikov? The head of the department that spies on foreign journalists, Vasily Dvornikov? (His department, I learn just days before I fly out, goes under the innocuous title of "assistance programming". It runs white programmes – the public stuff – and black programmes – the secret stuff.) Or someone else? There are many permutations. It's possible that a billionaire individual unhappy with something I'd written about his business affairs may simply have paid the FSB to chuck me out.

As the WikiLeaks cables make clear, the *siloviki* – the power guys – have been the chief opponents of the post-Obama "reset" between Moscow and

Washington. They are equally resistant to any similar thaw between the Kremlin and London. The FSB is still fuming, three years on, at the British government's decision to sever co-operation with the agency in the wake of the Litvinenko murder – an action the FSB regards as insulting.

Adding my name to a deportation list must have struck somebody as a tactical masterstroke. It's a way for the FSB to express its continuing contempt for Britain, to remove one of its more irritating house-guests, and to send an unambiguous message to other foreign journalists: obey the rules or suffer the same fate. But in PR terms, the move turns out to be a disastrous own goal.

On the flight back the crew find me an empty row at the back of the plane. The stewardesses are kind; they bring me tea, they offer reassurance. I try not to think about the scene in Moscow where – I discover later – Tilly is tearful, and my son Ruskin sobs himself to sleep. Phoebe drowns her sorrows with friends and vodka. The day has been, by any standards, surreal.

After five hours, I land in London. Sometime after midnight I check into the Premier Inn hotel near King's Cross, from where I had set off 18 hours previously. I have a new room. When I open the door I discover it's been arranged, as if by some mocking hand, for a family: two children's beds are laid out neatly on the floor next to a double. But my kids are far away. It's uncertain when I'll see them again. Our awaited family reunion didn't happen. I stare at the beds. In a day of dismal surprises and bitter reversals this is my blackest moment.

Over the next 24 hours, the British Foreign Office tries to find out why I've been unceremoniously sent back to London. William Hague, the foreign secretary, makes no public comment on my case. But privately diplomats at the Moscow embassy work hard to get an answer. The *Guardian*, meanwhile, prepares a story. We agree with the Foreign Office not to go public with news of my expulsion until the Russians have been given a chance to explain, and possibly reverse, their action.

But Sergei Lavrov, Russia's foreign minister and the chief exponent of the Kremlin's uncompromising foreign policy rhetoric, is in no rush to speak to his British counterpart. I'm deported on Saturday. On Sunday Lavrov is unavailable. On Monday lunchtime Hague manages to get through. Lavrov says that he knows nothing about my case. He promises to get back to Hague – the diplomatic equivalent of a polite brush-off.

After more than 48 hours, then, the Russian government still hasn't explained why it has deported me – in contravention of European norms and rules laid down by the Organisation for Security and Co-operation in Europe. Lavrov is unable to shed any light on this. We conclude we have no alternative but to publish. At 18.11 on Monday 7 February 2011 the *Guardian* website goes live with a story by media editor Dan Sabbagh.

It reads:

> The *Guardian*'s Moscow correspondent has been expelled from Russia, in what is believed to be the first removal of a British staff journalist from the country since the end of the cold war. Luke Harding's forced departure comes after the newspaper's reporting of the WikiLeaks cables, where he reported on allegations that Russia under the rule of Vladmir Putin had become a "virtual mafia state". The journalist flew back to Moscow at the weekend after a two-month stint reporting on the contents of leaked diplomatic cables from London, but was refused entry when his passport was checked on arrival.

In Britain, my treatment sparks concern. John Kampfner, the director of Index on Censorship says: "The Russian government's treatment of Luke Harding is petty and vindictive, and evidence – if more were needed – of the poor state of free expression in that country." Amnesty International UK suggests the expulsion "is another sign of the shrinking space for free speech in the country". Graham Jones, Amnesty's Russian country co-ordinator, points out: "Russia is becoming synonymous with intimidation of journalists as well as a spate of murders. It is already the third most deadly country in the world for journalists."

Martin Woollacott, the *Guardian*'s veteran analyst and former foreign editor, writes a thoughtful editorial, taking stock of Russia's progress – or lack of it – since the Soviet era. He writes:

> It is easy to guess at the "crimes" that led the Russian authorities to take this step, unprecedented since Soviet times. These were to report

on the many deficiencies that increasingly disfigure Russian politics and society, including the corruption of the state bureaucracy, the security establishment's links to organised crime, the counterproductive brutality of the government's policies in the Caucasus, the shrinking space for a free press, the hollowness of the country's democratic institutions, and the abuses of the judicial system. To name but a few.

Woolacott also wonders whether my association with the paper's story on what the WikiLeaks material revealed about the nature of the Russian system "as it has evolved, or rather devolved, under Vladimir Putin" was the "crowning offence":

> For a time it seemed that the Soviet Union's ways of controlling and managing the international press had disappeared for good in the new Russian Federation. There was an understandable prickliness about patronising foreigners, including those of the journalistic variety, and there was a lack of openness understandable in a society that has long seen curiosity as a dangerous commodity.
>
> But it was permissible to hope they would in time disappear. Instead, the old ways gradually returned. Rewards for the discreet, but punishment, and harassment, for those who crossed certain red lines. Is it as bad as the old days? No. But it is bad enough.

The *Guardian* story prompts an avalanche of calls from friends, colleagues, and Russian journalists, some based in London. Having spent my career writing the news, I have unexpectedly become the news: I'm front-page in the *Guardian* and the tail item on BBC news bulletins; my Facebook page overflows with messages. I take no pleasure in this. I am worried about the security of my family. When my children return from school they discover Russian journalists are camped next to the picket fence outside our cottage. My wife's mobile phone rings unceasingly.

One secret cable, written in April 2009 by the US ambassador John Beyrle, speaks of how Russia's deepening economic crisis and "uncertainty over the durability of the Medvedev-Putin political "tandem"' had crystallised divisions within the elite. This rift is between the hardline *siloviki* and what Beryle calls "more moderate proponents of Russia's political and economic development".

Since then, differences between the Medvedev and Putin camps seem to have grown. It's possible, then, that I've become a part of this murky intra-elite struggle, a football kicked between hardliners and moderates. But it's also possible that I've merely become a hate-object for an anonymous mid-ranking FSB colonel, trying to impress his superiors.

It is apparent that the Russian foreign ministry is entirely clueless about my expulsion. Sources protest that they know nothing of the FSB decision to put me on a blacklist. Russian newspapers report that the FSB had failed to consult: instead the organisation took a unilateral decision to declare me *persona non grata*.

According to *Kommersant*, which devotes a long article to my case, the deportation order was "unexpected" for the foreign ministry and even news for the Kremlin. One foreign ministry source describes the move as "unreasonable". He admits to *Kommersant*: "The *siloviki* took the decision without consulting anybody." Vladimir Putin's spokesman Dmitry Peskov also denies that Russia's prime minister has anything to do with it. "To link the deportation of the *Guardian* journalist with his critical articles about Vladimir Putin is absolutely inappropriate," Peskov says. This may be true. Or not.

Exactly who took the decision, then, is a mystery. But it is, nevertheless, embarrassing for the Russian authorities. It provides further evidence of just how dysfunctional Russia's warring political system has become – a Darwinian jungle of competing clans. It is left to Lavrov to make the best of the situation. Having not been informed, the foreign ministry now has to come up with a face-saving explanation. On Monday evening, three days after the event, Lavrov announces that I was refused entry to Russia because I had failed to pick up my new press card before leaving for London in November "despite knowing the necessity of doing so". It is an old Soviet trick: make up a bureaucratic excuse and blame the victim.

This announcement – of a rule that nobody knew existed – is so risible, so demonstrably feeble, as to be amusing. The *Guardian* points out that this is "manifestly not a plausible reason for my deportation", not least since the foreign ministry had already announced in November I had to leave. Lavrov's statement causes mirth among the Moscow foreign press corps. Phoebe receives a text from Tony Halpin, the bureau chief of the London *Times*. It says: "So Luke 1, Kremlin 0? Interesting development." Lavrov also claims I have "repeatedly violated" rules by travelling to forbidden counter-terrorism zones. This isn't true either, as Lavrov must surely know – it is, in fact, a lie.

But the minister's post-facto comments are enough for Russia's state-controlled press to dutifully report them as true, and to blame me for my unhappy experience at Domodedovo airport. With an eye to his forth-coming London trip, Lavrov suggests vaguely I can return to Russia if I "regulate" issues surrounding my accreditation.

It's left to the *Moscow Times*'s comment editor, Michael Bohm, to speculate further on the real reasons for my Kafkaesque removal. Bohm is unimpressed by Lavrov's explanations; he points out that other western journalists frequently travel to the north Caucasus without notifying in advance the security services, who have a reputation for picking up and harassing reporters. So why pick on me? He writes:

> Harding's explanation for his expulsion is much more convincing – that it was related to his articles about WikiLeaks cables that speak about corruption among top officials and Russia as a "mafia state", something that clearly irritated either the FSB or the Kremlin or both … The other likely explanations for Harding's expulsion is his 1 December article, referencing WikiLeaks cables, that then-President Putin likely knew about the plans to kill former FSB agent Alexander Litvinenko before he was poisoned in London.

Bohm suggests I was singled out "arbitrarily as a fall guy to intimidate other foreign journalists working in Russia".

He continues:

> The message the Kremlin and FSB want to send seems clear: if you write about sensitive issues, such as corruption among top officials or other

government abuses, you could be kicked out of the country. Every autocracy strives to enforce self-censorship any way it can. After all, self-censorship is a lot "cleaner" and more subtle than clumsy and crude government enforced censorship. When successfully implemented, it is self-regulating and requires little maintenance, apart from expelling a foreign journalist every now and then to remind them that they are guests in a country that doesn't take kindly to criticism – foreign or otherwise ... Russia truly is a closed society – and not only for Harding.

If the Kremlin continues to expel foreign journalists who write about corruption and other government abuses of power, Russia will close itself off not only from that irritating, insolent institution called the Fourth Estate, but from foreign investors and the entire western democratic world as well.

The *Moscow Times* piece strikes me as well judged. Undeniably, part of the reason I've been thrown out is *pour décourager les autres.*

My expulsion even spills into Britain's House of Commons, where I'm unwittingly responsible for a rare moment of cross-party unity. Chris Bryant, the former Labour Europe minister who leads the campaign to uncover phone-hacking at Rupert Murdoch's *News of the World* newspaper, raises my deportation in a parliamentary question.

I catch some of the debate from the offices of the *Guardian* – a strangely disembodying experience. Bryant describes me as a "thorough, meticulous and courageous journalist". He says my deportation amounts to a "pretty chilling state of affairs".

Bryant also claims my expulsion is part of a wider pattern of Russian state abuses that includes the harassment of the last British ambassador to Moscow, Tony Brenton, the recent rigged trial of Mikhail Khodorkovsky, and the unsolved murder of Anna Politkovskaya. "Does it not also accord with the revelation that the Russian security service press office which deals with journalists' inquiries has now been given authority to issue licences for the routine bugging and surveillance of all journalists operating in Russia?" he asks the house.

Bryant then makes his most telling point. He urges the British government to make clear that "Mr Lavrov is not welcome in this country while

British journalists are excluded from Russia." His comments allude to one of the few weapons Britain has at its disposal: the denial of visas to senior Kremlin officials, many of whom own lavish properties in London. He adds: "The United Kingdom has vast financial interests in Russia. Will not British business be nervous, fearing that this shows a return to the worst practices of the communist era? Will people not think that those who have suggested that Russia is a mafia state or a kleptocracy are not far off the mark?"

Jo Swinson, the Liberal Democrat junior education minister, says my deportation is "extremely concerning" and, for Russia, ultimately self-defeating. "Even if the Russians refuse to see morally or liberally this is totally unacceptable, can they at least be persuaded that it is hugely damaging to their own interests because of its impact on foreign trade, investment and their place in the world?" Robert Halfon, meanwhile, a Conservative backbencher, wonders whether Russia is on the way to becoming a "rogue state".

In Russia the debate is rather different. Russia's liberal establishment – that is, human rights groups like Memorial, independent newspapers, the opposition radio station Echo of Moscow – are all warmly supportive. *Vedomosti* even names me its "hero of the week". The FSB removed me, the paper says, to show "who in Russia is boss".

But politicians, pro-Kremlin newspaper editors and state-sponsored bloggers are critical or abusive. Borrowing an insinuation from Soviet times, several of them hint that my case is far from straightforward – in other words, that I'm a spy. Valery Fadeev, editor-in-chief at *Expert*, a magazine with connections to the ruling United Russia party, dubs me "a high-class propagandist" with links to "the British intelligence service".

Fadeev offers no evidence for this piece of make believe. He appears unfamiliar with British politics, and unaware that the left-leaning *Guardian* is an unlikely recruiting ground for MI6. (I console myself with the "high-class" bit. But the differences between me and James Bond are too ludicrous to ponder: I wear cracked trainers, don't own a car, let alone an Aston Martin, and take my children to school on the number 23 tram – an unusual if original spymobile.)

Other commentators are simply venomous. One blogger on Pravda.ru calls me "an anti-Russian scumbag". To my surprise a few Moscow-based western colleagues are mean-spirited. One calls me a "renegade" for daring to write about Kremlin corruption (surely an obvious topic for any journalist?). She quotes another Moscow correspondent who – anonymously – accuses me of attention-seeking conduct. The spy claim enters the echo chamber of Russia's news media but quickly disappears.

And within four days of my deportation the Russian foreign ministry performs an extraordinary U-turn. The ministry gets in touch again to say I can have a visa. The Russian ambassador in London even rings Rusbridger; the ambassador claims to know nothing about the FSB intrusions into my flat. The Russian government fails to explain my deportation but makes out it was an administrative error. If I am a spy, and a grave threat to Russian state security, why let me back in again?

The foreign ministry's change of heart looks like incompetence, muddle and disorder – a state of affairs captured in Russian by the word *bardak*. These are the kind of things that are supposed to have disappeared from Putin's rational, vertical, Prussian-style state.

Exactly a week after I'm deported I return to Moscow's Domodedovo airport. I take the same British Midland flight. I even watch the same film, *The Social Network*. At passport control there is no sniggering. After picking up my luggage and clearing customs, I set off past the banks of check in counters and across the terminals towards the airport express train. From behind I hear the words: "Gospodin Harding, Gospodin Harding!" A thin, wiry grey-haired figure appears breathlessly beside me. It's Alexander Kuznetsov, one of the two foreign ministry functionaries who announced my expulsion in November.

Kuznetsov solemnly produces an envelope. It contains my ministry press card. "You forgot this," he says handing me my accreditation. It's a moment of pure farce; I can't stop myself from laughing. I ask whether this now means I can stay in Russia indefinitely. Apparently it doesn't. My accreditation expires on 31 May 2011, I read – so the decision to grant me a new visa is merely an interim face-saving measure. In three months, when the scandal is quietly forgotten, I have to leave Russia again.

Back at our Moscow *dacha*, and reunited after more than a month apart, we hold an extraordinary family vote. Do we stay in Russia until the end of May? Or do we take the pragmatic decision, after four years of state-sponsored nastiness, to leave Russia sooner? The vote is 3-1 in favour of getting out. Only Phoebe votes to stay put. She has spent four years writing about the other Russia. While I've been immersed in the grim world of Kremlin politics Phoebe has been roaming around Moscow under an open sky. She has explored gold-domed churches, markets full of berries, museums with crazily enthusiastic curators, and wooden palaces under falling snow.

What's more she's planning a book of Moscow walks. Unlike my experiences, her encounters have been uplifting. She's chatted with grandmothers on local trains, curious villagers, and Pushkin-quoting walking companions. Moscow's weather hasn't put her off either: at one point she returns home with mild frostbite, having been out in 27C below zero temperatures. Her peculiar knack has been to look beyond Moscow's tower blocks and traffic jams and to winkle out the city's hidden beauty. She knows Moscow's secret places. She is understandably reluctant to give this up.

I reason that it's going to be difficult for me to continue as a correspondent under these circumstances. The FSB's scrutiny of our family is more intrusive than ever: our phones are bugged, emails are delayed or fail to arrive, our private sphere is non-existent – the only places left are the bottom of the garden or the noise-filled metro. I can't rule out further "provocations", to use the catchall Russian phrase denoting conspiracy. We prepare to leave again for the third time in four months. I also decide to smuggle out my old notebooks.

My last few days in Moscow are unlikely to reveal why I've become the target of sustained counter-intelligence procedures from my FSB friends, the ghosts. But I decide to say goodbye to my Russian contacts, and to ask them if they can shed light on why I've been treated with such hostility. A couple of days after my return to Moscow, I meet Olga Kryshtanovskaya again. Our rendezvous takes place in a cafe in the corner of the House of Books close to her flat. The bookshop is a cosy and anonymous venue – or at least it appears anonymous at the time.

Kryshtanovskaya says that it's clear my articles have infuriated the FSB. She points out I've trampled over numerous red lines: writing about the links between the FSB and the mafia, and publishing stories about Putin's team, and the money of his team. "From your point of view it's illogical to throw you out. But from the FSB's point of view it's entirely logical. They've found an enemy – you. And they've got rid of him."

According to Kryshtanovskaya, the Russian elite has been badly spooked by the Arab spring and the revolutions in Tunisia, Egypt and Libya. It is deeply fearful that a similar popular uprising could take place at home. I represent a threat to what the FSB sees as "constitutional order", she explains – in other words, the political monopoly as well as the private assets of the Putin regime, which now sits on increasingly shaky foundations. "They are terrified of being overthrown, like in Egypt. You represent a threat to power. That's why you are an enemy," Olga says.

I ask about the FSB's mystifying tactics. By repeatedly harassing me, and by breaking into my flat, the security services could only make my journalism tougher on the Kremlin than it might otherwise have been, I tell her. Why persevere with bone-headed and counter-productive operations? Kryshtanovskaya counters that the FSB's methods follow a prescribed pattern.

In my case, the security services decided to take what she calls "prophylactic action" against me. The term is specific to the FSB's strange lexicon. I ask Olga to write the word down in Russian: *profilaktirovat*. "The theory is that if you scare someone in time it will stop them from committing hostile actions. If that doesn't work you need to punish them in some other way."

It is widely believed the security and law enforcement services belong in Putin's domain, that they follow his orders rather than Medvedev's. But increasingly, it seems to me, they are enjoying near-total autonomy.

"Does Putin actually control them?" I ask.

Kryshtanovskaya says she doesn't know. "The answer is top secret."

The conversation is an interesting one. We've been sitting in the cafe for 20 minutes when Olga gestures at the young man who has slid – unnoticed by me – into a nearby leather bench seat. He is sitting at 90 degrees to us; he isn't visible but can hear our entire conversation. The young man wears a synthetic light grey suit and open-necked white shirt; he isn't drinking anything. The other tables are empty, yet he has chosen to sit next to us.

"He's from the FSB," Olga whispers.

"How can you be certain?"

"I know the type," she says. "When I mentioned the word *profilaktirovat* I noticed his reaction. He was eavesdropping."

Olga indicates there's no point in continuing with our chat; we leave the cafe separately then stroll together across an icy pavement to the metro station; the air is cold and sharp. The young man follows, makes a phone call, disappears. I ask her about relations between Medvedev and Putin. "Not very good," she says. "It's a struggle for power, a struggle to the death." And what about the FSB colonel, or general even, who brought such embarrassment on his bosses by deporting me – could he expect demotion? "The reverse," Kryshtanovskaya replies. "Promotion. And medals." The word in Russian is *nagrady*.

As we part, she again urges me to take care. "You are in danger," she says bluntly.

CHAPTER 17

The File

Zersetzung, die: Decomposition, Rotting, Subversion, Undermining.
OXFORD DUDEN GERMAN-ENGLISH DICTIONARY 1999

I have always admired Timothy Garton Ash's slim, elegant memoir *The File*, written after the collapse of the Berlin Wall, when Garton Ash reads his Stasi file. It is a model book. In it, Garton Ash heroically confronts his Stasi informers and grapples with his own early Oxford self and less-than-perfect memory. Garton Ash plays the role of post-cold war detective. He tracks down the *inoffizieller Mitarbeiter*, or unofficial collaborators, who passed information about him to the ministry for state security, communist East Germany's secret police. Much of it is wrong, ridiculous or inconsequential. The Stasi's appetite for detail turns out to be voracious. The service's motto was: "To know everything."

There are awkward encounters with retired secret policemen in Berlin's garden suburbs. Several of those who worked for The Firm – as the Stasi styled itself – now seem to be wearing synthetic tracksuits. One Stasi collaborator who informs on Garton Ash turns out to be a university lecturer in English literature. Another is in the insurance business. A third politely declines by letter to be interviewed. There is denial, obfuscation, defiance and – sometimes but not always – expressions of regret. The studious East Germans, one learns, had elaborated personal surveillance into a kind of perverse national group activity: with the spies and the spied upon. Even now, only a minority of those who participated in it recognise it for what it was: a morally repugnant form of terror.

Along the way, Garton Ash, the book's Virgil-like guide, consistently asks the right questions. Why inform? Or – better put – what is it in people's personal biographies that drives them into the arms of the secret police? Why does one person become a resistance fighter and another a faithful servant of dictatorship, one a Stauffenberg, the other a Speer, Garton Ash wonders. Could Britain, differently configured, have become a communist police state? And can we be confident that the methods of the security services in Britain – and the western world in general – are superior to those used in the former Soviet bloc?

In some ways, Garton Ash's personal history mirrors my own: the Stasi, like the FSB in my case, had him down as a British spy. In the 1980s the Stasi banned him from travelling to the GDR. Expulsion is the traditional method, as he puts it, of dealing with "lesser enemies". The assiduous East Germans also sent his details to Soviet Moscow, placing him on its System of Unified Registration of Data of the Enemy.

(Garton Ash writes that the system had 15 categories: secret agents, members of "subversive organisations" and "centres of political-ideological diversion", "provocateurs", "banned and undesirable persons", "hostile diplomats", "hostile correspondents", terrorists and smugglers. He was identified as category five: "Persons who execute commissions for subversive activity against the states of the socialist community on behalf of hostile intelligence services ..." Under this system I would, I suppose, be a "hostile correspondent".)

In the 1980s, as communism begins to totter, Garton Ash cunningly manages to evade the ban: he visits Poland and Czechoslovakia and even manages to slip into East Berlin for two days in 1984, and again the following year, accompanying the British foreign secretary, Geoffrey Howe. And then in 1989 the wall comes down. In 1992 Garton Ash gets to read his Stasi file. Suddenly the curtain is pulled away. From the debris of Europe's divided history, his old diaries, and the Stasi's buff-coloured binder on him he can fashion a kind of retrospective truth. Perhaps not *the* truth. But a convincing version of it. For Garton Ash, an academic, a historian, a journalist, an intellectual, and a student of eastern Europe's painful transition from former communist dictatorship to European normality, what joy! The file offers something all-too-rare in life: a moment of personal and professional closure.

But I can envisage no such moment of democratic awakening or truth telling in Russia. Rather, there is every sign the current ruling clique will hang on to power indefinitely, despite the protests against Putin's rule. If my FSB file were ever made public – something that will be possible only after another Russian revolution, the third in a century – it's unlikely I shall be around to read it. But my file exists. I can't see it. But I can imagine it. I can piece together the clues.

Two weeks after my expulsion I receive an email from Florian Knauer, a German post-doctoral researcher at Berlin's Humboldt University. Knauer says he is writing a book on stalking, bullying, psychological torture and what he calls "psychological disintegration". He says, by way of introduction: "I have just read in the *Frankfurter Allgemeine Zeitung* about your decision to leave Russia. The article says that members of the Russian secret service broke into your flat and that state authorities have bullied you and your family. These methods sound familiar to me."

Knauer goes on to explain that the Stasi used similar methods of repression against opposition members in former East Germany. In fact, these techniques were exported across the Soviet bloc. He points me to an article written by Herta Müller, the Romanian-born German novelist, who was awarded in 2009 the Nobel prize in literature.

Müller describes suffering dreadfully at the hands of the Securitate, Romania's secret police. At her factory they spread the slander that she was an informer. There were interrogations, beatings. And break-ins. I read: "The secret police came and went as they pleased when we weren't at home. Often they would deliberately leave signs: cigarette butts, pictures removed from the wall and left on the bed, chairs moved." The most uncanny incident, she writes, lasted weeks: the agents would cut bits off a fox skin lying on the floor, finally removing its head. Müller calls this "psychological terror". "Anything could happen, the flat was no longer private."

These seemingly harmless psychological tactics even have a name – *Zersetzung*, Knauer says. Could I tell him a little more about my experiences?

The word is a curious one. I speak fluent German, and spent four years in Berlin as the *Guardian*'s Germany correspondent, prior to Moscow. I hadn't come across *Zersetzung*, however. *Zersetzung*, I discover, is a scientific term borrowed from chemistry. It translates as "decomposition", "disintegration" or "corrosion". (To my English ear corrosion sounds best.) But it can also mean undermining, subversion, disruption, dissolution and corruption.

The Romantics, with their fascination for decay in the natural world, used the word metaphorically from the late 18th century onwards. Modern political groups also made use of the term: the Nazis referred to the "disintegrating influence" of the Jews, to justify their extinction; the communists talked of "disintegrating" their ideological enemies.

Knauer introduces me to the work of Sandra Pingel-Schliemann, a German writer and journalist. She has studied the use of *Zersetzung* in the former German Democratic Republic. She has interviewed victims and – like Garton Ash – spent months combing through the archives of the ministry for state security. I begin reading her book, *Disintegration: Strategy of a Dictatorship*, published in 2002 in Berlin. I am horrified, fascinated. My own curtain doesn't exactly open. But a small crack appears, and I can begin to peek through it.

I read that under Erich Honecker *Zersetzung* was used extensively. As applied by the Stasi, *Zersetzung* is a technique to subvert and undermine an opponent. The aim was to disrupt the target's private or family life so they are unable to continue their "hostile-negative" activities towards the state. Typically, the Stasi would use collaborators to garner details from a victim's private life. They would then devise a strategy to "disintegrate" the target's personal circumstances – their career, their relationship with their spouse, their reputation in the community. They would even seek to alienate them from their children.

Pingel-Schliemann cites the case of Herr J. First Herr J lost his driver's licence. Months later he found anonymous notes insulting him hanging on the trees of his village. Then rumours circulated that he was cheating on his wife. At work Herr J faced growing problems. Finally, the police arrested him and sentenced him for a theft he didn't commit. To Herr J, these events were disturbing, random and inexplicable. He had no inkling that the Stasi were behind them.

The security service's goal was to use *Zersetzung* to "switch off" regime opponents. After months and even years of *Zersetzung* a victim's domestic problems grew so large, so debilitating, and so psychologically burdensome that they would lose the will to struggle against the East German state. Best of all, the Stasi's role in the victim's personal misfortunes remained tantalisingly hidden. The Stasi operations were carried out in complete operational secrecy. The service acted like an unseen and malevolent god, manipulating the destinies of its victims.

It was in the mid-1970s that Honecker's secret police began to employ these perfidious methods. At that moment the GDR was finally achieving international respectability. (It joined the UN in 1973, opened up a dialogue with West Germany and in 1975 signed the Helsinki accords. It also desperately needed urgent financial assistance from the West German government in Bonn.) Honecker's predecessor, Walter Ulbricht, was an old-fashioned Stalinist thug. He used open terror methods to subdue his post-war population: show trials, mass arrests, camps, torture and the secret police.

But two decades after East Germany had become a communist paradise of workers and peasants, most citizens were acquiescent. When a new group of dissidents began to protest against the regime, Honecker came to the conclusion that different tactics were needed. Mass terror was no longer appropriate and might damage the GDR's international reputation. A cleverer strategy was called for.

Over in Leningrad, meanwhile, in 1975, Vladimir Putin had fulfilled his teenage dream and joined the KGB. Within a few years he would be breaking up the city's hippy communes. His KGB comrades nicknamed him "Moth", such was his skill at quietly picking away at targets.

And so the regime embarked on an unseen psychological war against its internal critics. This war was an unequal one since the other side – a relatively small section of East Germany's population – had no idea it was being fought. The targets were "enemies": artists like the dissident singer Wolf Biermann (expelled to West Germany in 1976); pastors; local church groups; peace activists; anyone who wanted to leave for the west. Pingel-Schliemann describes *Zersetzung* as "subtle", "anonymous", "noiseless" and "inscrutable". Its methods differ from officially recognisable forms of persecution such as torture, arrest and murder. *Zersetzung* is covert: usually the victim had no idea that the Stasi was behind it (although by the late 1980s the suspicion of Stasi involvement was widespread among opposition groups).

On page 197 I read about the case of Frau R. Stasi employees used duplicate keys to break into Frau R's flat. Once inside they removed the pictures from her walls. During the next secret break-in they shifted the spice pots in her kitchen. Then they replaced Frau R's favourite kind of tea with another variety. The Stasi officers were an enterprising bunch: they broke in again and again, each time coming up with something new. On one occasion they changed Frau R's hand towels. On another they rotated the flowerpots on her window-seat. In another case officers broke in at night while their victim was sleeping. They crept into the bathroom and switched on his electric razor. The victim woke up, terrified. He was unable to explain what was happening. "You can't tell these things to anybody. If you did, they would simply say: 'Sure, you were drunk,'" he said.

The most insidious aspect of *Zersetzung* is that its victims are almost invariably not believed. When Frau R told her friends what was happening they concluded that she was losing touch with reality: "We found it impossible to explain why someone would want to remove the hand towels," one of them admitted. Some *Zersetzung* victims think they are going mad or are ill; those affected suffer the reproach that they are hallucinating.

Superficially, the moving around of personal effects might seem harmless – little more than a puerile prank. But for the victims the results could be psychologically disastrous, I read. They could lead to withdrawal, psychosis, "the complete breakdown of a psyche", and even suicide. "The essential characteristic of *Zersetzung* is its anonymity," Pingel-Schliemann writes. "These *Zersetzung* activities are subtle. They can't be obviously identified as persecution measures by the Stasi." She adds: "Even now, it often happens that when those affected describe their experiences ... no one believes them. All too often, their personal descriptions are discounted as paranoia."

The Stasi boss Erich Mielke grew interested in psychological techniques in the 1960s. By 1971 – when Honecker replaced Ulbricht – Mielke's ministry began to transform *Zersetzung* from a thuggish tool into a pseudo-academic discipline. These methods of intimidation and anonymous harassment were classified as "operational psychology". Operational psychology is conventional psychology's dark twin: instead of healing people, the idea is to harm or damage them.

Mielke established a chair of operational psychology at the Juridical Higher School, the ministry for state security training academy in Potsdam. Here, students wrote papers on advanced psychological techniques: they learned, for example, that sleep deprivation and solitary confinement are more effective interrogation methods than beatings or electric shocks. For the mature totalitarian state, "hard" torture was no longer necessary. What was required was "soft" torture.

On 1 January 1976 Mielke issued secret policy directive 1/76. It regulated the use of psychology in "operational procedures". Ambitious Stasi officers penned theses on how concealed sanctions could be deployed against class enemies; one ran to 800 pages.

It said, in ponderous German:

The enemy becomes chiefly preoccupied with himself. The reasons for his misfortune, and for the need to renounce hostile activity, exist within a framework that he is unable to blame either the socialist state in its entirety or the security organs.

Enemies reacted "more slowly and hesitantly" to *Zersetzung* than to forms of open persecution, the paper noted. (These could strengthen an individual's self-confidence, and damage the political authority of the East German state. Open methods also risked leaving the Stasi open to "libel and discrimination in the western mass media".) For these reasons, *Zersetzung* operations had to be carried out in conditions of total conspiracy.

As I read, the similarities between Honecker's East Germany and Putin's Russia strike me as overwhelming. Both are, in effect, sophisticated modern dictatorships. Both appreciate that the subtle arts of repression are more effective than crude old-school methods. And Russia – like the defunct GDR – is greatly concerned about its international image, with the "elite" especially nervous about the fate of its assets in the west. And like the mature East Germans, Moscow has signed up to numerous human rights treaties and, in addition, is a signatory to the European convention on human rights. It has international obligations and is – or aspires to be – a respected, senior member of the global community.

Using *Zersetzung* techniques, then, is the perfect answer. At a time of growing domestic discontent in Russia the FSB's harassment of Russia's opposition – as well as the odd foreign enemy – is a useful secret tool. And after all, where is the evidence that human rights have been infringed? An open window, a strange alarm clock, a sex book by the bed – come off it! *Zersetzung*, carried out by the state's invisible emissaries, is difficult to observe and even harder for its victims to prove.

In her study Pingel-Schliemann concludes: "These days a total dictatorship doesn't need to use methods of open terror to subdue people for years and make them weak ... Moreover, developments in technology and communications offer future dictators ever more subtle possibilities for manipulation." Her comments strike me as prescient. In Herr J's case Stasi operatives had to creep round at night hanging individual notes in his village with the words: "Whore", "Drunkard", "Speeder" and "Bigmouth". Today's Kremlin bloggers and faceless state patriots have it much easier. They need only reach for their mouse.

Three weeks after I leave Moscow I travel to Berlin. I telephone Pingel-Schliemann. She is sympathetic. My experiences in Moscow are identical to other *Zersetzung* victims, she confirms. "You should write a book, Herr Harding. This is the best *Therapie* for you," she advises. She has information: the former chair of operational psychology at the Stasi's higher academy is still alive. His name is Jochen Girke. After the collapse of the Berlin Wall he has continued to work as a psychologist in Potsdam. He also advises Germany's Linkspartei (the "Left party"), which enjoys support from diehard East German communists, West German ultra-leftists and middle-aged radicals. Girke is in the phone book. I call him. I explain my own unusual circumstances. To my surprise, he agrees to meet.

We decide on a cup of coffee in Ganymed, an old-fashioned brasserie overlooking Schiffbauerdamm, a cobbled riverside street beneath Berlin's Freidrichstrasse station. The restaurant exudes pre-war charm: it has a solid wooden counter with brass railings; cherubs and angels decorate the bar, blowing bugles; the elderly waiter bears an uncanny resemblance to Albert Einstein. I perch on a stool next to a large, solemn-looking cake.

Girke is a few minutes late. He is a well-groomed, prosperous-looking man of 62, with grey hair, a classic German moustache and a modest paunch; he's wearing a black Hugo Boss shirt and jacket. I tell him of my experiences with the FSB in Moscow – the break-ins, the open windows, the strange noises in the middle of the night, and the literature advising me how to orgasm correctly. Girke nods. He smiles. There is recognition and – though I may be imagining this – a trace of professional pride. "These are typical *Zersetzung* methods," he begins.

According to Girke, all secret services, including western ones, use what he calls "grubby tools". "In our case it was ideologically justified. We were building a better Germany. The order legitimised the methods," he says. In Honecker's German Democratic Republic, as in Putin's Russian Federation, journalists were automatically considered to be enemies and spies, he explains. "When you come up against a journalist you assume he has connections with the security services. Journalists are classic examples of the *Feindbild*, the conception of the enemy ... It's perverse. But you were taught to always expect the enemy to attack."

I explain that the FSB have targeted me with puzzling zeal. As FSB chief, it was Putin in 1999 who stated that foreign espionage posed Russia's gravest threat. But Girke says this zealousness may simply be the work of an ambitious junior officer trying to climb his way up the greasy career pole: "The case officer has to show his superiors he's successful. He's not interested in whether someone is a good father, a good person, or a good journalist. He wants to find proof that the *Feindbild* is true."

In fact, the Stasi wanted to know everything about a target's private life, Girke says – whether he had a mistress, his relationship with his wife, what books he was reading, debts – anything that might have lent itself to manipulation. No detail was too frivolous. The Stasi was interested in the brand of cigarettes a person smoked, where he parked his van, how much he drank.

The Stasi's *Zersetzung* methods were astonishingly diverse and ingenious, he says – a "ballet of methods" that spoke of a dark creativity. "We would arrange for a pipe to burst in the floor above a target's flat, flooding it. The idea is to irritate you in your job or personal life. Eventually you get rid of them." On another occasion, the Stasi would arrange for the dispatch of a dozen strawberry flans to a victim's home; the victim would complain they hadn't ordered the cakes, but the order form would be filled in correctly, with the victim's name and address. The Stasi would also orchestrate the delivery of a child-sized coffin to the home of a target with a young family; the undertaker would offer his condolences for the child's death. In fact, nobody had died.

More usually, though, the methods were banal but grimly effective. Stasi officers would break into a target's car, then park it back in the same place but half-mounted on the kerb, Girke says. When its owner returned he found his car in a subtly different position. Had someone broken in? Or was he imagining things? Or was he going potty? "They [the secret services] do those things to show that they are all-powerful, omnipotent, and that they can enter your private sphere at any time," Girke explains.

But what about sex? Was anything in a target's personal life off limits? During our four years in Moscow we assumed that our marital bedroom was bugged; we would discuss anything sensitive at the bottom of the garden next to the plum tree. Bugging was one thing, but was there, well, video as well? Girke says that the Stasi would sometimes exploit a target's sexual weaknesses, and recalls the case of a homosexual West German businessman who travelled to Leipzig for a trade fair. (He says the Stasi greatly overestimated the businessman's significance, erroneously passing the file up to the level of a general.)

Leaving pornographic literature by someone's bed was another trademark Stasi tactic. It was used, for example, to discredit the reputation of Herr B, a member of a religious peace group in Mecklenburg – as was spreading false rumours that a target was cheating on their spouse. On one occasion the Stasi's department XX/4 (as Garton Ash notes, responsible for infiltrating church groups) in Berlin sent a vibrator to the wife of a target, acquired by an informer from West Berlin. With it came an anonymous note: "Better to use the vibrator than to cheat on your husband."

Generally, however, Girke says the secret police had no operational interest in sex, though I still find the voyeuristic possibilities discomforting. He says officers are more interested in pillow talk – the possibility that in the privacy of the bedroom a target would disclose something of great operational significance. "You have to see things through the lens of the FSB. You are in bed with your wife. You tell her that the first secretary at the British embassy has just given you a new assignment. It is of vital national interest. The FSB is listening in. Their ears start to ring."

It is this fantasy – the quest for the elusive piece of information, the spook's Holy Grail – that makes the job all apparently worthwhile. For the conscientious counter-intelligence agent, the hours of waiting and listening are all focussed on this one moment. Girke compares it to a knightly quest. It is, he suggests, a sort of cross between the medieval romances of Wolfram von Eschenbach and a modern spy-thriller. He explains: "Imagine that you are a hunter who sits patiently with his weapon in the meadow and waits for the appearance of a great white deer that everyone has been talking about it. The hunter fantasises he will shoot the deer dead with a golden bullet."

During Girke's time in the service, the Stasi developed sophisticated techniques of bugging and surveillance, he says. "We had advanced technical systems. You don't have to keep a cable hanging out of the window. Everything has been completely miniaturised. The bugs are no bigger than a pen-head, and are linked to a transmitter in the street," he says. Days before my departure from Russia, I had discovered the lock on the front door of my *dacha* to be stiff and damaged – signs of an FSB break-in. (The date is 17 February 2011. On this occasion the intruder seems to have been in a hurry. Or less concerned about leaving clues. Is this also in my file?) I suspect the budget-minded security services have come to collect their eavesdropping equipment. "That's entirely possible," Girke says.

Girke is unable to shed light on who originally invented "operational psychology". It was, he believes, the KGB who first developed the practice. After all, it was "the friends" from Moscow who in the 1950s established the GDR's fledgling secret police, with the two services – the East German and the Soviet – working closely together thereafter. The KGB discreetly placed liaison officers in key East German towns and in all eight Stasi directorates. One of them, from 1985-1990, was Vladimir Putin, who was based in city of Dresden. What precisely Putin got up to in Dresden is a mystery. Formally he was assigned to run a Soviet-German friendship house in

Leipzig. Presumably he had already learned about operational psychology from the KGB's own academy.

During the cold war years the KGB had two key preoccupations, Girke says. One was spying on Nato and the Bundesnachrichtendienst (BND), federal West Germany's foreign intelligence agency. The KGB's interest was in getting hold of blueprints of the missile systems of Nato countries and other defence matters. The second aim was ensuring that the East Germans (and other socialist Warsaw pact nations) remained loyal partners. "The liaison officers would give us concrete suggestions," Girke says. "There were always contacts and connections."

By the time of *perestroika* this once close relationship had degenerated into one of mistrust, with Honecker displeased by Mikhail Gorbachev's economic reforms and ideological backsliding. Still, at a personal level, relations remained friendly, Girke says. The KGB had their own house in Potsdam next to the Berlin Wall; the KGB and Stasi would play football matches on a grassy pitch near Schloss Cecilienhof, the palace where Churchill, Truman and Stalin held the Potsdam conference.

Around 1986 Girke says he had an unexpected phone call from his opposite number in the KGB, also a professor in operational psychology. The two men met on a bench in Schloss Sanssouci, Frederick the Great's baroque summer palace in Potsdam, not far from the Stasi's *Hochschule* in Potsdam-Eiche where Girke taught. (The academy appears in the *The Lives of Others*, the Oscar-winning film about the Stasi by the West German director Florian Henckel von Donnersmarck.) They discussed the scientific aspects of their work. Both secret services understood how psychological techniques could be applied to carefully chosen enemies. But it was the east Germans, Girke says, who transformed operational psychology into, as he saw it, a rigorous academic discipline. "We were the ones who refined *Zersetzung*. The German service used more refined techniques," he says. "The Russians were always more brutal."

Two decades later, Girke admits that the entire GDR project – and his role in it – was wrong. "I think it was a huge mistake. All of us – the chiefs, the party bosses, the service – all of us believed you could make people happy by compelling them. We thought we could build another Germany using these methods. It was an illusion. But we put so much energy into it, into making people's careers fail. I recognised this far too late." He says that he wasn't personally involved in hounding dissidents but accepts "collective responsibility" for what the service did. He is, he admits, a *Schreibtischtäter*. (The word translates literally as "desk perpetrator" and was originally coined to describe the pen-pushers – rather than the Gestapo – who made the Third Reich possible.)

Somewhere in Moscow, on someone's desk, in someone's dusty filing cabinet, on someone's encrypted data-stick, is my FSB file. I ask Girke what is likely to be in it. "You get a number. They put you in a category," he says. The Stasi has its own classification system depending on the seriousness of the case. Additionally, Girke says, the FSB will have given me a codename, an alias for use in secret operations. This codename is important: it depersonalises the target and makes it easier to carry out hostile measures against them. (Garton Ash is understandably delighted when he finds out the Stasi have christened him "Romeo".) Girke says the FSB will have included copies of my *Guardian* articles – I am, after all, a "hostile correspondent" – as well as details of the operations against me. He adds that files are never closed. Even though Russia has now ejected me, I apparently live on somewhere in the FSB's dusty archives.

The Potsdam Stasi academy may have shut down, but – so far as he knows – the FSB still has its own chair of "operative psychology" at its academy in Moscow. Why, though, would the Russians persist with such methods long after the supposed end of the cold war? Or, more accurately, why has Putin revived the use of KGB tactics long after the battle for power and influence between east and west has disappeared? Girke has a simple answer. "*Wladimir Putin macht was er kennt,*" he says. "Vladimir Putin does what he knows." He adds: "It's obvious. He wants to hang on to power and so he uses secret service methods."

The day before our departure snow still blankets our *dacha* home. A light white powder covers the plum tree and the red sugar maple. The great tits are at our bird feeder again, five or six of them, vividly pecking away. Soon there will be nobody left to feed them. We send the children off separately: Tilly to Geneva for a skiing holiday and Ruskin with Phoebe's cousin Alice back to London. The precaution may appear overblown. But at this stage it seems better to be cautious.

Packing up to leave, I ponder Russia's fate since the collapse of the Soviet Union and the end of communism. There are many unattractive aspects – the feudal arrogance of Russia's "elite", for one; the lack of legal protection for ordinary Russians from arbitrary bureaucratic overlords, for another. This has long been the case. The historian Richard Pipes calls this the "singular chasm" that has existed across the ages in Russia between the rulers and ruled. Isaiah Berlin refers to "two nations" – the "class of the governed" who "behave as humans do everywhere" and the "governing class" who are "feared, admired, detested, and accepted as inevitable by the entire population".

I know which nation I prefer. Among the class of the governed there is much to admire: the indomitable spirit of the Russian people in the face of insuperable obstacles and daily frustrations; the rich literary and theatrical culture; the intense friendships. Our leaving party is a classically Russian affair. We drink vodka. We eat gherkins. We make tearful toasts. We laugh with our Russian and western friends. And at some point long after dawn we collapse groggily into bed.

But the biggest failing of the current Russian regime, I feel, is intellectual. Like the ghosts who broke into my apartment, using an old KGB tactic from a manual written long ago, Lieutenant Colonel Putin has gone back to his comfort zone. As a young spy he had twin mentors. They were the KGB and the Stasi. It shows. The result is a profound lack of empathy for anyone who disagrees with him. Hence his slur against demonstrators protesting in massive numbers against election fraud. Under his tutelage Russia has become bullying, violent, cruel and – above all – inhuman.

By 2011, after over a decade in power Putin has completed a giddy counter-revolution. He has replaced the semi-democratic structures of the 1990s with a power vertical. He has fostered corruption, since corruption ensures loyalty. He has given the FSB unprecedented powers. And he has restored the agency to its old KGB role as guardian of the state. But opposition to his rule is growing. Soon it may become unstoppable. And he has failed, utterly failed, to come up with anything new.

An English Spring

Hertfordshire, England
April 2011

If Winter comes, can Spring be far behind?
PERCY BYSSHE SHELLEY, 'ODE TO THE WEST WIND'

After a Moscow winter, an English spring. From the window of my study in Hertfordshire, I can see a Scots pine and a wayfaring tree, flowering white. Daffodils and primroses carpet the neighbouring gardens; there are pink cherry trees and magnolias in creamy blossom. My new jogging route takes me past an allotment and a cabbage field to Hatfield forest. Here, in the early evening, I spy a fox. The fox sizes me up before slinking off among the oaks and hornbeams. There are rabbits, too many to count, and deer.

In fact, our new modern-built home is more suburban than pastoral. It has little in common with our now-empty Moscow *dacha*. The house backs onto a hospital car park; one balcony overlooks Stansted airport's flight path. We've inherited a satellite TV dish. Unlike Moscow, with its communal Soviet-era apartment blocs built in the 70s and 80s, the British appear to live in individual Lego houses, each a mini-Eden. We have a garden. It is a small strip of turf identical to that of our neighbours. There is a shed. After a decade away we are slowly relearning the grammar, the orderly and discrete architectural spacing, of British life.

And yet, in the early weeks I find it hard to unlearn Moscow rules. When inside I immediately deadlock the front door. In cafes and restaurants I glance over my shoulder, on the lookout for young men wearing cheap ill-fitting suits and brown shoes. Once, I hear Russian voices outside on the street. I find myself following two men. They disappear innocently into the local hospital. In Moscow, there are blizzards and snowfalls; but here there is warmth – it's 19C in April – and birdsong. In the early morning I hear wood pigeons clatter in the pines outside my bedroom; I watch as they pad down the deserted street.

Over time, it appears that the old world has gone for good. When I return to the house the white patio doors – bolted when I left – are still bolted. Household objects remain where we left them. The window of my son's new bedroom is not a warning, a gesture, or a dark hint – it's just a window. There are no inexplicable night-time noises, and no sex manuals. After a month our household furniture arrives from Russia in a large van. I discover the Putin-Medvedev clock. We decide to leave it – and them – in a cardboard box. They remain there.

My daughter is at the international school we promised her after the Russian foreign ministry announced we had to leave Moscow. My son goes to a local primary school: his uniform is a green sweatshirt, and for the first time in his life he has to wear a tie. Both children seem happy – though Tilly complains that her new life is *boring*, compared to the excitement of the old. Still, we are anonymous again. And – I think – safe. I walk my son to school through a small wood. He does the last stretch on his own.

ACKNOWLEDGEMENTS

The author would like to thank:

Stanislav Belkovsky

Irina Borogan

Tony Brenton

Robert Chandler

Victoria Chumirina

Lisa Darnell

Martin Dewhirst

Charlie English

Orlando Figes

Richard Galpin

John Harding

Felicity Harding

David Hearst

Alice Hodge

Ian Katz

Yulia Koval-Molodtsova

Olga Kryshtanovskaya

Alexander Lebedev

David Leigh

Clifford Levy

Toby Manhire

Sara Montgomery

Tom Parfitt

Lika Peradze

Katie Roden

Alan Rusbridger

Andrei Soldatov

Martin Seddon

Phoebe Taplin

Jan Thompson

Giles Tremlett

Sergei Vasilyev

Penelope Vogler

INDEX

(the initials LH in subentries refer to Luke Harding)